FATAL ERRORS; OR POOR MARY-ANNE.
A TALE OF THE LAST CENTURY

FATAL ERRORS; OR POOR MARY-ANNE. A TALE OF THE LAST CENTURY

By Elizabeth Hays Lanfear

Edited by Timothy Whelan and Felicity James

LONDON AND NEW YORK

First published 2020
by Routledge
2 Park Square, Milton Park, Abingdon, Oxon OX14 4RN

and by Routledge
52 Vanderbilt Avenue, New York, NY 10017

Routledge is an imprint of the Taylor & Francis Group, an informa business

© 2020 selection and editorial matter, Timothy Whelan and Felicity James; individual owners retain copyright in their own material.

The right of Timothy Whelan and Felicity James to be identified as the authors of the editorial material, and of the authors for their individual chapters, has been asserted in accordance with sections 77 and 78 of the Copyright, Designs and Patents Act 1988.

All rights reserved. No part of this book may be reprinted or reproduced or utilised in any form or by any electronic, mechanical, or other means, now known or hereafter invented, including photocopying and recording, or in any information storage or retrieval system, without permission in writing from the publishers.

Trademark notice: Product or corporate names may be trademarks or registered trademarks, and are used only for identification and explanation without intent to infringe.

British Library Cataloguing-in-Publication Data
A catalogue record for this book is available from the British Library

Library of Congress Cataloging-in-Publication Data
A catalog record for this book has been requested

ISBN: 978-1-138-54461-1
eISBN: 978-1-351-00310-0

Typeset in Times New Roman
by Apex CoVantage, LLC

Publisher's Note
References within each chapter are as they appear in the original complete work

CONTENTS

Acknowledgements	vii
Chronology for Elizabeth Hays Lanfear	viii
Introduction	xii
Bibliography	xl
Note on the Text	xliii

FATAL ERRORS; OR POOR MARY-ANNE (1819)   1

   Dedicatory Epistle   2
   to Mrs. Wm. Hills

   Preface   3

   List of Subscribers   4

   Text of *Fatal Errors*   9

APPENDICES   69

A. **Two Tales by Elizabeth Hays, in *Letters and Essays, Moral and Miscellaneous*, by Mary Hays (1793)**   71
   No. X. Cleora, or the Misery attending Unsuitable Connections 71
   No. XI. Josepha, or the Pernicious Effects of Early Indulgence 75

CONTENTS

B. Selections from Elizabeth Hays Lanfear's *Letters to Young Ladies on their Entrance into the World; to which are added Sketches from Real Life* (1824)   **83**
Introductory Letter 85
Letter II. On the Motives for Female Improvement 88
Letter III. On the Motives for Female Improvement (continued) *91*
Letter VII. On the Single Life 94
Sketches from Real Life: Sketch I. Louisa the Indulged 98

C. Letters of Elizabeth Hays Lanfear   **111**
 1. Elizabeth Hays, Gainsford Street, to Mary Hays, 30 Kirby Street, Wednesday morning, undated [c. January 1796] 111
 2. Elizabeth Hays, Chelmsford, Essex, to Mary Hays, 22 Hatton Street [Hatton garden], Holborn, 4 February 1801 112
 3. Elizabeth Hays, Ingatestone, Essex, to Mary Hays, George Row [9 St. George's Place], Camberwell, 14 August 1803 114

Notes   117

ACKNOWLEDGEMENTS

Our thanks to the British Library for permission to use their copy of *Fatal Errors*, the only extant copy, as the copy-text for this edition. Our thanks as well to the directors, librarians, curators, and staff of the New York Historical Society, The Carl H. Pforzheimer Collection of Shelley and his Circle, New York Public Library, Astor, Lenox, and Tilden Foundations, and Dr Williams's Library, London, for permission to consult, quote, and publish selected materials from their collections of manuscripts relating to Elizabeth Hays, Mary Hays, William Godwin, Mary Wollstonecraft, and other figures appearing in this volume whose letters belong to their collections. Information about Mary Hays's family and her activities within the Godwin circle has been significantly expanded in recent years by two online publications: *The Diary of William Godwin* (eds), Victoria Myers, David O'Shaughnessy, and Mark Philp (Oxford: Oxford Digital Library, 2010) (http://godwindiary.bodleian.ox.ac.uk), and *Ed Pope History* (http://edpopehistory.co.uk), an invaluable resource by Ed Pope which provides students and scholars with access to information on some 3,000 individuals in and around London between 1780 and 1810. Our appreciation goes as well to the staff of the Angus Library, Regent's Park College, Oxford, for access to various Baptist church books relating to Southwark and London during the late eighteenth and early nineteenth centuries, and to the staff of the London Metropolitan Archives, the Public Record Office, and the Southwark, Lambeth, Wandsworth, Greenwich, Islington, and Surrey Local Studies Libraries in the Greater London area, for important genealogical information related to Elizabeth and Mary Hays. We also wish to thank two graduate students at Georgia Southern University, Breanna Harris and Jessica Branton, for their assistance in typing various portions of the text. In particular, Felicity James would like to thank her doctoral student, Emma Probett, for assistance and enlightening discussion of the conduct novel, and her final-year students on the 'Sex and Sensibility' module at the University of Leicester for being such enthusiastic early readers of Lanfear. Timothy Whelan wishes to thank Professor Gina Luria Walker of the New School, New York, for her assistance and encouragement in the publication of this volume and in furthering our knowledge of Mary Hays and her sister, Elizabeth, through reconstructing more expansive models of women's biography. Whelan also wishes to thank Marilyn Gaull of the Editorial Institute, Boston University, who, in her impressive tenure as editor of the *Wordsworth Circle*, has graciously embraced this new exploration of Mary and Elizabeth Hays in the pages of that publication.

CHRONOLOGY FOR ELIZABETH HAYS LANFEAR

1754	Birth of Joanna Hays (d. 1805), eldest sister of Mary and Elizabeth Hays.
1756	Birth of Sarah Hays (d. 1836), sister of Mary and Elizabeth Hays.
1759	Birth of Mary Hays (d. 1843).
1765/66	Birth of Elizabeth Hays. She died in early February 1825, in her 59th year (according to the death entry for the cemetery at St Mary's, Islington); most likely she would have turned 60 in 1825, and thus would have been born in 1765; it is possible, however, that her birthday was in January, and thus she could have turned 59 shortly before her death, placing the year of her birth as 1766.
1768	Birth of John Hays (d. 1862), brother of Mary and Elizabeth Hays.
1772	Birth of Thomas Hays (d. 1856), brother of Mary and Elizabeth Hays.
1773	Birth of Marianna Hays (d. 1797), youngest sister of Mary and Elizabeth Hays.
1774	Death of John Hays, father of Mary and Elizabeth Hays; marriage of Joanna Hays and John Dunkin, Jr (1753–1827), who move next door to Mrs Hays and family in Gainsford Street.
1779–80	Courtship of Mary Hays and John Eccles (1755–80), chronicled in their extensive correspondence, in which Elizabeth Hays appears often.
1783	Publication of John Dunkin, Jr's, *The Divinity of the Son of God, and the Complete Atonement for Sin . . . in a Letter to a Friend*.
1784–86	Publication of several poems and prose pieces by Mary Hays in the *Universal Magazine*.
1788–92	A friendship develops between the daughters of Robert Robinson of Cambridge and Elizabeth and Mary Hays, the latter corresponding with Robinson between 1782 and 1789.
1792	Mary and Elizabeth Hays leave the Baptist chapel in Gainsford Street (Blackfields) and join the Unitarian congregation in Salter's Hall.

CHRONOLOGY FOR ELIZABETH HAYS LANFEAR

1792–95	Friendships and correspondences flourish between Mary and Elizabeth Hays and several leading Unitarian ministers and laypersons, including George Dyer, Hugh Worthington, Jr, Theophilus Lindsey, John Disney, John Evans, and Joseph Priestley.
1792	Mary Hays commences a friendship with Mary Wollstonecraft and publishes her pamphlet, *Cursory Remarks on an Enquiry into the Expediency and Propriety of Public or Social Worship*.
1793	Mary Hays's *Letters and Essays, Moral and Miscellaneous*, appears, with two chapters (fictional tales) composed by Elizabeth Hays.
1794–96	Mary Hays's friendship with William Frend turns into a romantic affair; she also commences her important friendship and correspondence with William Godwin.
1795	In October, Mary Hays leaves her family in Southwark and takes rooms in Kirby Street in the home of Ann Cole; Mary and Elizabeth meet Mary and John Reid of Leicester.
1796	Mary Hays's *Memoirs of Emma Courtney* is published; Elizabeth Hays's first complete draft of *Fatal Errors* is read and critiqued by Mary Wollstonecraft, but not published. Mary Hays commences a five-year career as a contributor to the *Monthly Magazine* and the *Analytical Review*. Marianna Hays marries Edward Palmer in June, and by early fall Mary Hays becomes a resident in their home in John Street.
1797	Elizabeth Hays lives in the family home in Gainsford Street, Southwark; Mary Hays lives with her sister, Marianna, until the latter's death (December 1797), after which she returns to Miss Cole's house in Kirby Street; Mary Wollstonecraft dies in September.
1798	Publication of *Appeal to the Men of Great Britain in behalf of Women*, a feminist tract generally attributed to Mary Hays; Hays begins her long friendship and correspondence with Eliza Fenwick.
1799	Publication of Mary Hays's second novel, *The Victim of Prejudice*; Hays meets Henry Crabb Robinson *c*. March.
1800	In the aftermath of the Charles Lloyd affair, Mary Hays seeks a more retired life in her quarters in Miss Cole's new house in Hatton Garden, where she will stay until 1803; Elizabeth Hays begins a long residence with her brother, John, in Essex; Mary Hays's 'Memoir of Mary Wollstonecraft' appears in Richard Phillips's *Annual Necrology, for 1797–98* (published in 1800).
1801	Mary Hays's biographical sketch of Charlotte Smith appears in Phillips's *Public Characters of 1800–1801*.
1803	Mary Hays moves into her own house at 9 St George's Place, Camberwell, covering her expenses from the proceeds of her important work, *Female Biography* (6 vols); Elizabeth Hays returns to London from Essex and meets Ambrose Lanfear.

CHRONOLOGY FOR ELIZABETH HAYS LANFEAR

1804   Elizabeth Hays and Ambrose Lanfear marry on 14 March at Maldon and move into his house in Islington. Mary Hays, still at Camberwell, publishes *Harry Clinton*, a novel for young readers.

1805   Elizabeth Lanfear's son, John Hays Lanfear, is born on 22 April; Joanna Hays Dunkin, eldest sister of Mary and Elizabeth Hays, dies in December. It is probable Elizabeth Lanfear taught for a time in a local school for young girls; she also composed several articles for publication in a periodical, but they remain untraced.

1806   Mary Hays completes the third volume of Charlotte Smith's *The History of England, from the Earliest Records to the Peace of Amiens* and publishes the first volume of her *Historical Dialogues for Young Persons*. In February she moves from Camberwell to Islington, once again occupying her own house; she later takes in three of John Dunkin Jr's youngest daughters as boarders and students; Elizabeth Lanfear gives birth to her second son, Francis, on 19 September.

1807   Mary Hays publishes the second and third volumes of her *Historical Dialogues*; Eliza Fenwick is a frequent guest of Hays and Lanfear in Islington.

1809   Ambrose Lanfear commits suicide as a result of severe financial setbacks; John Dunkin's daughters return to Essex and Mary Hays leaves Islington for Wandsworth, where she lives for the next four years with her brother, Thomas.

1810   Elizabeth Lanfear and her two sons move into a house in Church Street, Islington, where she is joined by her mother, who assists her daughter in the management of her household; Emma Dunkin and William Hills, a niece and nephew of Mary and Elizabeth, marry and take up residence nearby in Canonbury Square, Islington.

1812   John Hays, younger brother of Mary and Elizabeth, marries Elizabeth Atkinson Breese on 4 April in London; Mrs Hays dies on 5 August and is buried in Southwark; George Wedd and Sarah Dunkin (a niece of Mary Hays and Elizabeth Lanfear), marry on 20 August at Maldon.

1813   Mary Hays leaves her brother's house in Wandsworth and boards for a year with a Mrs Mackie at her school in Oundle, Northamptonshire; Sarah Hays Hills, a widow since 1803, moves with her unmarried daughter, Mary, from the Minories to a house in Felix Terrace, Islington, not far from William and Emma Hills (her son and daughter-in-law) in Canonbury Square, and Elizabeth Lanfear (her sister) in Church Street.

1814   Mary Hays returns to London for several months and then removes to Bristol to board in the home of Penelope Pennington in Dowry Square, Hot Wells, Clifton; Elizabeth Lanfear remains in Church Street, Islington, with her two sons.

CHRONOLOGY FOR ELIZABETH HAYS LANFEAR

1815–16	In Bristol, Mary Hays joins the Committee for the Prudent Man's Friend Society, and, as an outgrowth of her work on the Committee, publishes her dramatic narrative, *The Brothers; or, Consequences: A Story of What Happens Every Day; Addressed to that Most Useful Part of the Community, the Labouring Poor*, printed for and sold by her old friend from Southwark, the Baptist minister William Button.
1817	John Hays Lanfear, Elizabeth's eldest son, dies on 16 August; Mary Hays's novel, *Family Annals, or The Sisters*, is published in London.
1818	Publication of the second edition of Hays's *The Brothers* in London and in Dublin; Emma Dunkin Hills urges her aunt, Elizabeth Lanfear, to publish her manuscript of *Fatal Errors*.
1819	*Fatal Errors; or Poor Mary-Anne. A Tale of the Last Century*, is published in London by A. J. Valpy.
1820	Matilda Mary Hays (d. 1897), niece of Mary and Elizabeth, is born in Doughty Street on 8 September, the daughter of John and Elizabeth Breese Hays.
1821	Publication of Hays's *Memoirs of Queens: Illustrious and Celebrated*, her last known work.
1823	Lanfear is still living in Islington; Mary Hays takes rooms in Vanbrugh Castle, near her two nieces, Sarah Dunkin Francis (1787–1825) and Marianne Dunkin Bennett (b. *c.* 1792).
1824	Publication of Lanfear's *Letters to Young Ladies on their Entrance into the World; to which are added Sketches from Real Life*, and John Hays's *Observations on the Existing Corn Laws*.
1825	Elizabeth Dunkin Francis, living near her aunt Mary Hays at Maze Hill, Greenwich, dies in late January; Elizabeth Hays Lanfear dies in early February and is buried in the church yard at St Mary's, Islington.
1828	Publication of the second edition of Lanfear's *Letters to Young Ladies*.
1843	Mary Hays dies in Clapton, north London, on 19 February and is buried at Abney Park Cemetery, Stoke Newington.
1846	Publication of Matilda Mary Hays's first novel, *Helen Stanley*.
1847	Publication of John Hays's *Remarks on the Late Crisis in the Corn Trade* in 1847; publication of Matilda Mary Hays's translations of *The Works of George Sand*, volumes 1–6, assisted by Eliza Ashurst and Edmund Larken.
1866	Publication of Matilda Mary Hays's last novel, *Adrienne Hope*, ending more than 80 years of publishing by members of the Hays family.

INTRODUCTION

Though Mary Hays is recognized as a major figure among Romantic women writers, her younger sister, Elizabeth, has received little attention, an unfortunate occurrence for women's literary history.[1] In 1796, when Mary Hays and Mary Wollstonecraft were composing *Memoirs of Emma Courtney* and *Maria; or, The Wrongs of Woman*, Elizabeth Hays was also writing a radical novel as she moved with her sister in a circle that included such figures as Wollstonecraft, William Godwin, Thomas Holcroft, George Dyer, Elizabeth Inchbald, Elizabeth Hamilton, Eliza Fenwick, Amelia Alderson, and Mary Robinson. For reasons unknown, Elizabeth Hays did not publish her novel at that time, despite having it critiqued by Wollstonecraft.[2] An 1820 letter to Mary Hays from a Miss Smyth in Bath revealed that Elizabeth's novel had finally been published, but the letter provided no title or date of publication, omissions for which A. F. Wedd, Lanfear's descendant, failed to supply an answer in her publications of Hays's correspondence in the 1920s, allowing the novel to elude detection by literary scholars and historians for nearly another century.[3] As Smyth's letter suggests, Elizabeth Hays's novel, *Fatal Errors; or Poor Mary-Anne*, had indeed been published in London in 1819, with the preface signed 'Eliz. Lanfear', her married name, a major reason for the novel's ability to elude modern scholarship. The novel was never reviewed, and only one known copy exists,[4] two more factors contributing to the novel's obscurity and lack of authorial identity. A year before her death, Elizabeth Hays Lanfear further established herself as an author in her own right with the publication of *Letters to Young Ladies on their Entrance into the World* (1824), with 'Elizabeth Lanfear' appearing on the title page as the 'author of "Fatal Errors", etc', but still without any attribution to her familial relationship with Mary Hays. Had Elizabeth Hays published *Fatal Errors* in 1797 under her name, she would long ago have joined her sister and Wollstonecraft in a select group of women Jacobin novelists, members of Godwin's circle of free-thinking individuals, and important contributors to the developing genre of conduct literature for adolescent girls in the late eighteenth and early nineteenth century. This edition, marking the 200th anniversary of the original publication of *Fatal Errors*, not only situates Elizabeth Hays Lanfear within that circle but, along with her sister, distinguishes her as one

INTRODUCTION

of the first two women novelists in British history to live the entirety of her life as a religious Dissenter.[5]

I

Elizabeth Hays (*c.* 1765–1825) was the daughter of John (1729–1774) and Elizabeth Judge Hays (*c.* 1730–1812). Her elder sisters – Joanna (1754–1805), Sarah (1756–1836), and Mary (1759–1843) – were joined by three younger siblings – John (1768–1862), Thomas (1772–1856), and Marianna (1773–1797).[6] As a mariner and ship's captain, John Hays worked primarily out of the Southwark wharves along Shad Thames, where Mary and Elizabeth Hays were born. They may have attended boarding school in their early years, but no record exists for such an experience.[7] By 1776, two years after her husband's death and about the time of the marriage of Sarah Hays to Thomas Hills (1753–1803), Mrs Hays was operating as a wine merchant out of her home in Gainsford Street, a short street running parallel with Shad Thames to the south and adjacent to the open fields known as 'Blackfields', which bordered Gainsford Street and what was then Fair Street and New Street to the south. This area of Southwark experienced considerable development in the 1770s and 1780s as the businesses and warehouses along the wharves expanded into Gainsford Street and along Shad Thames to the edge of Bermondsey. Among the primary beneficiaries of this development were cornfactors like John Dunkin, Sr (1729–1809), and his son, John Dunkin, Jr (1753–1827), who were also, like the Hays and Hills families, devout Dissenters of the Baptist persuasion, all attending the Blackfields chapel located at the end of Gainsford street during the ministries of John Langford (1765–77) and Michael Brown (1778–1820). Mrs Hays operated as a wine merchant until *c.* 1803, supplementing her income from her husband's legacy through her own labour, something many working-class widows did at this time, especially when unmarried children remained at home well past the normal marrying age. This was particularly apropos to Mrs Hays, for Mary Hays never married; Elizabeth married in 1804 at the age of 39, and John in 1812 at the age of 44.

In their youth, Mary and Elizabeth Hays developed a closeness they did not share with their older sisters Joanna and Sarah, the latter two having children only a few years younger than their two youngest siblings, Thomas and Marianna Hays. Joanna married John Dunkin, Jr, in 1774; their first child, John Hays Dunkin, was born the following year. By 1776, the Dunkins were living next door to Mrs Hays and her children in Gainsford Street; John Dunkin, Jr, would eventually become a deacon in the Gainsford Street chapel and serve as guardian to Mary and Elizabeth and a surrogate father to their three younger siblings. John Dunkin and his brother Christopher, along with William and Sarah Hills, siblings of Thomas Hills, attended Baptist academies in Northampton for boys and girls operated by the Rev. John Collett Ryland (1723–1792) and Martha Trinder (d. 1790), the latter a member of Ryland's Baptist congregation in College Lane.[8] Not long after their marriage, Thomas and Sarah Hays Hills moved across the Thames to the Minories, just above Tower Hill, where their first child was born in 1777. The Hills transferred their memberships from the Baptist chapel in Gainsford Street to the Independent congregation at White Row, Spitalfields, the same congregation that was home to the family of Benjamin Flower (1755–1829), another classmate at Northampton with the Dunkin and Hills children who later became the politically radical publisher of the *Cambridge Intelligencer* and was known to Mary Hays and other members of the Godwin circle in the 1790s.[9] Flower and the young people from Gainsford Street were joined at Ryland's academy by William Button (1754–1821), who in 1775 became minister to the Particular Baptist congregation in Dean Street, Southwark (where the Dunkin and Hays families most likely attended in the 1790s) and who later published Mary Hays's short moral-didactic work, *The Brothers* (1815).[10]

The little that is known of Elizabeth Hays's youth is derived from the correspondence that passed between Mary Hays and her ill-fated lover, John Eccles (1755–1780), between 1779 and 1780. Elizabeth appears 14 times in these letters, nearly always as 'Betsy' (Mary was known as 'Polly', both common nicknames at the time). Elizabeth was about 14 when Hays and Eccles commenced their correspondence; her main role was to stealthily convey the forbidden letters between the two lovers, for they did not receive familial approval until just prior to Eccles's death. At times, letters were abruptly ended by Eccles, conscious that his messenger Elizabeth might be forced to leave with the letter still unfinished, for fear her presence outside his window or absence from her home would be noticed by other family members. Mary Hays's usual ploy was to lean a book against her bedroom window and then walk by Eccles's window, after which he would know that Elizabeth would soon be bringing him a letter. When Elizabeth was ill, the flow of letters would temporarily cease, much to the couple's chagrin. Since Eccles could not always engage Hays in public without drawing unwanted attention to his interest in her, he would often walk home from church with Elizabeth, using her as a conduit for his thoughts about her sister and gaining similar insights from Elizabeth about Mary's thoughts and feelings towards him. Her services were so appreciated by Eccles that he wrote to Mary Hays on 4 August 1779:

> I am much affected with Miss Betsy's generous and kind offices; they convince me, I have not formed a wrong opinion of her; how seldom is the confidence, how rarely the friendship of those of her age to be depended on: may she be rewarded according to her desert; may she never feel distress like mine; if she should, may she find some pitying friend to assist her, and alleviate her affliction.[11]

Elizabeth sometimes relayed news concerning Mary's health and at other times served as a convenient chaperone for the flirtatious couple who cleverly sought ways to escape the confines and suspicious eyes of Gainsford Street for other

INTRODUCTION

locales more romantic and free, such as Greenwich Park, Vauxhall Gardens, Lark Hall in Lambeth, or the gardens at St Helena in nearby Rotherhithe.[12]

Nothing is known of Elizabeth Hays's activities during the 1780s, for she is absent from the letters that passed between Mary Hays and Robert Robinson (1735–1790), the controversial Baptist minister at Cambridge, although he, along with various members of his family, visited the Hayses in Gainsford Street on several occasions in the 1780s and knew many of their Southwark friends among the Particular Baptists. By 1790 Elizabeth had joined her sister in sharing friendships with Robinson's daughters, especially Mary Robinson and her husband Samuel Brown, a wine merchant, after their settlement in London in the late 1780s. Though raised as Calvinistic Baptists in the chapel in Gainsford Street, by the early 1790s Mary and Elizabeth Hays had embraced Unitarianism and 'rational Christianity', with Robert Robinson serving as one of their primary influences. Their two older sisters, however, remained evangelical Calvinists (Joanna a Particular Baptist and Sarah an Independent), as did their youngest sister, Marianna, the latter clearly protected by the watchful eye of Mrs Hays and John Dunkin, Jr.

Between 1791 and 1795, Mary and Elizabeth Hays moved among some of London's leading Unitarian ministers and laypersons, such as Joseph Johnson (1738–1809), George Dyer (1755–1841), William Frend (1757–1841), Theophilus Lindsey (1723–1808), John Disney (1746–1816), Robert Winter (1762–1833), Hugh Worthington, Jr (1752–1813) (Mary and Elizabeth joined his congregation at Salter's Hall in 1792), John Evans (1767–1827) (Elizabeth would maintain a connection with Evans and his congregation at Worship Street into the 1820s), and, after 1799, with Henry Crabb Robinson (1775–1867). Elizabeth Hays appears five times in Worthington's letters between November 1791 and September 1792. On 15 November 1791, Worthington praises the two sisters for their 'united kindness', promising 'to assist y^r enquiries after truth in general, or the sense of Revelation in particular', fully aware as a liberal Dissenting minister that 'no 2 persons think exactly alike in every point of moral & theological opinion, & it is not necessary they should. Let us agree to differ. Unity in charity is much better than unity in sentiment'.[13] In a similar nod to their budding ecumenism, Ann Robinson, daughter of Robert Robinson, noted the following May the importance of the Hays sisters joining Worthington's congregation and of the similarity of his religious opinions in relation to those of 'the great Priestley's', insuring their freedom 'from that load of superstition and errour which is abroad in the world' and keeping their minds 'superior to vulgar errours, and popular prejudice'.[14] Worthington drank tea with the two sisters in Gainsford Street in July 1792, and that August, after reading a manuscript version of Hays's *Letters and Essays, Moral and Miscellaneous* (published in 1793), recommended Hays proceed with the book and 'get y^r sister to dip her pen in ye same inkstand'.[15] Elizabeth Hays would heed her pastor's advice and composed two tales that her sister inserted into *Letters and Essays*: 'Cleora, or the Misery attending unsuitable Connections' and 'Josepha, or the Pernicious Effects of Early Indulgence', both tales reprinted in this volume (see Appendix A). Worthington wrote to the two sisters again in September 1792, during a visit to his parents at Leicester, and in May 1793, after the publication of *Letters and Essays*, he requested Hays to 'tell [her] sister Authoress, & in so doing tell y^rself, that a *venerable old Critic* pronounced a high Encomium on the good sense & good stile of y^r late volume';[16] quite a compliment for two single women in Southwark to receive from Worthington's father, Hugh Worthington, Sr (1712–1797), minister at the Great Meeting in Leicester from 1743 to 1797, the same congregation in which Mary Reid (1769–1839), who became a friend of Mary and Elizabeth Hays in 1795, worshiped until 1807.

Upon his arrival in London from Cambridge in 1792, George Dyer, a former associate of Robert Robinson and member of his congregation in St Andrew's Street, became a frequent companion and correspondent of Mary and Elizabeth Hays. On two occasions he escorted them from Gainsford Street to Joseph Priestley's home in Hackney for afternoon tea, once in late January 1793 and again in February 1794, the latter instance accompanied by William Frend, Mary Hays's future lover, shortly before Priestley's immigration to America.[17] Previous to her introduction to Frend that year (he too had been an associate of Robert Robinson at Cambridge during his time as a fellow at Jesus College), the two had corresponded just after the publication of her *Cursory Remarks on an Enquiry into the Expediency and Propriety of Public or Social Worship* (1792), a copy of which had been given to Frend by their mutual friend, Samuel Brown, Robert Robinson's son-in-law.[18] Hays's formal introduction to Frend led to an on-again, off-again romantic relationship that lasted for more than a decade, ending with his marriage to Sarah Blackburne in 1808.

From Frend to Godwin was a logical progression for Mary Hays in 1794. A few weeks after her first meeting with Godwin, she invited him on 1 January 1795 to a family dinner at the home of her brother-in-law, John Dunkin, Jr, at 2 Paragon Place, Walworth, hoping that Godwin would respond quickly enough for her to have the 'opportunity of making a Brother & Sister participators in the satisfaction I promise myself'.[19] Hays had left the family home in Gainsford Street sometime in late summer or early autumn 1794 and moved in with the Dunkins in their spacious residence at the Paragon, along what was then known as Surrey Road (Kent Road today), a lavish crescent of large townhouses linked by Coadestone colonnades and built by the Southwark architect, Michael Searles (1750–1813), who seems to have developed a connection with the Dunkin and Hays family in the 1790s.[20] Between 1790 and 1796, Joanna Dunkin bore four children, which explains the need for the larger home and Mary's presence to assist in the care of such a large family (nine children). Mrs Hays, along with Elizabeth, Marianna, Thomas, and John, remained at Gainsford Street, probably Elizabeth's first extended separation from her older sister. As Mary Hays's letter reveals, Elizabeth and one of her brothers appeared more than willing to walk to the Paragon for dinner with Godwin that January evening in 1795.

Other Unitarian friends of the Hays sisters at this time included the bookseller/publisher Joseph Johnson, who, like Mary and Elizabeth, was a former Particular Baptist; the poet Ann Batten Christall (1769–1848), whose subscribers to *Poetical*

INTRODUCTION

Sketches (published by Johnson in 1795) included Mary, Elizabeth, and either John or Thomas Hays;[21] Dr John Reid (1773–1822) of Leicester, who visited London with his sister, Mary, in 1795 and settled there late in 1798, both Reids becoming friends of the Hays sisters and moving in the Godwin circle; and a young Henry Crabb Robinson (1775–1867), who met Mary Hays in early spring 1799 and who recorded much of her history and that of her sister Elizabeth in his diary, letters, and reminiscences.[22] Two other individuals from Norfolk are also worth mentioning: Thomas Martin, the Congregationalist minister turned Unitarian who later relocated to Liverpool;[23] and Stephen Weaver Browne (*c*. 1769–1832), an Anglican who became a Dissenting minister and whose friends included Mary and Elizabeth Hays as well as Amelia Alderson, Robert Southey, Samuel Taylor Coleridge, John Tobin, and Charles Lloyd.[24] Lloyd (1775–1839) was originally from Birmingham and lived for a time with Coleridge in the West Country; he published *Poems on Various Subjects* in 1795, which Mary Hays presented to Reid upon her departure from London for Leicester in January 1797. By 1798 he was living in London and had met Hays and many of the young Romantic figures residing there, including Browne and John Reid. He would have an ugly public encounter with Hays in late 1798 and charge her with scandalous behaviour that greatly damaged her reputation into the next century.[25]

Elizabeth Hays experienced a second separation from her older sister in October 1795 when Mary Hays left the Dunkin home at the Paragon and moved across the Thames into the Kirby Street home of Ann Cole, a single woman like Hays who had assumed the business of her recently deceased father, George Cole, a long-time engraver and printer to the Bank of England.[26] Now, either for financial or social reasons (few women lived alone at this time), Cole decided to take in at least one boarder in the person of Mary Hays. Elizabeth Hays remained at the Gainsford Street home with her mother and two unmarried brothers (Marianna appears to have taken Mary Hays's place at the Paragon with the Dunkins). Nevertheless, Elizabeth Hays maintained close contact with her sister and her many friends within the Godwin circle despite the expanded geographical distance created by Mary's departure from Southwark. Godwin's diary entries are cryptic at times, and his references to Mary Hays usually suggest that during his visits she was the only Hays present ('Miss Hayes'), but on many occasions Godwin writes 'Miss Hayes's', which could be merely the possessive use of her name or a way of suggesting that both Mary and Elizabeth were present.

Elizabeth most likely appeared with her sister for tea with Godwin on 29 January and on 14 May 1795, for, given their dates, both events would have occurred in the Dunkin home at the Paragon during Mary Hays's residence there. The May meeting was shared with a bevy of individuals known to both sisters, including William Frend, George Dyer, and Stephen Weaver Browne. Others present were denoted by Godwin as '&c', such as John Dunkin and his wife or Mrs Hays and Marianna Hays, whose presence as orthodox Baptists surrounded by Unitarians and a famous sceptic formed a fitting gloss to Godwin's closing comment about

xvii

there being much 'talk of God' that day. Godwin dined at the 'Hayes's' again on 24 August 1795, most likely another meeting in the Dunkin home at the Paragon or the Gainsford Street home with Mrs Hays and family. After Mary Hays moved to Kirby Street in October 1795, Godwin's visits increased due to his close proximity. Elizabeth Hays would not have been present at all of those meetings since she was still living in Southwark. She appears to be present, however, on Thursday, 9 June 1796, when Godwin has tea at 'Hayes's, w. Wolstencraft [Mary Wollstonecraft], A. A. [Amelia Alderson], Brown [Stephen Weaver Browne], Tookes [William Tooke, Jr and his father, most likely] & Hayes's [suggesting both Mary and Elizabeth]'. A similar reference to the 'Hayes's' and 'Tookes' occurs on 12 November 1796, this time with Elizabeth Hamilton and Wollstonecraft present as well. On 13 August 1797 Godwin writes that 'Hayses dine', another indication that both sisters were present with him.[27]

In the year after Mary Hays's removal from South London to Kirby Street, several other changes occurred in the Hays household that affected Elizabeth's situation. In December 1796, Thomas Hays married Elizabeth Dunkin (*c.* 1775–1832), half-sister to his brother-in-law, John Dunkin. Thomas and his new wife lived in Gainsford Street for a time, most likely sharing the family home with Elizabeth and possibly John Hays. Mrs Hays appears to have moved in with the Dunkins at the Paragon (she is absent from the Poor Rate Books for Gainsford Street between 1796 and 1798) after the marriage that June of Marianna Hays, Elizabeth's youngest sister, to Edward Palmer (1770–1831), a marriage that formed a connection between the Hays family and the Palmers of Walworth that would continue into the 1840s. In June 1798, Edward's brother, Nathaniel (1774–1840), married Joanna Dunkin (b. *c.* 1777), John Dunkin's daughter and Mary and Elizabeth Hays's eldest niece. Edward's other brother, Samuel (1775–1848), became the father of Samuel Palmer, Jr (1805–1881), the Romantic artist and friend of William Blake and acquaintance of Crabb Robinson.[28] Edward and Marianna Palmer settled into a house in John Street, a short street extending south from Doughty Street to Theobalds Road (what was then known as Kings Road), running parallel with Grays Inn Road.[29] In the fall of 1796, Mary Hays left Miss Cole and moved in with the Palmers (they were only a short distance from Kirby Street), most likely answering a call for help from her youngest sister because of a pregnancy. What happened after that is not fully known, but things did not go well. Marianna died in early December 1797, only three months after Mary Hays witnessed the death of Mary Wollstonecraft under similar circumstances.[30] By mid-December 1797, Hays was back at Miss Cole's, and not long thereafter Mrs Hays returned from the Paragon to the family home in Gainsford Street, with Thomas Hays taking a separate residence nearby.

In 1798, John Dunkin moved his family from the Paragon in Walworth to a mansion in Champion Hill, Camberwell, a new development inhabited by wealthy London merchants and professional men.[31] During the 1790s, he and his father (they were both cornfactors and owned businesses along Shad Thames) purchased several farms around Chelmsford and Maldon and at least one mill in Essex (Beeleigh), acquisitions that became central to their business endeavours.

INTRODUCTION

John Dunkin, Jr, grew wealthy from his business and retired in 1804 to Woodham-Mortimer Lodge in Essex, not far from Maldon, where five of his remaining daughters, as well as Elizabeth Hays, were married in the parish chapel. Between 1801 and 1806, John Hays lived primarily at Chelmsford, probably managing Dunkin's farms and mills and building his own business as a cornfactor. For a portion of that time (1801–3) Elizabeth Hays lived with him and was prepared, she confessed to her sister, to live with him thereafter as the domestic head of his household had they both remained single. Writing to Mary Hays on 4 February 1801, one of three letters by Elizabeth Hays to her sister that have survived within the Hays Correspondence (see Appendix C for the texts of these letters), she laments how necessity requires 'old maids' to live with either their mothers, brothers, or another female companion:

> Though I have now no wish to change it, I perfectly agree with you in pronouncing a state of celibacy to be but little favourable either to virtue or happiness – I wonder not that old maids generally speaking have been objects of censure or ridicule – Perhaps there is no character, which it is so difficult for a woman to maintain with propriety. . . . Pride (& it may be want of that very soft sensibility which some of my sex possess) will now preserve me from one of those evils, whether I shall entirely escape the other time & future events must determine.[32]

She continues with an even more poignant passage, especially given her sister's persistent emotional scars from her long-running relationship with William Frend:

> There are more or less I should suppose in the life of every one particularly trying periods, periods in which the mind undergoes a sort of revolution. The last two or three years *has* been one of those to me. – The struggle is over, & now that I have resigned for ever the sweet illusions of youth, I shall endeavour to reconcile my mind to the world as it is, & daily more & more cultivate a taste for those rational & simple pleasures, which if they do not afford any very lively interest, leave no sting behind. It is well as you observe that each prefers his own burthen to that of his neighbour. I wish not to be again under the dominion of the passions, & would not for worlds exchange my situation for yours.

Elizabeth closed her letter with a warning about withdrawing from polite circles of sociability (the aftermath of the Lloyd affair), especially for those who, like her sister, did not move easily within society's norms, sentiments that would surface later in Elizabeth's letter, 'On the Single Life', in *Letters to Young Ladies* (see Appendix B):

> I am sorry the unmerited calumny you have incurred should have given you a distaste to general society – The narrow cir[cles] to which most

women are confined is [I] believe one great cause of their unhappiness and of their errors. I seldom go into company my self, however averse I may have been to making the effort, without finding my self the better for it. The more we see of, & compare the different lots of our fellow creatures, the less we are inclined to repine at our own & the more we expand our feelings in general benevolence, the less danger there is our becoming a prey to concentrated passion, or selfish misanthropy – both of which originate in the same sourse [sic] – *Sickly & Distorted Sensibility*.

Elizabeth's letter reveals a penetrating intellect and unabashed individualism that establishes her as a fitting counterpart to Mary Hays and the other women who circulated around Godwin and Wollstonecraft during the previous decade. Her critique of her sister, however, would soon reverberate in a strangely prophetic way in her own life.

Elizabeth Hays returned to London in 1803, most likely joining her mother at the Dunkins' home in Champion Hill, for that year Mrs Hays disappeared from the Poor Rate books in Gainsford Street. She retained ownership of the family home until her death in 1812, when it may have passed on to one of her sons or to George Wedd, her nephew, or was sold as part of her estate. Mary Hays stayed at Champion Hill on several occasions, probably because her mother was there as well as several of the Dunkin children with whom Hays had been close since their birth in the early 1790s. To maintain that closeness even more, in 1803 Hays left Hatton Garden for a house of her own in South London at 9 St George's Place, Camberwell, not far from Elephant and Castle along Walworth Road about halfway between Blackfriars Bridge to the north and Champion Hill to the south. This marks an important epoch in Hays's life, for now she could experience the independence she had so desired since her initial departure from Gainsford Street and the Dunkins' home at the Paragon in 1795. That year she wrote to Godwin, explaining to him that her radical decision to leave home was driven by

> the idea of *being free*, a wish to break by the *necessity* of greater exertion, (I acknowledge the weakness which this implies) & even by local change, certain fatal, connected, trains of thinking, a desire of strengthening my mind by standing alone, & of relieving the relations I love of the burthen of my wayward fancies, also, I will own, a latent hope of enjoying, occasionally, more of the intercourse & conversation that pleases me.[33]

Mary Hays relied on a small annuity and monies from her publications to pay her bills during her time in Camberwell (1803–6) and later in Islington (1806–9), after which she would never live in such an independent manner again.

Elizabeth Hays's situation also changed in 1803, for that year she became engaged to Ambrose Lanfear (*c.* 1750–1809), a man who had already buried two wives. While visiting friends or relations at Ingatestone, Essex, that August, she informed her sister about the 'prospect of a change in my situation, which on the maturest reflection & deliberation entirely meets with my approbation',[34] fully aware of the shock it would produce and, possibly, some pain as well for her sister. Elizabeth Hays was introduced to Ambrose Lanfear by her niece, Joanna Dunkin Palmer, who lived in Aldermanbury, in the City of London. At the time of Elizabeth's first meeting with Lanfear, he was living at 4 Upper Terrace, Islington, the only Lanfear listed in *Holden's 1805 London Directory*. He was a freeman of the Cordwainer Company and operated as a haberdasher at 32 Cheapside from the 1780s until his death in 1809. His first marriage was to Sarah Smith on 7 June 1781, a marriage that produced one son, also named Ambrose (1787–1870). After the death of his first wife, Lanfear married Sarah Stanfield (Stanfeld) (*c.* 1767–1802) on 21 July 1792. The marriage produced one son, Joseph (b. 1795), prior to Sarah's death on 10 April 1802.[35] At the time of Elizabeth Hays's letter to Mary Hays (August 1803), both sons were living with their father, provoking Elizabeth to remark to her sister that she was now ready to 'perform every duty, & love those boys . . . so pathetically recommended to my attention'.[36]

In her letter, dated 14 August 1803, Elizabeth Hays offers her sister, who must have been reading with some level of surprise and, given Elizabeth's age, no small degree of apprehension, an initial critique of her future husband:

> M[r] L appears to be a man of virtuous principles, liberal sentiments & good, though not a polish'd understanding but if I am not deceived in him he possesses what is still dearer to me, an excellent temper, & great sensibility of heart – goodness seems to be his characteristic, as I believe it is that of every branch of his family, to all of whom, M[rs] J Dunkin & Martha Lanfear in particular, I feel more than ever inclined to attach my self. . . . [W]ould to God that you were happy, calmly rationally happy, it is an alloy to my own satisfaction that you are not so. My heart is too full of complicated & various emotions to permit me to say any more.[37]

Besides the allusion to her sister's ongoing relationship with William Frend, the preceding passage reveals the extensive familial network Elizabeth and her sister enjoyed throughout their adult lives. 'M[rs] J. Dunkin' is not Elizabeth's older sister Joanna but rather Sarah Francis Dunkin, who in 1799 married Elizabeth's nephew, John Hays Dunkin (1775–1858), eldest son of John and Joanna Hays Dunkin. The younger Dunkins lived for a time at Beeleigh, near Maldon, Essex, and most likely grew close to Elizabeth during her time in Essex when she lived with her brother John. Sarah Francis Dunkin was the sister of Henry Francis (1781–1857), who married Elizabeth Dunkin (1787–1825), Sarah's sister, on 17 May 1803, a few months before the composition of the above letter. It appears Henry Francis knew Ambrose Lanfear prior to the latter's engagement to Elizabeth Hays, as did his sister-in-law, Joanna Dunkin Palmer.[38]

INTRODUCTION

Elizabeth Hays married Ambrose Lanfear at Maldon, Essex, on 14 March 1804, and settled into his home in Upper Terrace, Islington. She soon gave birth to two sons: John Hays Lanfear on 22 April 1805, and Francis Lanfear on 19 September 1806.[39] During these two years, many changes occurred in her extended family. Within a year of her removal to Woodham-Mortimer Lodge in Essex, Joanna Hays Dunkin, her eldest sister, died in December 1805, leaving John Dunkin, Jr, with several young daughters still at home. His retirement to Essex, however, allowed Elizabeth's brother, John, to return to London, where he took a house at 54 Great Coram Street, near Brunswick Square, and signed in the Poor Rate Books for Islington for a second house at 3 Park Street (actually 'Park Place' according to the Rate Book), a row of houses located at the west end of Park Street facing what was then known as Back Street (currently Liverpool Street).[40] In mid-February 1806 Mary Hays, along with her servant from Camberwell, moved into the Park Street house, only a short distance from her sister Elizabeth, who was just beginning her second pregnancy (which may have been a motivating factor for Hays's removal to Islington). Shortly after her arrival at Park Street, Mary Hays informed Crabb Robinson that he would still find her, 'as at Camberwell, surrounded not by affluence & elegance, but by cleanliness, external comforts & exact order; & these, I believe, in a degree, I should still retain, though in a garret or in a clay-built cot'.[41]

Elizabeth Lanfear's house may have been similarly modest, for her husband's business habits never gained him the financial security John Dunkin enjoyed. This may explain comments by George Dyer in an undated letter (*c.* spring 1806) to the editors of the publishing firm of Vernor and Hood concerning Lanfear's interest in supplementing her family income through writing. Some time prior to his letter, Dyer had introduced Lanfear to the editors and told them she had prepared a body of material, under the signature 'E. L.', that she wished to send them. 'With respect to this Lady', Dyer writes,

> I have not been acquainted with her or her literary pursuits for some years: but when I formerly was more acquainted with her, I thought very favourably of her genius, from some early specimens, and I knew her to be seriously employed in literary pursuits, and from what her brother said, I concluded that she had been much so employed since I had the pleasure of more acquaintance with her. How her papers may have been received I know not: – I think she and I should differ now in our sentiments in many subjects; but still I think well of her intentions and her abilities: tho' I think it very probable, that she is engaged so much in her school, (the principal labour of w[ch] lies on her) as well as by her attention to an afflicted sister who perhaps may now be dead,) that she may not be able to answer either her own expectations, or yours; – She expressed some fears of this kind by letter before I left London – Be these matters as they may, I was influenced by the kindest motives in introducing her to you, supposing it would be the means of engaging her in some

agreeable exercises in her own way, and that some time or other literary engagements might be formed between you and her, which might prove mutually agreeable and beneficial.[42]

Her lack of response to Dyer and the editors might have been precipitated by the fatal illness of Joanna Dunkin the previous December, or possibly from the demands of teaching, in which, Dyer implies, she was currently or had recently been employed, or from her first pregnancy and, by the time of Dyer's letter, her second pregnancy. Most likely the latter was the reason for her lack of response, for her second pregnancy would have terminated her teaching and writing by the spring of 1806, not long after Mary Hays's arrival in Islington. No publications by Lanfear from this period have surfaced, nor is there any record of Lanfear operating a school in Islington. It is more probable that Lanfear taught for a time at a boarding school for young ladies located just a few doors down from her residence in Upper Terrace and operated for many years by Alice Flowerdew (1759–1830), a widow and writer best known for her *Poems, on Moral and Religious Subjects* (1803), a volume that circulated widely within London's Dissenting community. Flowerdew and the Lanfears attended the General Baptist meeting in Worship Street during the ministry of Mary Hays's friend and correspondent from the 1790s, John Evans.[43] Dyer's letter provides both a fascinating account of Lanfear *c.* 1806 as well as evidence of his continued appreciation of his friendships from the previous decade with Elizabeth and Mary Hays.

About the time Elizabeth Lanfear ceased teaching, Mary Hays informally entered the same profession, supplementing her income by writing historical texts for young readers and by taking in as boarders and pupils in late 1806 or early 1807 the three youngest (and now motherless) teenage daughters of John Dunkin – Emma (b. *c.* 1792), Sarah (1793–1875), and Marianne (b. *c.* 1795). They remained with her through the end of 1808.[44] They may have boarded previously at Flowerdew's finishing school and, if Lanfear did indeed teach there, could easily have been instructed by Lanfear herself prior to her second pregnancy. If so, the three girls would have been transferred only a short distance away to Mary Hays's house to finish their education. During these years, Eliza Fenwick and Crabb Robinson walked on several occasions to Islington to see Hays and Lanfear. Fenwick called at the Lanfears in Upper Terrace one day in early April 1806, and that October proposed making another visit to Hays but wanted to make sure it would be a convenient time for she did not wish 'to rob M[rs] Lanfear of you on the day of y[r] usual visit there', which would seem to suggest that Lanfear was not employed at that time.[45] Crabb Robinson visited Hays on Sunday, 4 May 1806, and after church ate at Hays's home with one of Ambrose Lanfear's sons (which one is unclear). Two weeks later he visited Hays again and they all drank tea with Ambrose Lanfear, Sr.[46] In 1809, having accomplished her mission with her nieces, Hays left Islington and moved into Thomas Hays's large home on Wandsworth Common, near Clapham, where she would stay until 1813 when she removed to a school for girls in Oundle, Northamptonshire, living there for a year as a boarder,

INTRODUCTION

not a teacher. While in Wandsworth, Hays tutored several of her brother's young children, especially his daughter Elizabeth (b. 1801), a role Hays was now adept at fulfilling. She even served as a surrogate mother/teacher for Orlando Fenwick (1798–1816), Eliza Fenwick's son, during his time as a boarder at Mr. Wilkinson's school near Wandsworth in 1811–12.[47]

Hays's removal from Islington coincided with another major event in Elizabeth Lanfear's life. In February 1809 Ambrose Lanfear committed suicide due to a series of financial setbacks and an impending bankruptcy. In Crabb Robinson's Reminiscences for 1809 (written on 22 August 1848), after recording a visit to Anna Letitia Barbauld (who had recently lost her husband due to drowning as a result of his dementia, a death Robinson describes as 'a relief to her'), Robinson was reminded of the suicide of Ambrose Lanfear that same year due to a 'commercial embarrassment'.[48] Eliza Fenwick would not learn about 'poor Mrs Lanfear' until July 1810, wondering if the suicide was the reason for Mary Hays's recent silence as a correspondent. 'Were your circumstances or your spirits so affected by that event as to induce you to quit or change the nature of your home?' she writes to Hays at Wandsworth.[49] Whether Mary Hays's circumstances were affected by the event is not known, but Elizabeth Hays's situation was altered dramatically. She was now single, like her sister Mary; a widow, like her mother and sister Sarah; and, like Eliza Fenwick, a single mother attempting to maintain two children but without the financial means necessary to live as comfortably as she wished.

Lanfear's familial deprivation soon ended, for Mrs Hays (who may have been living with her son Thomas and whose place was now taken by Mary Hays) removed to Islington, most likely to assist her daughter in the care of her two young boys in her new residence in Church Street, a short distance from Upper Terrace and just below St Mary's Church. In 1810, Emma Dunkin, one of Elizabeth's three nieces who had lived with Mary Hays in Park Place *c*. 1806–08, married her cousin William Hills (b. 1784), the son of Sarah Hays Hills. They soon moved into a new home in Canonbury Square, a beautifully preserved square in the heart of Islington on the south side of Upper Street, about three blocks from the house where Mary Hays had once lived at the end of Park Street. In April 1812 Lanfear's familial connections further expanded with the marriage of John Hays, her brother, to Elizabeth Atkinson Breese (*c*. 1781–1832) (her second marriage), followed by their removal to a spacious home at the Paragon in Blackheath.[50] A few months later, a third event occurred, the death of Mrs Elizabeth Hays at the age of 81. When her will was proved in January 1813, Mary Hays and Elizabeth Lanfear each received £800, enabling them to maintain their independence with more security and ease than they experienced prior to Mrs Hays's death.[51] That same year, Sarah Hays Hills, a widow for 10 years at this point, left her home in the Minories and, with her unmarried daughter Mary (1792–1832), settled at 5 Felix Terrace, Islington, a short distance from her son and daughter-in-law in Canonbury Square and her sister in Church Street.

INTRODUCTION

Shortly after the death of Mrs Hays, a significant reference to Elizabeth Lanfear appears in Crabb Robinson's diary. In September 1812, Robinson attended a dinner party in the Bermondsey home of the newlyweds George Wedd (1785–1854) and Sarah Dunkin (1793–1875). Wedd was a nephew of John Towill Rutt (1760–1841), a friend of and distant relation of Crabb Robinson, and Sarah was one of the three daughters of John Dunkin, Jr, who had lived with Mary Hays in Islington. Robinson was accompanied by two friends, Mordecai Andrews III (1781–1821) and his sister, Eliza Julia Andrews (1792–1861), a nephew and niece of J. T. Rutt and cousins of George Wedd. Eliza Julia would later join a party of immigrants to America in 1817 led by George Flower (1786–1862), Benjamin Flower's nephew, who married her along the way to Illinois, despite the fact that he was still married to his first wife in England, an indiscretion for which Robinson never forgave Eliza Julia Andrews.[52] Robinson writes on 5 September 1812:

> At 4 Mord: And[rews]: drove me in a gig to Geo. Wedd's with whom I dined his bride looked exceedingly well And Harriet Wedd his Sister very pretty. Miss Hill[s], the other brides maid a very agreeable girl. There were besides Mr Hill[s] a nephew of Miss Hayes & Mr Lanfere [sic] the Son in Law of Miss H. I was not much pleased with either; H. is a coarse man in language & manrs but is good humoured ... L. has more stuff in him. He has travelled And Miss H. speaks of him very highly for his exemplary conduct to his Mother in law [Elizabeth Lanfear] in very trying Situations; but he is forward & makes pretensions beyond what he is entitled to – It was a day of effort. I resolved to amuse myself & others And I believe I succeeded. Andrews drove me & his Sister home late[.][53]

William Hills arrived at the party that day accompanied by his unmarried sister, Mary, and their friend, Ambrose Lanfear, Jr, Elizabeth Lanfear's unmarried stepson. Fourteen years later Lanfear, Jr, would marry Mary Hills and shortly thereafter immigrate to New York, where she died on 9 February 1832 from complications arising from the birth of her daughter, Emily Francis Lanfear (1832–1917). Ambrose Lanfear would later remove to New Orleans, where he became a prominent banker.

Elizabeth Lanfear suffered a second family tragedy on 16 August 1817, when her eldest son, John, died just prior to his 13th birthday. The news traveled quickly through the various circles of her family and friends, even reaching Miss Smyth, Mary Hays's Irish friend who had been a fellow boarder with her at Penelope Pennington's home in Bristol during Hays's residence there between 1814 and 1817. Smyth wrote to Hays on 4 November 1817, asking to be remembered to Lanfear and hoped 'that by this time her grief has subsided and that the very promising child that remains will console her for the one she has lost'.[54] Smyth's next letter, dated 9 January 1818, was sent to Hays at the Gainsford Street residence of

INTRODUCTION

George Wedd and family, not far from Thomas Hays's home in Mill Street, Dockhead. 'I was delighted', Smyth writes,

> with your manner of passing your time at your nieces [Sarah Wedd] & look on it as one of I trust many advantages of your present residence that you are within reasonable distance of your own family so many of whom appear to be both estimable & agreeable I hope your sister has by this time recovered her health & spirits[.][55]

Lanfear continued to make news in the West Country, but not because of her personal problems. On 21 February 1820, Smyth wrote again to Hays, this time from Bath, confessing that she was 'surprized to hear' that Lanfear 'had commenced authoress I am sure whatever she wrote would be marked with good sense & good feeling. I have not been able to procure her book but the libraries here I do not think so good or at least so well regulated as Barrys at Bristol', the first reference to Elizabeth Hays Lanfear as a published writer in the correspondence of Mary Hays and the first reference to her as a writer in any capacity since comments by Wollstonecraft in two of her letters to Mary Hays in 1796 and the George Dyer letter of 1806.[56]

A few months later, Crabb Robinson dined with the family of John Hays in his home in Doughty Street, not far from Brunswick Square, joined by Lanfear and her surviving son, Francis. Robinson's diary entry is surprisingly negative concerning the widow-turned-feminist novelist (most likely he had seen or heard of her novel), their conversation that day reminding Robinson of similar conversations he shared with Mary Hays and her friends during their radical phase in the late 1790s. After commenting on her son, he wrote the following about Elizabeth Lanfear on 5 May 1820:

> His mother did not please me. She is a *radical* And offensively violent in the expression of her opinions – A vulgar declaimer, adopting all the commonplace notions So that the very words were familiar to me – There is an unfeminine severity in her manner as well as a char[r] of her opinions themselves not suited to the fair sex so that she gave me no pleasure – But she is a strong minded clever woman I have no doubt.[57]

Given Robinson's devoted friendship with Mary Hays and his frequent avowal of her intellect and character, his critique of Lanfear as 'unfeminine' seems more apropos of Richard Polwhele's harsh description of Hays in *The Unsex'd Females* (1798) than Robinson's usually sympathetic appreciation of strong-minded women in his diary and letters. Possibly Lanfear's novel and her conversation that day reminded Robinson of a time he now viewed through a more conservative political and social lens, judging her radicalism in 1820 more harshly than he did her sister's in 1799. Eliza Fenwick, a former radical herself, was more sympathetic, for hardships had altered her perspective on life considerably, leaving her

INTRODUCTION

ample empathy for Lanfear (Fenwick had lost her only son, Orlando, in 1816). Fenwick closed her letter to Mary Hays in December 1821 with condolences concerning the death of Hays's niece, Sarah Wheeler, and that of Lanfear's son, adding, 'who than myself can more truly appreciate their affliction'.[58]

By 7 November 1824, Robinson's attitude towards Lanfear had softened. During a visit to Mary Hays at Vanbrugh Castle in Greenwich, where she lived between 1823 and 1832 as a boarder in a school operated by Robert Browne and his wife, Robinson discovered that Lanfear 'has a cancer And it threatens her with an early death. Probably it is of a . . . malignant nature. . . . At least the surgeons hold a much more serious language about it'.[59] On 1 January 1825, he visited Hays again, this time in the home of William and Emma Hills in Canonbury Square, the same William Hills that Robinson had met at George Wedd's home in September 1812. Hays was in Islington to see her dying sister, who, Robinson would later write in his diary, 'is still alive but in a deplorable state'.[60] A month later, on 6 February, he walked to Greenwich and found 'Miss Hays in deep affliction at the death of her niece M^{rs} [Elizabeth Dunkin] Francis, and the dying condition of her sister Mrs Lanfere [sic] – rather a melancholy visit'.[61] Henry and Elizabeth Dunkin Francis had moved to Maze Hill, Greenwich, adjacent to Vanbrugh Castle, in 1819, joined by William and Marianne Bennett, Elizabeth's younger sister and, like Sarah Wedd and Emma Hills, one of the three Dunkin girls who had lived with Mary Hays in Islington c. 1806–8. Less than a month after the death of Elizabeth Francis, Elizabeth Hays Lanfear died in her home in Islington, in her 59th year, and was buried on 25 February 1825 in the cemetery at St Mary's, Islington, alongside her son John. Among the named individuals in her will are her stepson Ambrose (she left him 'three silver watches, a silver Cross and a silver Fish Knife; also the twenty two volumes of the Encyclopedia Britannica'), her surviving son Francis, her two brothers, and her sister Mary.[62]

II

Mary Hays declared to William Godwin in early February 1796, 'Between one sister, Elizabeth, & myself, every thought has been, from infancy in common'.[63] By that date the two sisters had explored Rousseau and sentimental fiction, revolted against orthodox Calvinism, devoured Helvétius, read through Godwin's *Political Justice*,[64] and turned from writing short moral tales to composing epistolary novels that promoted the values of their rational faith and their social, educational, and psychological ideals. A few weeks before Hays's letter to Godwin, Elizabeth Hays, after a day of reading Rousseau (the volumes had been borrowed from Mary), offered a perceptive critique of the controversial French writer:

> The farther I proceed, the more I am charm'd – yet I find in it a thousand things to disapprove, – many of their principles are false – their ideas of duty erronious [sic] – their sexual distinctions absurd – their loves

though trebly refined, the extreme of voluptuousness. It has enervated me beyond measure – but this will soon be over, my mind will shortly regain its elasticity – I return to Helvetius with new vigour.[65]

Though inspired and intrigued by Rousseau and Godwin, Mary and Elizabeth Hays considered Helvétius the best teacher on human nature and the role of gender in education. Mary opined on his views in several periodical pieces in the *Monthly Magazine* in 1796, and both sisters incorporated his theories into their novels.[66]

If powerful feelings could lead to proper thinking and virtuous action, then even Mary Hays's affair with William Frend, at least while it lasted, was sufficient, she believed, to prove such theories, though whether Elizabeth took matters that far seems doubtful. Mary Hays wrote to Godwin on 20 November 1795:

> The affections ^& sentiments^ which arise out of the sympathies of our nature (or, if you prefer the phrase, are generated by our habits) are not the less real, tho' the supposed excellence on which they are founded shou'd be merely the work of an erroneous fancy: the mind capable of sketching the picture is brought forward by the effort, & sacrifices (as Rousseau observes) every sordid feeling to the imaginary model. What ever exalts the passions & raises the imagination gives birth to talents, to great & heroic exertions. . . . The source of all my pleasures & of all my improvements has been in my attachments – I love to find excellence, to admire, & to emulate, it – when I lose this ardour I shall sink into apathy & lassitude![67]

Within the Wollstonecraft circle of feminist novelists, opinions about sentiment and sensibility often surfaced. 'You sometimes reproach me with want of sensibility', Elizabeth wrote to Mary in early 1796, but

> in this you do me injustice – I much doubt whether my feelings are not equally strong with your own – though various circumstances may have rendered them less irritably acute, the only difference between you, & me, is this, – that terrified by your example, it has been the business of my life, to repress sentiments, which it has been too much yours, to indulge – in avoiding one extreme, I may sometimes have run into the other, – & vainly boasted of a philosophy which in an hour of temptation would have avail'd me nothing. You know my heart to be capable both of love, & friendship – though a more indiscriminate mixture with society than you experience, may have made me less romantic – I am neither cold – nor selfish – I am only more cheerful – more rational & not quite such a maniac as my favourite sister.[68]

Is this passage, Elizabeth embraced a feminist model that balanced sentimental and rational expectations for women, a balance she felt her sister did not always

INTRODUCTION

exhibit in her writings and actions. Elizabeth warned Mary of the dangers she faced in pursuing Frend, especially after he rejected her at the close of 1795. 'My sister ever tried to discourage me', Hays explains to Godwin that February, 'with a degree of impatience, at times, bordering on asperity – "She hated the name of the man who had robbed her of her friend".'[69]

The contrast between the 'less romantic' and 'more rational' younger sister and the 'unfortunate' older 'maniac' sister is evident in the contrasting style and tone of *Emma Courtney* and *Fatal Errors*. *Fatal Errors* was composed *c.* 1796–97, about the same time as Mary Hays's *Memoirs of Emma Courtney*, Eliza Fenwick's *Secresy*, Elizabeth Inchbald's *Nature and Art*, Mary Robinson's *Walsingham: or, The Pupil of Nature*, and Wollstonecraft's *Maria: or, The Wrongs of Woman*, and serves as an important addition to this influential group of early feminist novels. Like these novels, *Fatal Errors* is a cautionary tale about the consequences of making bad decisions in matters of love and marriage, decisions that too often left young women bound to a state of financial dependence and social isolation. If Hays's aim in *Emma Courtney* was to show 'the possible effects of the present system of things, & the contradictory principles which have bewilder'd mankind, upon private character, & private happiness',[70] Lanfear's 'plain and simple relation of what does, or may happen every day' to women, as she writes in her Preface to *Fatal Errors*, is a fitting companion piece. The language and tone are more restrained than in *Emma Courtney*, and Lanfear's heroine more measured in her attempt to balance the demands of reason and feeling than Courtney, yet neither woman achieves the education, independence, or equality they desire.

These shared themes did not escape Wollstonecraft, though her remarks to Mary Hays in September 1796 after reading Elizabeth's manuscript seem faint praise at best: 'your Sisters M.S. . . . has merit; but displays more rectitude of mind than warmth of imagination',[71] another indication of Elizabeth's reserved tone and style. Wollstonecraft writes again on September 20: 'I return your Sister's M.S. with some observations which appear to me important'.[72] Wollstonecraft was not the only reader of her manuscript, however. Eliza Fenwick also saw a version of it in the summer of 1800, which reflects the post-1796 date of some of the allusions in the text and reveals Elizabeth's continued editing of the manuscript after Wollstonecraft's comments. Fenwick requested that Hays 'avoid giving your sister my opinion of her manuscript. I respect her too much to be reluctant to give her that pain',[73] suggesting an even more severe response than Wollstonecraft's. Whether Wollstonecraft's 'observations', Fenwick's silence, or Elizabeth Hays's own insecurities contributed to her hesitation to publish at that time cannot be known, but what is certain is that she buried the manuscript for nearly two decades.

Lanfear's title – *Fatal Errors; or Poor Mary-Anne. A Tale of the Last Century. In a Series of Letters* – suggests the novel's 1790s biographical and literary origins, while also engaging, as we will see, with a longer eighteenth-century tradition of writing by and about women. The title page is anonymous and undated, but the dedicatory epistle is signed 'Eliz. Lanfear' and dated 31 May 1819, from Islington. Lines from poems by John Langhorne and William Wordsworth grace the title page, with Wordsworth's selection taken from 'Simon Lee: The Old Huntsman', a poem from the 1798 *Lyrical Ballads*:

> O Reader! had you in your mind
> Such stores as silent thought can bring,
> O gentle Reader! you would find
> A tale in every thing.

The novel was dedicated to Lanfear's niece Emma Dunkin Hills, who, after her marriage to her cousin, William Hills, in 1810, settled in Canonbury Square, only a short distance from Lanfear's home in Church Street. As mentioned previously, Emma had lived with and was tutored (along with her sisters Sarah and Marianne) for a time by Mary Hays in Islington. In her dedicatory epistle, Lanfear attributed the publication of the novel to her recent discovery of the manuscript buried among some old letters 'which had for the last twenty years reposed quietly in my portfolio'. Based on her niece's favourable opinion of the manuscript and her confidence in her aunt's literary abilities, Lanfear finally agreed to publish the manuscript, despite noting in her Preface that the novel would, 'like its author, make at present but a petty and antiquated appearance'. She even asserts that the masquerade ball near the end of the book was based upon an account provided her 'by a gentleman who was present when it occurred'. In the British Library's copy of *Fatal Errors*, an annotation in pencil at the foot of the page reads 'by RS', a tantalizing though cryptic suggestion that the 'gentleman' might have been Robert Southey, who became acquainted with Mary and Elizabeth Hays in the early months of 1797.

In her Preface, Lanfear poses as an editor of a collection of letters rather than the creator of a novel, ascribing authorship to an unnamed 'young and single lady' 'towards the close of the last century'. In the intervening decades, Lanfear's quiet life may have shielded her from some of the repercussions of publishing a feminist novel from the 1790s once read and critiqued by Mary Wollstonecraft, for few outside her immediate circle of family and friends in 1819 would have associated 'Mrs Lanfear' or even 'Eliz. Lanfear' with Mary Hays and their radical literary friends from the previous century. Lanfear may also have been spared the opprobrium her sister experienced in the late 1790s by correctly noting the 'petty and antiquated appearance', as she puts it, of Jacobin novels in 1819. As a result, the novel attracted little public notice, for no known reviews exist. Fortunately, a glimpse at the novel's circulation can be partially reconstituted through the subscription list, which contains names and locations of more than 20 individuals related by blood or marriage to Elizabeth and Mary Hays as well as numerous friends in London and beyond, many of whom were associated with Unitarian circles. Some of these individuals had been known to the two sisters since the 1790s – Stephen Weaver Browne, George Dyer, John Evans, Dr John Reid, Sampson Kingsford, and William Tooke – and others after 1800, including the Unitarian MP William Smith, the publisher A. J. Valpy, and the wife of Daniel Whittle Harvey (1786–1863), founder of the *Sunday Times* and London's first Chief of Police (1840).

INTRODUCTION

In 1824 Lanfear published her second work, *Letters to Young Ladies on their Entrance into the World; to which are added Sketches from Real Life* (a second edition, without any additions or alterations, appeared posthumously in 1828).[74] Included in the volume are chapters titled 'On the Motives for Female Improvement' (a topic of interest to Lanfear and Hays since the late 1770s) and 'On the Single Life', the latter possessing passages strikingly apropos to Mary Hays. These letters have been reprinted in this edition, as well as 'Louisa, the Indulged', a moral tale from Part II of the volume (see Appendix B). In this volume, Lanfear returned to the short cautionary tales for adolescent girls (especially concerning their choice of marriage partners) she had employed 30 years earlier in her two pieces that appeared in Mary Hays's *Letters and Essays* (see Appendix A) and, in some respects, in *Fatal Errors*. The title page of *Letters to Young Ladies* announces Lanfear as the author of *Fatal Errors*, but the poetic inscription from Lord Lyttleton's 'Advice to a Lady' suggests that, unlike her novel, there would be no 'unfeminine' displays in this work of conduct literature:

Seek to be good, but aim not to be great:
A woman's noblest station is retreat;
Her fairest virtues fly from public sight –
Domestic worth, – that shuns too strong a light.

These lines would have reminded readers of similar sentiments found in James Fordyce's popular *Sermons to Young Women* (1766) or John Gregory's *A Father's Legacy to his Daughters* (1774).

In her introductory epistle, Lanfear presents education as a vehicle for helping teenage girls 'regulate their hearts, their understandings, their tempers, and their duties, by [acquiring] fixed and steady principles of religion and morality'. She reminds her readers to study the Bible, especially the Old Testament, for the Jews were 'chosen' 'to preserve the knowledge of the Divine Unity in times of great ignorance' and to display God's 'benevolent designs to all mankind', two hallmarks of the Unitarianism she and her sister had espoused for more than three decades. Besides religion, young ladies should explore history and proper literature. 'Poetry and novels may be read occasionally', she admits, 'but not indiscriminately or too frequently'. 'Indulging too often in works of fancy', she argues, 'or what is commonly called light reading, vitiates the taste, promotes indolence, and deters young persons from pursuing graver and more important studies'.[75] Though an odd comment from the author of *Fatal Errors*, it may be that in the intervening years since her original composition of *Fatal Errors*, Elizabeth Lanfear's appreciation of sentimental novels had declined, an attitude her sister seems to have shared, for Mary Hays devoted herself after 1799 to biography, history, and moral fiction designed for young and working-class readers. Despite Lanfear's conservative aims and attitudes towards the proper development of young women, her letters and tales are nevertheless marked by an underlying feminism reflecting similar concerns expressed in *Fatal Errors* and her sister's two novels from the 1790s.

Shortly before her marriage to Ambrose Lanfear in 1804, Elizabeth Hays described her future husband as 'a man of virtuous principles, liberal sentiments & good, though not a pollish'd understanding but if I am not deceived ^in him^ he possesses what is still dearer to me, an excellent temper, & great sensibility of heart',[76] ideals shared by her fictional heroine, Mary-Anne Southerdon. Elizabeth Hays may or may not have been deceived when she composed that letter, but certainly the heroine of *Fatal Errors* found deception pervasive in courtship and marriage, suffering greatly at the hands of male oppressors. The limitations of her education and the strictures of society forced her into a catastrophic causal chain that Elizabeth and Mary Hays, as well as their feminist contemporaries Mary Wollstonecraft and Eliza Fenwick, knew was a far greater likelihood for a young woman at that time than romantic visions of domestic bliss within an egalitarian, companionate marriage. As *Fatal Errors* demonstrates, by 1819 Elizabeth Hays Lanfear had not forgotten the power or prevalence of that debilitating chain and unrealistic dream.

III

The story of *Fatal Errors* could, on one level, be seen as the story of the reception of women's writing of the eighteenth and early nineteenth centuries – one of dispossession and obscurity. It narrates the difficulty of establishing female identity, as the central character struggles to find a place in the world. The novel opens with Mary-Anne Southerdon displaced from her home through the death of her parents, setting out into an uncertain future, 'all at present a blank before me'. It closes with her own death, homeless, outcast, betrayed, and a blank space where we might expect the intricacies of the plot to be explained. A 'concluding note by the editor' raises questions around the ending only to evade them: 'the correspondence here ending,' comments the editor, 'it is not in my power fully to answer these inquiries'. Mary-Anne's quest for a place in the world – through reading, intellectual enquiry, writing, marriage – has ended in disillusionment and loss.

But the story of *Fatal Errors* is also one of survival and recovery. Recent research in reconstructing the networks of religious Dissent around Mary Hays has fortuitously uncovered the single known copy of the novel. A central feature of this cultural and genealogically based research is its precise attention to local detail – house moves, familial and business relationships, worship practices – which has recovered not only a larger context for the Hays sisters, but for women's writing more broadly in the period.[77] Its discovery indicates the rich possibilities of concentrated research into the literary, religious, and kinship cultures of Dissent, a specific example of what might be uncovered in 'attending to the myriad thoughts and feelings produced and structured by religious Dissenting publics', as Daniel White puts it.[78]

INTRODUCTION

As critical interest in this area grows, we are beginning to move towards a more nuanced understanding of the part women played in the intellectual and textual cultures of religious Dissent. Whereas Mary Hays was once primarily discussed as a disciple of Wollstonecraft, the work of scholars such as Gina Luria Walker, Eleanor Ty, and Mary Spongberg, among others, has enabled her long and complex literary career to come to light.[79] Scholarly attention has broadened from a focus on *Emma Courtney* to include serious consideration of her intellectual philosophy, her experimental approach to life-writing, and the negotiations of female experience in *Female Biography* (1803) and *Memoirs of Queens: Celebrated and Illustrious* (1821). Now the work of Elizabeth Hays Lanfear can be set alongside her sister's writing in its exploration of self-definition and 'sexual distinction', and her strange, belated 'Jacobin' novel can once again be placed in dialogue with the writers it was initially created alongside. In this closing section, we want to explore some critical readings of *Fatal Errors*, and to suggest why and how this novel can be contextualized in longer traditions of, and perspectives on, writing of the era.

Lanfear herself showed an intense awareness of the ways in which her work might be critically situated and judged. Each detail of the novel, from its title onwards, offers an insight into the ways in which women's writing tried to find a place for itself in changing literary culture at the turn of the nineteenth century. At the time of publication, this was already a 'tale of the last century' in several ways – personal, literary, cultural. As we have seen, it belonged to Lanfear's past, and the Hays sisters' intimacy with other intellectual novelists and radical thinkers, rethinking social and literary norms: Mary Wollstonecraft, Eliza Fenwick, William Godwin, Thomas Holcroft. But that time of intense intellectual Revolutionary fervour, for Lanfear, was gone. The novel had, as she tells her niece in the dedication, 'for the last twenty years reposed quietly in my portfolio'. Those 20 years had also seen the novel develop in different ways. Novels 'in a series of letters' were becoming outmoded as the epistolary form had begun to fade from popularity, and Lanfear's dedication betrays her nervousness about the ways in which her work might, 'like its author, make at present but a petty and antiquated appearance'. This time lag, however, which Lanfear suggests is a weakness, is also a great strength of the novel, because it allows us a retrospect on the work of the 1790s, a self-conscious reflection on earlier modes of female writing and behaviour, and also on the development of a genre.

As such, the key title phrase, *Fatal Errors*, is particularly revealing of the ways in which we might see Lanfear as a woman writer negotiating with a longer literary tradition. It sums up a key question of the novel: how is a woman's fate determined? Through destiny, circumstance, or her own actions? The phrase is, of course, a common one: but in using it, Lanfear links herself to a larger tradition of writing by and about women, as well as a particular effort in the 1790s to think through, as Wollstonecraft has it in the *Wrongs of Woman*, the 'peculiar fate' of woman.[80] We might trace it through a variety of works relating to female behaviour in the period, most prominently Samuel Richardson's *Clarissa*. Clarissa's 'posthumous letters' to her parents twice use the phrase, imploring forgiveness from her father 'especially of that fatal error which threw her out of your protection', and ruing 'the grief which my fatal error has given to you both'.[81] Richardson's use of the phrase echoed through the eighteenth century to evoke the problems caused by hostile men to naïve women. For Sarah Pennington, in *An Unfortunate Mother's Advice to her Absent Daughters, in a Letter to Miss Pennington* (1761), the 'fatal error' her daughters must guard against is the choice of a husband with 'a bad heart, and a morose temper'.[82] Written after Pennington's painful marital separation, when she was debarred from seeing her daughters, the work is a mixture of self-defence, memoir, and conduct manual, which roundly vindicates her private virtue despite the 'latitude of behaviour' she admits she may have displayed in public. Virtuous but credulous women, she warns, lay themselves open to misconstruction and gossip in a 'world full of deceit and falsehood'.[83] The slander she complains about might bear some parallel to Vernon's malign interpretations of his wife's 'six months residence, as he invidiously called it, in the house of Mr. Howard'. For Pennington, the 'fatal error' consists in women's poor appraisal of men, the one aspect in which they might have agency, were they educated properly. Similarly, in Sophia Lee's *The Recess* (1781), Matilda bemoans not the villainy of the man who is tricking her into a forced marriage, but her own 'extravagant credulity': 'my *innocence*, ah rather say *ignorance*, groaned I mentally, that fatal error which ever too severely punishes itself'.[84] Mary Wollstonecraft, too, emphasizes Maria's 'extreme credulity' as a key factor in her misreading of her husband's character: a misreading she describes as a 'fatal error!'[85] Meanwhile, Amelia Opie's optimistically credulous Adeline Mowbray eventually admits her 'fatal error of opinion' in her youthful opposition to marriage.[86]

Lanfear's choice of title, then, suggests the ways in which she was navigating the novel and conduct book traditions of the eighteenth century alongside the legacies of the 1790s. This adds further depth to our understanding of women Jacobin writers' participation in the conduct literature tradition: early works such as Wollstonecraft's *Thoughts on the Education of Daughters* (1787) and Mary Hays' *Letters and Essays, Moral and Miscellaneous* (1793) exist in a continuum with later work such as Lanfear's *Letters to Young Ladies on their Entrance into the World* (1824). Instead of viewing such volumes either as apprentice work or, conversely, as the conservative withdrawal of later life, they should, instead, be seen as an ongoing exploration of the ways in which women might negotiate social and sexual conventions. In the case of Lanfear, as Gary Kelly first noted, they also show an ambiguity: discussing the two early pieces reprinted in this edition, 'Cleora' and 'Josepha', he suggests that they present 'two contrasting women – one in tune with Mary Hays's Revolutionary feminism, the other reminiscent of moralistic, conservative, and pessimistic conduct-books of previous decades'.[87]

While *Fatal Errors* does go some way towards dispelling Kelly's general concept of Elizabeth's writing as 'more narrowly didactic, socially conservative, and gloomy' than that of her sister, his intuition of her work as double-edged seems correct.[88] *Fatal Errors* swings between optimism and pessimism, between radical and sensual possibilities and, on the other hand, cruelty, oppression, and death. In format, it retains the epistolary fashion of its 1790s peers – but towards the close, appears to betray its doubts about this choice. While the major part of the novel is written in letters from Mary-Anne's perspective alone, giving it a claustrophobic intensity, the epistolary sequence breaks down in the final stages, leaving the editor to intervene to narrate some, if not all, the complications of the plot. Even moving between individual letters can yield differences in tone and style. In the first letter the heroine establishes herself, in Emma Courtney mode, as a creature both of intellect and emotion, seeking a correspondence which will allow her to 'pour forth with my accustomed frankness, the reflections of my mind, or the feelings of my heart'. The next letter, however, shows her prosaically engaged in her housekeeper duties, 'fatting turkeys, making mince pies &c &c' for her uncle's visitors, and ends with a mention of her cousin Sarah, 'at present confined'. This contrast nicely shows the range of women's experience, and the shifting tone of the novel, as it fluctuates between the larger emotional and intellectual landscape of women, and the details of lived female experience.

Fatal Errors also shows Lanfear in the process of negotiating changed generic expectations and also, perhaps, her own changed perspectives. While at times we can hear an echo of the politicized Jacobin voice – as when Mary-Anne feebly comments on the 'gilded chains' to which women are subject – at others, the novel appears to offer a regretful, backward look at the repercussions of the Revolutionary years. Mary-Anne is abducted to France, where her bigamous second marriage takes place, and her situation when Malvern deserts her – pregnant, spurned for another mistress – seems to invite deliberate parallels with Wollstonecraft's desertion by Gilbert Imlay in Paris in 1794. Yet Mary-Anne is no Wollstonecraft. For all her earlier interest in 'liberty' she shows little inclination to muse on the 'state of public affairs in France', and is chided for her 'old-fashioned English notions of morality'. We are told that 'the revolution had already commenced', and we see its traces everywhere in this novel. Yet we never look at it directly, and Lanfear's negotiations with the revolutionary ideas of her own circle are similarly hard to read.

The novel's most obvious link to a radical 1790s context comes with the introduction of Algernon Howard in letter five. He shares his initials with Emma Courtney's love interest, Augustus Harley, but in behaviour, he is closer to Emma's older mentor, Mr Francis, not afraid to instruct and to contradict. He is at once a love interest and an intellectual and political challenge, since he immediately questions Mary-Anne's views on 'sexual distinction' and the 'liberty' of women. Mary-Anne is a more hesitant, less articulate version of Wollstonecraft and Hays: 'I did, though timidly, venture to complain of the many and various evils to which our sex are, in every country, more or less exposed'. Howard, on the contrary, argues from a Burkean standpoint: women are distinguished by their gentleness and modesty, and in return 'enjoy the inestimable privilege of being universally treated with kindness, tenderness and respect'. Although Mary-Anne privately describes this as characterized by 'gallantry', rather than 'truth', she also acknowledges the strange effect of sexual attraction on her perspective, which forces her to abandon her attempt to argue with Howard in confusion: 'I felt embarrassed, and all of a glow!'

In articulating her attraction to Howard, Mary-Anne joins the ranks of 1790s women who seek to govern their own seduction plots: Hays' Emma Courtney; Fenwick's Sibella; Wollstonecraft's Maria. Heirs, as Nicola Watson points out, to Rousseau's Julie, these heroines show women writers wrestling 'with the problem of how to authorize a revolutionary female subjectivity premised upon the authenticity of individual feeling'.[89] Female feelings – sentimental, sexual – became intimately entangled with political anxieties in these novels of the Revolutionary decade. Mary-Anne shares a good deal with these earlier heroines, but from the vantage point of 1819, offers us a more rueful viewpoint. Overtly, we are told that she does not have a sexual relationship with Howard, but we are privy to her 'irresistible fascination' with him, registered in breathless sensual confusion much like Emma Courtney's protestations to Augustus: ' – my heart flutters – I breathe with difficulty – *My friend – I would give myself to you* – the gift is not worthless'.[90] She insinuates herself into his house, taking a position as his housekeeper without his knowledge, an arrangement which clearly oversteps the purely domestic. This is reminiscent of Fenwick's free-thinking Sibella, and of Godwin's assertion of Wollstonecraft's sexual independence in the *Memoirs*: 'We did not marry . . . Mary felt an entire conviction of the propriety of her conduct'.[91]

The difference is that Mary-Anne is pessimistic from the start about the consequences of her actions, and cautious about her own anarchic desires: 'I am wandering in devious ways', she exclaims, 'sporting on a precipice'. She is conscious of the ways in which attraction towards Howard overwhelms her power of argument. His words put her into a 'delirium': and she reports a 'sort of fascination in his eloquence which could be better felt than described'. A 'delirium': not rational, intellectual response but a collapse into unmanageable feeling. Howard's conversation is repeatedly evoked – 'that voice which still vibrates in my ear', 'those honied accents which have sunk so deep into my soul' – alongside telling allusions to *Paradise Lost*, as the two comment on a picture of Milton's Satan. As Lanfear attempts to rewrite male traditions, Mary-Anne appears to be struggling with the same questions which beset both Wollstonecraft and Mary Hays: can a woman both think *and* feel? Can sensual and emotional arousal really co-exist with rational intellectual engagement?

Moreover, given Howard's association with Burkean gallantry, Mary-Anne's sexual attraction might seem to have counter-Revolutionary impulses. That said, we are repeatedly informed of the traits Mary-Anne and Howard share, particularly an urge towards benevolence coupled with a sceptical approach towards charity, which might well have stemmed from Elizabeth Hays' reading of George Dyer's *Complaints of the Poor People of England* (1793). Howard, like Mary-Anne, and in keeping with his reformist name-sake, argues for 'a more radical cure, than incidental charity could perform'. He is also given a speech in praise of 'genuine sensibility, when united with good sense and artless simplicity', and is very nearly won over by Mary-Anne's charms as she sings on a moonlit night. Howard's capacity for feeling response thus complicates any straightforwardly gendered or politicized reading of this seduction narrative.

But this strand of the story is set aside, as Howard transpires to be only indirectly responsible for later plot development. Instead, Mary-Anne's downfall comes from her lawful husband, Vernon, who secretly trades her for his gambling debts to his friend Malvern. The real dangers in the novel stem not from sexual feeling but from corruption, greed, and the pressure of social convention in a patriarchal society. Yet the novel deals relatively sympathetically with its array of weak male characters, themselves overset by financial catastrophe and poor education. Meanwhile, even women of feeling are not immune to mercenary impulse. 'How difficult is the science of self-knowledge!' Mary-Anne laments, when Vernon has been disinherited, 'I feel that I never should have married Mr. Vernon, had I not considered him as the promised heir of Mrs. Blount's very ample fortune'.

This awareness of mixed motives and human frailty is also evident in Lanfear's reworking of the seduction plot. Mary-Anne, deceived and abducted to France, at first 'falls lifeless', and endures 'acute suffering'. She slowly softens, however, giving way 'to love and to hope', and accepts the second marriage she has been tricked into, believing Vernon to have died. It is only after a miscarriage and the discovery that Vernon is still alive that she breaks down. As for so many sentimental heroines before her, death is the only possible conclusion – and we might also be reminded of the Richardsonian origins of the title. But although *Fatal Errors* ends, inevitably, by killing off its heroine, it also offers a more complicated reading of *Clarissa* and the seduction narrative more broadly. 'My health was now perfectly re-established', Mary-Anne tells us after marrying her abductor, 'and my spirits, though occasionally depressed, had in some measure recovered their usual tone'. This is some way from the 'dauntless intrepidity' with which her sister's 'victim of prejudice', Mary Raymond, struggles against her seducer, and her eventual despair and 'deadly torpor'.[92] And as opposed to the continual victimization of Mary Raymond, Mary-Anne's downfall is a more ambiguous narrative. Her musings on her marriage to Vernon suggest her uncertainty over her own agency: 'With a clear perception of right and wrong in the abstract, in every important action of my life, circumstances have hitherto led me to act against my better judgment'.

This alertness to the ways in which circumstances might press up against ideals may also point back to the novel's post-Revolutionary status. By 1819, both the political landscape and the literary marketplace had changed; so, too, had the lives of the Hays sisters, as they endured bereavements and disappointments. The frustrated, partial ending of the novel points to the limits of the epistolary genre, as does the worn-out trope of the masquerade. Symbolically, we are being asked to consider a larger metaphor of identity, as Mary-Anne and Howard remove their masks for a climactic – and, for Mary-Anne, ultimately fatal – moment of recognition and desire. Yet in its perfunctory and unconvincing treatment of the masquerade, the novel itself might be seen to show some awareness of the limits it has reached, confronting its own history and coming to a dead-end. On the one hand we might see this simply as a sign of the novel's 'ineptitude', to quote Terry Castle's review of Fenwick's *Secresy*.[93] But as Castle goes on to discuss, the strange, 'dissociated' qualities of *Secresy* tell their own story; as Nicola Watson analyzes, Fenwick's novel both represents and is trapped in a 'peculiar aesthetic and political deadlock'.[94] This is a good lens through which to view the obscurities and uncertainties of *Fatal Errors*, in particular the strangely skimped, compressed, and contradictory ending. At the close of a novel dedicated to exploring the pressure of circumstances, the editor admits that 'it is not in my power' to disclose all circumstances of the plot; the closing paragraph of this novel dedicated to the difficulties of female self-definition is given over to a description of Mary-Anne's luxurious chestnut hair and dark blue eyes. Perhaps the best way to view this uncertain, contradictory ending is to see it as a reflection of the double nature of the novel – belonging at once to the 1790s and the late 1810s, evoking but not examining its Revolutionary context, a survivor in a different age.

Yet the novel did survive. The reason for that rests largely with the network of Dissenting relatives and supporters on show in the subscription list and detailed in the footnotes. The Hays sisters were intellectually nourished by the 'unusually articulate, theologically aware' writing community of Dissent, to which *Fatal Errors* owes its questioning approach to convention, as well as its exploration of the friction between reason and emotion.[95] Moreover, the additional biographical material detailed in this edition adds further weight to Gina Luria Walker's re-reading of the later years of the Hays sisters, who far from withdrawing from society, instead enjoyed an older age 'filled with family, marriages, parties and supportive learned female communities'.[96] This is borne out by the novel's belated publication, with its loving familial dedication, and supported by an extensive list of subscribers. Thus, both in its content, and its contexts, *Fatal Errors* gives an insight into the ways Dissent nurtured its female writers and helped them to live on past the 1790s.

The edition thus answers recent critical calls for 'new ways of reading relationships between literary women both in and out of print'.[97] Recovering *Fatal Errors* helps us towards a growing understanding of Romanticism as an intricately, messily, sociably connected creative era, which nurtured women's writing in different ways, and which cannot easily be categorized by period, or by politics. We now hope that further connections might be uncovered – with women's writing, with novels of the 1790s and beyond, or with Dissenting culture more broadly. We might see parallels to another writer extensively revising her manuscripts of the

INTRODUCTION

late 1790s for publication in the 1810s – Jane Austen. Indeed, there are some tempting echoes in *Fatal Errors* to *Sense and Sensibility*, and to *Pride and Prejudice*, suggesting Lanfear's immersion in contemporary literature, and another parallel for the struggles of *Fatal Errors* with the legacies both of sensibility and the epistolary form. But this edition also makes the case for understanding less well-known patterns of influence and inheritance, such as the importance of the Hays–Dunkin network, and later nineteenth-century figures it produced like the unsung Matilda Mary Hays. *Fatal Errors* is a story of dispossession and loss, followed by a long period of obscurity in the archives – but this Chawton House edition provides an appropriate home for Lanfear's work, and a chance for her to find her place in the world again.

BIBLIOGRAPHY

Manuscript resources

East Lane Church Book, 1806–19, MS Angus Library, Regent's Park College, Oxford.
Fenwick Family Correspondence, 1798–1855, MS 211, New York Historical Society, New York.
Godwin, William, MS G, Carl H. Pforzheimer Collection of Shelley and His Circle, The New York Public Library, Astor, Lenox and Tilden Foundations, New York.
Hays, Mary, MS A. F. Wedd Collection, Shelfmark 24.93, Dr. Williams's Library, London.
Hays, Mary, MS MH and Misc. MS, Carl H. Pforzheimer Collection of Shelley and His Circle, The New York Public Library, Astor, Lenox and Tilden Foundations, New York.
Horsleydown and Carter Lane Church Book, MS Metropolitan Tabernacle, London.
Keppel Street Church Book, 1795–1826, MS Angus Library, Regent's Park College, Oxford.
Robinson, Henry Crabb, MS Diary, Reminiscences, Correspondence, and Notebooks, Crabb Robinson Archive, Dr. Williams's Library, London.
White Row, Spitalfields, Baptism Book, MS X099/303, N/C025/001, 1756–1891, London Metropolitan Archives, London.
Wollstonecraft, Mary, MS MW, Carl H. Pforzheimer Collection of Shelley and His Circle, The New York Public Library, Astor, Lenox and Tilden Foundations, New York.

Primary sources

Alliston, A. (ed.), *The Recess; or, A Tale of Other Times* (Lexington, KY: University of Kentucky, 2000).
Brooks, M. (ed.), *The Correspondence (1779–1843) of Mary Hays, British Novelist* (Lewiston, ME: Edwin Mellen Press, 2004).
Clemit, P., and G. Luria Walker (eds.), William Godwin, *Memoirs of the Author of a Vindication of the Rights of Woman* (Peterborough: Broadview Press, 2001).
Hays, M., *Letters and Essays, Moral and Miscellaneous* (London: T. Knott, 1793).
Hays, M., *Memoirs of Emma Courtney* (London: G. G. and J. Robinson, 1796).
Hays, M., *An Appeal to the Men of Great Britain in Behalf of Women* (London: J. Johnson and J. Bell, 1798).
Hays, M., *The Victim of Prejudice* (London: J. Johnson, 1799).
Hoagwood, T. A. (ed.), *The Victim of Prejudice* (Delmar, NY: Scholars' Facsimiles & Reprints, 1990).
Kelly, G. (ed.), *Mary and the Wrongs of Woman* (Oxford: Oxford University Press, 2009).

Lanfear, E. H., *Fatal Errors; or Poor Mary-Anne. A Tale of the Last Century: In a Series of Letters* (London: A. J. Valpy, 1819).

Lanfear, E. H., *Letters to Young Ladies on their Entrance into the World; to which are added Sketches from Real Life* (London: J. Robins and Co., 1824; 2nd ed., 1828).

McWhir, A. (ed.), *Adeline Mowbray, or, The Mother and Daughter; A Tale* (Peterborough: Broadview Press, 2010).

Myers, V., D. O'Shaughnessy, and M. Philp (eds.), *The Diary of William Godwin* (Oxford: Oxford Digital Library, 2010) (http://godwindiary.bodleian.ox.ac.uk).

Pennington, S., *An Unfortunate Mother's Advice to Her Absent Daughters, in a Letter to Miss Pennington* (London: S. Chandler, 1761).

Todd, J. (ed.), *Collected Letters of Mary Wollstonecraft* (Chichester: Columbia University Press, 2003).

Ty, E. (ed.), *The Victim of Prejudice* (Peterborough: Broadview Press, 1995).

Wedd, A. F. (ed.), *The Fate of the Fenwicks* (London: Methuen, 1927).

Wedd, A. F. (ed.), *The Love-Letters of Mary Hays (1779–1780)* (London: Methuen, 1925).

Whelan, T. (ed.), *Mary Hays: Life, Writings and Correspondence* (www.maryhayslifewritingscorrespondence.com).

Secondary sources

Brooks, M., 'Mary Hays: Finding a Voice in Dissent', *Enlightenment and Dissent*, 14 (1995), pp. 3–24.

Castle, T., '"Sublimely Bad": Review of Secresy; or, The Ruin on the Rock', *London Review of Books*, 17.4 (1995), pp. 18–19.

James, F., *Religious Dissent and the Aikin-Barbauld Circle, 1740–1860* (Cambridge: Cambridge University Press, 2011).

James, F., 'Writing Female Biography: Mary Hays and the Life-Writing of Religious Dissent', in D. Cook and A. Culley (eds.), *Women's Life Writing, 1700–1850* (Basingstoke: Palgrave Macmillan, 2012), pp. 117–32.

Kell, E., 'Memoir of Mary Hays: With Some Unpublished Letters Addressed to Her by Robert Robinson, of Cambridge, and Others', *Christian Reformer*, 11 (1844), pp. 813–20.

Kelly, G., *Women, Writing, and Revolution, 1790–1827* (Oxford: Clarendon Press, 1993).

Pedersen, J. S., 'Friendship in the Life and Work of Mary Wollstonecraft: The Making of a Liberal Feminist Tradition', *Literature and History*, 17 (2008), pp. 19–35.

Pollin, B. R., 'Mary Hays on Women's Rights in the Monthly Magazine', *Etudes Anglaises*, 24 (1971), pp. 271–82.

Reeves, M., *Pursuing the Muses: Female Education and Nonconformist Culture 1700–1900* (London and Washington: Leicester University Press, 1997).

Spongberg, M., 'Mary Hays and Mary Wollstonecraft and the Evolution of Dissenting Feminism', *Enlightenment and Dissent*, 26 (2010), pp. 230–58.

Spongberg, M., and G. L. Walker (eds.), 'Female Biography', special issue of *Women's Writing*, 25.2 (2018).

Ty, E., *Unsex'd Revolutionaries: Five Women Novelists of the 1790s* (Toronto and London: University of Toronto Press, 1993).

Walker, G. L. (ed.), *The Idea of Being Free: A Mary Hays Reader* (Peterborough: Broadview Press, 2006).

Walker, G. L., *Mary Hays (1759–1843): The Growth of a Woman's Mind* (Aldershot: Ashgate, 2006).

Walker, G. L., 'I Sought & Made to Myself an Extraordinary Destiny', *Women's Writing*, 25 (2018), pp. 124–49.

Watson, N. J., *Revolution and the Form of the British Novel, 1790–1825: Intercepted Letters, Interrupted Seductions* (Oxford: Clarendon Press, 1994).

Whelan, T. (gen. ed.), *Nonconformist Women Writers 1720–1840*, 8 vols (London: Pickering & Chatto, 2011).

Whelan, T., 'Mary Hays and Henry Crabb Robinson', *Wordsworth Circle*, 46 (2015), pp. 178–80.

Whelan, T., 'Mary Steele, Mary Hays and the Convergence of Women's Literary Circles in the 1790s', *Journal for Eighteenth-Century Studies*, 38 (2015), pp. 511–24.

Whelan, T., *Other British Voices: Women, Poetry, and Religion, 1766–1840* (New York: Palgrave Macmillan, 2015).

Whelan, T., 'Elizabeth Hays and the 1790s Feminist Novel', *Wordsworth Circle*, 48 (2017), pp. 137–51.

White, D. E., *Early Romanticism and Religious Dissent* (New York and Cambridge: Cambridge University Press, 2006).

Winckles, A. O., and A. Rehbein, *Women's Literary Networks and Romanticism: 'A Tribe of Authoresses'* (Liverpool: Liverpool University Press, 2017).

NOTE ON THE TEXT

This edition of *Fatal Errors* follows as closely as possible the 1819 text, taken from the only known surviving copy of the novel, now residing in the British Library. A few silent emendations have been employed to keep spellings, punctuations, or capitalizations consistent within the text and clear to the modern reader. In a few cases, where a spelling has been altered, the original spelling has been placed in an editorial note. Otherwise, spellings and punctuation have been left as they are in the original text. Mistakenly omitted words within a sentence by the author have been corrected by the editors and placed within square brackets. Quotation marks duplicated for each line of a poetic selection have been deleted, with inverted commas affixed only to the opening and closing words of the selection. In a few instances, missing quotation marks within a dialogue have been silently added. Lanfear's notes appear at the foot of the page and are marked by an asterisk (*); all other editorial notes appear at the end of the text.

FATAL ERRORS;
OR
POOR MARY-ANNE.
A TALE OF THE LAST CENTURY.

In a Series of Letters.

"O Reader, had you in your mind
"The stores, which silent thought can bring,
"O gentle Reader, you would find
"A Tale, in every thing!"
       · Wordsworth.[1]

"But stranger 'tis no Tale for thee,
"Unless thou lov'st Simplicity!"
       Langhorne.[2]

London:
Printed by A. J. Valpy, Tooke's Court, Chancery Lane;
Sold by
Sherwood, Neely and Jones, Paternoster-Row,
And T. Wiche, Beech Street, Barbican.

To Mrs Wm. Hills.[3]

My Dear Niece,

 To divert my thoughts from dwelling too constantly on a subject of deep and recent affliction,[4] I some time ago had recourse to the looking over of old letters and papers, which had for the last twenty years reposed quietly in my portfolio[5] – more quietly than myself; for during that period my heart has been pierced with many sorrows.[6] Among my papers, I found the manuscript, which in deference to your opinion, and in conformity to your advice, is now ushered into the great world, where, notwithstanding my confidence in your taste, I much fear it will, like its author, make at present but a petty and antiquated appearance; but such as it is, your partiality to your aunt, which may possibly in this instance have misled your judgment, will permit her to inscribe it to you, as a small, but sincere tribute of affection and esteem.

ELIZ. LANFEAR

Islington,
May 31st, 1819.

PREFACE

From the title prefixed to this little volume my friends and subscribers may possibly be led to expect a didactic and admonitory production. In this expectation, if such has been formed, I am sorry to say they will in some measure be disappointed.[7]

The tale, which is now with some diffidence respectfully offered to the novel-reading public, and from which I must beg my young and fair readers each to find a moral of their own, was written towards the close of the last century, by a then young and single lady, for the amusement of an idle hour, without any immediate view to publication.[8]

The scene described at the masquerade, is founded on a fact, related to her by a gentleman who was present when it occurred.[9] Of the circumstance which threw into her hands the correspondence from which the letters are selected, it would be unnecessary to inform the reader. In preparing them for the press much has been curtailed from the original manuscript, through the fear of wearying the reader by a too frequent recurrence of mere sentiment, grave reflections, or by humble attempts at picturesque and local description. These curtailments have reduced the work to a smaller compass than was first intended; but though many of the letters have been abridged, such passages only have been suppressed as, having no immediate connection with the narrative, could be spared, without injury to the story, which not being a romance, but merely a plain and simple relation of what does, or may happen every day, may still appear tedious and insipid to those, who on opening a book professedly written for amusement, expect to find its pages filled with high-wrought characters, marvellous incidents, or romantic and chivalrous adventures.[10]

May 31st, 1819.

LIST OF SUBSCRIBERS

A
Agnis, Mrs. Langford, Essex
Allen, Miss, Southend, Kent[11]
Appelgath, Mrs. James St. Covent Garden[12]   3 Copies
Armstrong, Mr. Cross Street, Islington
Ashley, J. Mrs. Ramsbury, Wilts
Atkinson, Mrs. Mint, Tower Hill[13]   3 Copies

B
Backhouse, Miss
Ball, J. Esq. Winkworth Place, City Road
Belsham, Miss, Essex Street, Strand[14]
Bennett, Mrs. W. Vanburgh [sic] House, Blackheath[15]   3 Copies
Blackman, Dr. M.D. Ramsbury, Wilts
Blake, Mrs. River Terrace, Islington
Bowring, Mr. I. G. Leadenhall Street
Bromley, Mrs. W. Bernard Street, Russell Square
Browne, Rev. S. W. Birmingham[16]
Brown, Mrs. Great Forley, Berks
Brown, Mrs. Lockhinge, Berks
Brown, Miss, Idstone, Berks

C
Canning, Mrs. Park Farm, Wilts   3 Copies
Chamberlain, Mrs. Tindal Place, Islington
Chamberlain, Mrs. Jos. Milk Street, Cheapside
Chemenant, Mrs. Greenwich
Clarke, R. Mrs. Tooting
Collins, J. Esq. Spital Square, and Stamford Hill[17]
Collins, Miss, do.[18]
Collins, Miss Louisa, do.

Coope, Mrs. J. Lay-Spring
Coope, Miss, Grove, Hackney
Copeland, Mr. I. Amen Corner

D

Derric, Charles, Esq. Tindal Place, Islington
Domville, Mrs. Clapton
Drinkwater, Miss   2 Copies
Dunkin, J. Esq. Bath Hampton[19]   3 Copies
Dunkin, Mrs. Beeleigh, Essex[20]
Dyer, G. Mr. B.A. Clifford's Inn[21]

E

Evans, J. Rev. A.M. Pullens Row, Islington[22]
Evans, Mrs. do.
Evans, J. Jun. A.M. do.
Evans, Caleb, Mr. do.
Evans, Hugh, Mr. do.
Evans, G. Mr. do.

F

Fitchett, R. Esq. Yeovil
Forster, Mrs. Mount Street, Westminster   3 Copies
Forster, Mrs. Lewisham
Forster, Miss, do.
Francis, Mrs. Maldon   2 Copies
Francis, R. Mr.
Francis, R. Mrs.
Francis, H. Mrs. Finsbury[23]   3 Copies

G

Good, W. Mr. Coleman Street
Gray, Miss, Hart St. Bloomsbury

H

Harvey, D. W. Mrs. Essex St. Strand[24]
Hays, Mr. Doughty St.[25]   6 Copies
Hays, Mrs. do.   6 Copies
Hays, T. Mr. Mill St. Bermondsey[26]   3 Copies
Hays, M. Mrs. Peckham[27]
Helps, J. Mr. Wood St.
Hewet, Mrs.
Higgs, Miss, Church St. Kensington

Hill, Mrs. —— Wilts
Hills, W. Mrs. Canonbury Sq. Islington[28]   6 Copies
Hooper, D. Esq. Hampstead

J
Jeaffreson, Mr. Upper St. Islington[29]   2 Copies
Johnston, Mr. Lewisham, Sussex
Johnston, Mrs. Muswell Hill
Jones, Mrs. St. Mary Axe

K
Kingsford, Sampson, Rev. Canterbury[30]
Kingsford, Mrs. Kensworth Vicarage
Kingsford, Kennet, Mrs. Beeleigh, Essex[31]

L
Large, Mrs. —— Wilts
Large, Miss, Do.
Lanfear, Mr. Woolley, Berks
Lanfear, Miss, Do.
Lanfear, Martha, Miss, Do.
Lanfear, Wm. Mrs. Ramsbury, Wilts
Lanfear, Miss, Do.
Lanfear, E. Miss, Do.
Lanfear, A. Mr. Do.[32]
Lanfear, Mrs. Dun Mill, Berks
Lanfear, Walter Mrs. Radley, Berks
Lanfear, Jos. Mrs. Woddon Court, Surrey[33]
Laurie, Mrs. Leith and Berwick Wharf
Lee, Mrs. Brunswick Place[34]
Lee, Eyre, Mrs. Birmingham
Lepard, Mr. Lambeth[35]   3 Copies
Lepard, Mrs. Strand
Lockner, Capt. Forty Hill, Enfield[36]   3 Copies
Lockner, Wm. Mr. Coleman Street

M
Masey, Mrs. Highbury Place, Islington
Maynard, Mrs. Bennett Street, Blackfriars
Merriman, Mr. Marlborough
Meyer, Mrs. Enfield[37]

N
Nalder, Mrs. Burwick, Wilts
Nind, Mrs. B. Leytonstone

P
Palmer, N. Mrs. Aldermanbury[38]   6 Copies
Patten, R. Mr. Hatton Garden
Peak, Mrs. Berner Street
Pearson, Mrs. Tooting, Surrey
Pine, Benjamin, Mrs. Maidstone
Pine, Mary, Miss, do.
Pocock, Mrs. Stortford[39]
Powell, Mrs. Bedford Place
Preston, Mrs. Strand

R
Rainier, Mrs. Highbury Grove
Reid, Dr. M. D. Grenville Street[40]
Russell, Mrs. Ramsbury, Wilts
Rutt, N. Mr. Coleman Street[41]

S
Sharp, R. Esq. M. P. Mansion House Place[42]
Shaw, Samuel, Esq. Brunswick Place
Shuter, John, Mrs. Gainsford Street[43]
Shuter, T. A. Mrs. Southend, Kent
Shuter, Miss, Lewisham
Shuter, James, Mr.
Slipper, Mrs. Lower Street, Islington
Smith, Mrs.
Smith, Wm. Esq. Old Jewry[44]
Solly, Mrs. Layton House
Stephens, M. Miss, Dorset Square
Stock, Charles, M. Mrs.   2 Copies
Stutzer, Mrs. River Terrace, City Road
Syer, Mr. Upper Street, Islington

T
Tanner, Mrs. —— Wilts
Tate, John, Esq. Islington
Taunton, Mrs. Chancery Lane

Tooke, Wm. Rev. F. R. S. Great Ormond St.[45]
Tooke, Mrs. do.
Tooke, Miss, do.
Tooke, T. Esq. Russell Square
Tooke, Mrs. do.
Turner, J. Mr. Coleman Street
Tyrrell, Miss, Guildhall
Tyrrell, E. D. Miss, do.

V
Valpy, A. J. Esq. Chancery Lane[46]   6 Copies

W
Wainewright, Mrs. Church Row, Islington
Wedd, G. Mrs. Gainsford Street[47]   3 Copies
Wheeler, Wm. Mrs. Canonbury[48]   3 Copies
Winter, Mrs. Belsize Grove, Hampstead
Wroughton, Mrs. Woolley Park, Berks.   3 Copies

Letter I.

Miss Southerdon to Miss F—.

Sussex.

Write to me frequently, said my beloved Eliza, as Mr. Dennet handed me into the chaise that was to convey me from the beloved village which filial affection, friendship, and a thousand tender, but melancholy recollections, had rendered dearer than ever to my almost breaking heart. You may depend upon my obeying your injunction; for now that my dearest mother is no more, to whom but yourself can I pour forth with my accustomed frankness, the reflections of my mind, or the feelings of my heart, – a heart which at present seems cold, and dead to every sentiment but that of sorrow? You tell me that time will ameliorate my affliction, and that at some future period, new duties, new affections may call forth new energies, and reanimate my bosom. It may be so; but I still feel that nothing can ever obliterate from my mind the fond, the grateful remembrance of a mother so tenderly beloved, of a father so justly respected. The world is to me an untried path, and all at present a blank before me. Mr. Dennet, though only an uncle by marriage, is, since the death of my parents, my nearest relation: I was too much engrossed by my own sorrows to have much conversation with him during our journey, but have since talked with him several times on the subject of my affairs.* He tells me, what I indeed knew before, that the principal part of my parents' income arising from an annuity on my mother's life, which of course expired with her, my fortune will be very small; but, he added, if I would entrust it in his hands, he would endeavor to make the most of it for me: in the mean time he begged me to consider his house as my home, where I should be welcome to reside as long as I continued single, or till I could find a more agreeable place of residence. "Your company," he continued, "will be to me an acquisition: for since the death of Mrs. Dennet, and the marriage of Sarah, my darling, and only child,[49] I have been very dull, and much at a loss for a good housekeeper." I thanked him for his kindness, and acquiesced in this arrangement. What better could I do? So here I am, and here for a while I am like to continue; for in our days there are no giants who run away with unfortunate damsels; and if there were, I have no sworn knight, no constant lover, to come to my assistance.

Letter II.

You desire me to write to you with the same freedom, the same fulness of communication, with which in times past we were accustomed to converse. I assure you it is my intention so to do, but at present I have little or nothing to inform

---

* Mr. Southerdon was educated for the church, but being prevented by some scruple of conscience from taking orders, he retired on a small annuity, with his wife and daughter, then an infant, into a distant county in the West of England. He died before his daughter had completed her eighteenth year, and Mrs. Southerdon did not long survive him.

you of, worth your attention; for though the sphere in which I formerly moved was narrow, my circle here is still more contracted. Our family party consists of Mr. Dennet, myself, one man servant, two female ones, a cat, and a dog; and in the few visits which I have either received or paid since I have been here, I have not yet met with one person who at all interests me: but as my uncle is very kind, very good-natured, and leaves me at entire liberty to employ my time, in any way I think proper, I ought not, and will not complain. He informs me that he is expecting very shortly some visitors from London, which I assure you we consider as quite an event, and are at present busily engaged in fatting turkeys, making mince pies, &c. &c. for the occasion. Our expected guests, who have promised to spend their Christmas with us, are a Mr. and Mrs. Cooper, distant relations of the late Mrs. Dennet. When they come down, I will write to you again. I was in the hope of seeing my cousin Sarah this winter, but she is at present confined.

Letter III.

Our expected guests arrived on Christmas eve, and since they have been with us, my time, which has been fully engaged, has passed very pleasantly. Mr. Cooper, who from his appearance I should judge to be about forty-five years of age, is an agreeable, gentlemanly man. His lady, a few years younger, may still be called a fine woman: her manners affable and genteel, but not so interesting as those of her husband, whom I find both a pleasant and intelligent companion. We are, in this short time, already become great friends, and they have given me an invitation to return with them to London, and to spend the ensuing spring at their house, where Mr. Cooper, having a large acquaintance, has promised to introduce me to a variety of different characters, and to many persons in whose society, he tells me, I shall be much gratified. Mr. Dennet not objecting to my leaving him for a short time, I have consented to this arrangement; and shall next week accompany my new friends to Berner Street.[50] Though I promise myself both pleasure and improvement from the excursion, having never been in London, I cannot help feeling some agitation at the thought of going there; but this will soon subside; and it would be a pity to lose the opportunity which now offers of going to town, as I may never have such another, and I could not possibly visit the metropolis under better protection.

Letter IV.

Since my last,[*] which informed you of my safe arrival, with Mr. and Mrs. Cooper, in Berner Street, I have not had one hour which I could spare for writing. My friends, who are exceedingly kind, do all in their power to entertain me. Our mornings have been occupied in running after fine sights, and our evenings in

---

[*] This letter does not appear.

visiting most of the principal theatres, and various other places of public amusement. Mr. Cooper, agreeably to his promise, has also introduced me into several private parties, in which at different times, I have been in company with authors, philosophers, and divines. In short in this little month I have both seen and heard more of this great world than ever I did before, or perhaps ever may again; and have gained from observation and experience, that species of knowledge which mere speculation can never afford. Whether I am happier or the better for my newly acquired wisdom, is a question which at present I have not time to ask myself. Yet there are moments, when my heart tells me, that "all is vanity and vexation of spirit;"[51] and it sometimes sickens within me at the sight of those vices and follies which everywhere abound in this overgrown metropolis. Among the higher classes, with a very few exceptions, interest and pleasure appear to be the Baals to which all bow the knee; and even among the literary circles, into which Mr. Cooper has been so good as to take me, though generally amused, I have not unfrequently been disgusted; and am at last, though reluctantly, obliged to confess that I like books better than book-makers, philosophy than philosophers, and tell Mr. Cooper, who sometimes talks with me on the subject of religion, that divinity must not be confounded with divines. The fault which most offends me in the philosopher, as well as in the priest, and of which I find them equally guilty, is a bigotted attachment to their own systems, and a want of liberality and candor to those whose opinions differ, though ever so minutely, from their own. Yet I am sometimes diverted at hearing in one party, writings and sentiments treated with the utmost contempt, which the next I go into may possibly extol as the highest effort of human genius. In short I find every one full of themselves, and ready to pronounce their own judgment a criterion from which they allow of no appeal.

I must confess upon the whole I feel myself both hurt and disappointed, at meeting with so much dogmatism, and vanity among those whom, when in solitude, I had pictured in my own imagination, as the wisest, and the best of men. I now own that I expected too much; and will for the future learn to take human nature as I find it, though my soul still pants after that ideal good, that visionary perfection, which nothing I have yet seen realises.

Letter V.

Never, my dear friend, did I more earnestly wish for a little chat with you, than I do this morning. I feel as if I had a world of intelligence to communicate, and yet, now that I have taken up my pen, I scarcely know what it is I wish to say. There is an awkwardness in committing one's thoughts to paper, which in conversation we do not feel, – at least so it appears to me at present, still I must try to give you an account of our yesterday's visit, or rather of a gentleman whom we met with at that visit; the rest of the company were mere nothings; – I mean comparatively. In the morning, Mrs. Cooper told me that we were engaged to dinner at a Mr. Smith's. "I am sorry for it," said I; "my spirits are exhausted: I am not quite well to-day, and am almost tired of racketing about." "We shall not stay late in the evening," cried Mr. Cooper, "and I think you will be pleased with the party. Mr. Smith is himself a clever man, and we generally meet very good company at his house." I wished to have been left at home; but feeling that it would appear rude and ungrateful in me, to oppose, what was designed by my friends to give me pleasure, I made no farther objection. As the day advanced, my reluctance to going out increased. The weather was cold, wet and gloomy. I was in melancholy mood, disinclined to dress: in short I was out of spirits, and every exertion appeared a burden to me: but go I must; and before I had finished the business of the toilette, the coach was at the door. At Mr. Smith's we were introduced to a genteel, but small party of ladies and gentlemen; and informed at the same time, that we were to have met there a gentleman of the name of Howard, who had been invited, but unfortunately was previously engaged: "But," added Mr. Smith, "he has promised if possible to join us in the evening." The name of Howard was familiar to me, having frequently heard Mr. Cooper speak of this Mr. Howard as a very superior man; but I had no wish to see him, no anxiety lest he should not come. My desire to be introduced to men of talents was abated; those whom I had already seen had disappointed me. I expected gods, and had found men.

A polite and agreeable young man of the name of Wansey, sat next to me at table. His attentions, added to the amusing conversation of the rest of the company, dissipated by degrees my ill humour. My vapours were flown, and had left in their stead a not unpleasing languor, from which I was in some measure roused by Mrs. Smith's saying to her husband, "Do you think Mr. Howard will be here at tea?" I at that minute had forgotten he was expected; and when his name was mentioned, wished, I knew not why, that he might not come. We now left the dinner-room, and soon after a loud rap at the gate occasioned me to start. "This is Mr. Howard," said Mr. Smith; and so it proved. In a few minutes the drawing-room door was opened, and a gentleman apparently about five and thirty, entered, with an air so genteel, so unceremonious, and yet so perfectly well bred, that I know not how to describe it. I gazed on him for a few moments in silence. He could not be called handsome; yet he appeared to me of a superior order of beings from any I had before seen. I know not what was the charm; yet the very first time that he addressed me, I found in the very tone of his voice, an attraction which riveted my attention. Conversation, which the entrance of Mr. Howard had a little interrupted, was soon renewed. Among other subjects, the propriety of a sexual distinction in character and manners, happened to be discussed; and I soon found that Mr. Howard carried his ideas of that distinction much farther than you and I allow of.[52] Yet do not smile when I tell you, that I felt no inclination to defend my own opinions, when I saw that they did not exactly coincide with his. Yet I did, though timidly, venture to complain of the many and various evils to which our sex are, in every country, more or less exposed; and added, "If the history of man, which I believed to be the case, was a melancholy one – that of woman, I was afraid on inquiry, would be found to be still more so." "I am not sure whether I shall grant that," cried Mr. Howard; "both sexes necessarily suffer some degree of oppression under every form of government; but while our sex are in a continual state of hostility with each other, yours, in civilised countries at least, enjoy the inestimable privilege of being universally treated with kindness, tenderness, and respect;" and he added, "that he should be sorry to witness the time, when we should be addressed by the other sex, with the same look, the same manner, the same tone of voice, as man to man." This speech had certainly more of a gallantry in it, than of truth; and had any other person in company made it, I should not have let it pass without a comment. As it was, I only observed, "that men everywhere enjoyed a much greater degree of liberty than was allowed to women." "Political liberty, do you mean?" replied Mr. Howard, "or do you complain of the domestic tyranny to which your sex are sometimes subjected?" I answered, "Neither:" looked down, and I believe very silly, for I felt embarrassed, and all of a glow! "Of what then?" said he, with a smile, which increased my confusion. "You have the liberty of a choice in the most important action of life, a liberty which we are denied." "That liberty," he replied, "is partly ideal: very few men are united to the woman of their choice;" and I thought, or it was my fancy, that he looked grave as he said so. He then added, "that he did not mean to deny that his sex possessed many advantages of which ours were deprived. He only wished to remind me that we enjoyed various exclusive privileges, which tended to preserve the balance; – privileges of which he never wished to see us deprived."

Alas, my dear Eliza, when will women be free? Never, I am afraid, while their chains are so sweetly gilded.[53] With men of real understanding, it is nonsense to contend for equality. They allow us all that is requisite to make us amiable, all that is necessary to render us happy. It is the coxcomb, the half-witted only, who pretend to treat woman with contempt, priding themselves on their sexual superiority, because they are conscious of not possessing any other.

Mr. Howard then said, – but it would be in vain to attempt to tell you the one half of what he said, though the recollection of the conversation kept me waking the greater part of the night. Then his manner was so conciliating, his smile so benevolent, the tone of his voice so manly, yet so harmonious, his language so elegant, so correct, that on whatever subject he gave us his opinion, those of the company who, before he came, had been most eager to speak, appeared now equally willing to listen, and by the most respectful attention, tacitly acknowledge his superiority. In short there was a sort of fascination in his eloquence which could be better felt than described.

As for myself, I have been in a delirium ever since. On our return, Mr. Cooper asked me my opinion of Mr. Howard. "I think him," I replied, "both the scholar and gentleman. He appears to me to possess virtue, talents, fine sense, exquisite taste: in short, every excellent as well as engaging quality." Mr. Cooper rallied me on the warmth with which I expressed myself, while he smiled at the extravagance, I suppose, of my panegyric. "Though," he answered, "Mr. Howard is, I assure you, all that you think him, he is also a man of large fortune; one who has travelled, seen a great deal of life, and has at different periods mixed in the very first circles: yet he is not a gay man, and I know of no one who is more generally respected." "I wonder," cried Mrs. Cooper, "that he is not married; but I suppose he has never yet met with a woman clever enough to suit him." "I dare say that is not the reason," replied Mr. C. "for we frequently see men of the first talents united, and that by choice, to very silly women." "Why is that?" I asked. "It may be accounted for, said he, on various grounds; but now we are on the subject of matrimony, pray what did you think of Mr. Wansey? I remarked that he paid you uncommon attention: and I intend asking him to dine with us very shortly, on purpose to give you the opportunity of completing your conquest. He is a young man of independent, though not large property, and one for whom I entertain a particular esteem." "I have not the vanity," said I, "to suppose that Mr. Wansey's attentions to me were any other, than what most young men think it incumbent on them to pay to single ladies; and so little impression did they make on me, that I assure you I had quite forgotten them:" and so I really had. Before Mr. Howard entered, I believe I had thought Mr. Wansey an agreeable young man; though by the side of him – but if I rant any more about this same Mr. Howard, you will certainly conclude that I have lost either my heart or my senses: the latter I give you leave to think, but not the former. Believe me, my dear Eliza, I consider him as too exalted, as moving in too high a sphere, to be loved by your forlorn, your orphaned friend.

Letter VI.

Mr. Wansey, the young man whom I mentioned to you in my last letter, after escorting us to the Park, the following Sunday, on Mr. Cooper's invitation, came home with us to dinner: since which time he has become a frequent visitor. My friends here, who place his more than usual attention to my account, are continually rallying me on the subject; and yesterday evening after he had left us, Mr. Cooper said to me, in a graver tone than he usually assumes, "that he congratulated me on having gained, in Mr. Wansey, a lover worthy of my acceptance." I answered seriously, "I should be sorry if I thought Mr. Wansey had formed any serious attachment to me, or had any intention of making me an offer of his hand." "Why so?" cried Mrs. Cooper. "Because," I replied, "it would give me no satisfaction to gain a heart, unless I could give my own in return." And why should you not give your own in return?" asked Mr. Cooper. "Because, though I consider Mr. Wansey as an agreeable acquaintance, and might in time esteem him as a friend, I could never think of him as a lover." "That is odd, may I add, a little perverse," replied Mr. Cooper: "when a young lady's affections are quite disengaged, (which, when you first came to my house, you assured me yours were,) from regarding a worthy young man, as an agreeable acquaintance, I should imagine it would be no very difficult, nor unnatural transition to receive him as a lover." "Our discussion," I returned, "at least as far as it applies to Mr. Wansey, is at present I think rather premature; so I shall say no more on the subject, but wish you a good night." The next morning, while we were at breakfast, Mr. Wansey was announced: the consciousness of what had passed between Mr. Cooper and myself the preceding evening, made me change colour as he entered the room. I hope he did not observe it; for I cannot love him, and should be truly sorry to mislead him. Mr. Cooper had said something, the night before, about going to the play. Mr. Wansey offered to join our party, and called in the morning to know our determination. "I should excessively like to go to-night," said Mrs. Cooper. "Agreed then," said Mr. C.: "and, Wansey, you take your dinner with us; a corner in our coach will be much at your service. Mr. Wansey accepted the invitation, and appeared to be in high spirits. At dinner he was to me, even more than usually attentive; at the play he seated himself by my side, and was during the whole evening so gallant, so polite, and so fearful lest I should be any ways incommoded, that I really could not help smiling at his well-meant, though over-anxiety. Towards the close of the third act, Mr. Cooper directed my eye to a box on the other side of the house, in which one glance told me was Mr. Howard. He saw us, smiled, and bowed: the mere sight of him, was to me as an electric shock: I know not how otherwise to describe the instantaneous effect which it produced on my feelings. I no longer attended either to the play or to Mr. Wansey, whose civilities became troublesome to me. I grew peevish, while I regretted the loss of that superior entertainment which I should have received had I been with those from whose criticism, whose refined taste, I might have improved my own. Thinking what I might have gained, I lost what it was still in my power to secure, and when the curtain dropt, so confused, so abstracted were my thoughts, I knew not that the play was finished, till Mr. Wansey roused me from my reverie, by asking me if I were not well. I hastily withdrew my eyes from the box, to which I fear they had been but too frequently directed, and standing up, complained of the insufferable heat of the house. "You wish to leave it," cried Mr. Wansey, "and will not like to stay the after-piece." "I have no choice," I replied, "and will do just what is agreeable to the rest of the party." "Let us stay the entertainment by all means," cried Mr. Cooper. I reseated myself, and once more ventured to steal a glance at the opposite side-box. He whom my eye sought, had left the house. The entertainment appeared to me very insipid: my head ached, and I was glad when it was over.

Letter VII.

We yesterday had the Smiths, with other company to dine with us: our party was select; and Mr. Howard, though last, not least, was of the number. The conversation during the whole of the day was extremely animated; but my attention was too much engrossed by one individual, to do justice to the rest; for when Mr. Howard is present, it is impossible to listen with patience to any one beside. Let him speak on what he will, he is so perfectly the master of his subject, that every interruption, or even observation from any one else appears impertinent: then to our sex he is so well-bred, so truly polite, and his flattery, if flattery it may be called, so delicate, that we almost mistake it for truth. In the course of conversation I ventured to ask him, "whether he did not think that women in general were too much the slaves of opinion?"[54] "I would not wish you to be indifferent to opinion." "But do you not think our respect for it may be carried too far?"

"Certainly." – "Do you allow," said Mrs. Smith, interrupting him, "of the natural equality of the sexes; or do you contend, that as men have more physical strength than women, they have also more mental capacity?" "I am not of the opinion," he replied, "that physical strength and mental capacity have any necessary connexion; for even granting that the faculties of the mind depend on the organisation of the body, it must be the fineness, and delicacy of the machine, and not the mere muscular strength, which constitutes its superior powers.[55] In delicacy of organisation, your sex," turning towards me, "certainly have the advantage over ours, and I have no doubt of your being equally with us capable of attaining every branch of knowledge, had you the same opportunities of acquiring it."

"But these we are denied," returned Mrs. Smith; "for, waving the difference of what is termed education, how narrow, comparatively, is the circle to which we are, generally speaking, confined; how many the prejudices by which we are shackled; and, out of our own families and immediate connexions, how few are the opportunities which we possess of gaining knowledge of any description!" "That is true," replied Mr. Howard, "but still the domestic occupations of females are, in my opinion, greatly superior to the mechanical employments of men of business: for surely the regulation of a family, the bringing up of children, the management of servants, are all higher departments, and require more of mind to conduct them properly, than the mere sordid pursuit of getting money." "But how few families," said I, "are conducted properly, nor has every woman a family to conduct," and I sighed; the sigh, though gentle, and scarcely audible, did not escape unnoticed. There was a something at that instant in the look and manner of Mr. Howard which told me he had heard, and understood it. Nothing eludes his penetration. I am sometimes in fear that he should read my thoughts. "Words," I once heard him say, "were the least part of conversation." Mr. Wansey, to my great relief, is gone out of town: he called on us before he set off, and said as he took his leave, that he should depend on finding me in Berner Street on his return. I am glad he was not of our party; his attentions would both have wearied and distressed me.

Letter VIII.

I have been nearly three months in London, and must now very shortly return into Sussex: my spirits sink at the thought. Since I have tasted the pleasure of more polished society, the sameness, and insipidity of our country neighbours appear to me insupportable. On my first coming to town, I felt a little disappointed; my ideas were confused, my head in a whirl; we were too dissipated, and viewing mankind in a mass, I not unfrequently turned with disgust from the gaudy, and sometimes odious picture which society presented. On a nearer and more minute inspection, I discern the nicer shades of individual merit; and by degrees lose my sense of general corruption, in the more pleasing contemplation of private excellence. Since my last letter to you, I have several times, in different parties, met with Mr. Howard; and every interview has added to the high opinion which I had previously entertained of his merit; while several anecdotes of his private life, related to me by Mr. Cooper, have increased the favourable judgment which I had before formed of his character and disposition. The first time I was in company with him, I was sure that he was amiable, or I should not have felt so strong a predilection in his favour. Talents may dazzle, but mere talents never touch the heart. I sometimes think, that I should respect him even more than I do at present, were his manners and conversation less brilliant. Mr. and Mrs. Cooper went yesterday morning to look at a collection of pictures:[56] I was not quite well, and declined accompanying them. Before their return Mr. Howard called on us, and was introduced into the drawing-room, where I was sitting alone, absorbed in meditation. Gilpin's Western Tour[57] was lying on the table: he took it up, and after reading aloud a few passages, entered into a conversation with me on the beauties of nature. He then spoke of the peculiar pleasure which travelling affords to persons of a cultivated taste, and gave me an account of several tours which he had himself made to different parts of England, and described some of the views which he had seen, and the places which he had visited, in such elegant and glowing language, that, listening to him, I forgot where I was, or how the minutes flew, till the entrance of Mr. and Mrs. Cooper dissolved the charm, and restored to me my recollection.

The conversation now took a different turn. Mr. Cooper talked of the paintings which he had been looking at, and mentioned in particular a large picture of Milton's Satan, which he thought very fine. Mr. Howard had seen it, but did not admire it: he thought it badly conceived: the portrait was too hideous: the artist ought to have represented Satan as beautiful, though fallen; and turning to Mrs. Cooper and myself, added, "I am sure the ladies will be of my opinion." "Certainly," I replied, "he ought to be represented beautiful, as the seducer of men." "As the seducer of women also," he replied.[58] "Eve," I answered quickly, "was, we are told, seduced by her ear." He smiled, and I felt, and I dare say looked, very silly; but that is what, in his company, I very frequently do. The strong sense which I entertain of his superiority to myself in every point of view, over-powers and oppresses me: never, I fear, do I appear to so little advantage as in his presence. Before him, all self-conceit, all self-possession are annihilated; and after having been in his company, I feel restless, mortified, and unhappy.

Letter IX.

Beware, beware, are the concluding words of your last grave and admonitory letter. The admonition comes too late: I do love him. I can no longer deceive myself: why therefore should I attempt to deceive my friend? Were I never to see him again, never again to hear the sound of that voice which still vibrates in my ear, or listen to those honied accents which have sunk so deep into my soul, I should never forget him. I both feel and acknowledge all the absurdity, all the hopelessness, of the sentiment which I still love to cherish. But you shall be obeyed. I will soon, very soon seek for safety in flight; yet could I but for one moment think it possible that – but no more – I will not cherish so idle, so vain a hope; yet "love will hope, where reason would despair."[59]

Letter X.

He is gone, gone from me for ever! I am sick at heart; my mind, which so lately was agitated with vague hopes, and restless uncertainty, is now enveloped in the thick gloom of despair. I shall never see him again; and whilst I can never for a single moment banish his adored image from my memory, mine is by him perhaps already forgotten. In vain I summon reason to my aid; – but I have not yet told you what has occasioned my present disquiet. Mr. Cooper this morning informed me that he expected a few friends at dinner; "and," he added, "I wished to have had Mr. Howard of our party, but he is gone out of town: he set off on a journey yesterday morning at an early hour, and I understand it is uncertain when he will return." Some person at that minute coming into the room, prevented my gaining at that time any farther information; so I hurried into my own room, that I might there conceal the painful emotion, which I found I had not the power to suppress.

At dinner, Mr. Howard's name having been mentioned, a lady who sat opposite to me, said, "I wonder whether there is any truth in the report which I have heard of Mr. Howard's being engaged to the rich and the beautiful Miss C—." "I cannot tell," replied Mr. Cooper, "but I do not know where the lady could bestow either her beauty or her fortune better." "I hear it is publicly talked of by many persons," cried a gentleman, who had before spoken of Mr. Howard as his particular friend, "but I believe without sufficient authority: I do not think Mr. Howard a marrying man." I was at this instant paring an apple, which I attempted to divide, without knowing what I was about; the knife slipped, and cut my finger: this accident, though a trifling one, being observed, interrupted the conversation, a conversation by which I had already been sufficiently excruciated. I felt as if I were going to faint; and availing myself of the excuse which my accident afforded, left the room. Mrs. Cooper followed me; and while she bound up my finger, which was still bleeding, told me, she thought I had possessed more courage, than to be so much disconcerted by so slight a wound. Glad to find my sudden indisposition attributed to a wrong cause, I sought not to exculpate myself from the charge of cowardice, though I could have told her that it was a wound deeper, and more severe than what the knife had inflicted, which had occasioned my sudden disorder. It is late, and I must lay down my pen: when I retired for the night, not feeling any inclination to sleep, I would not go to bed till I had relieved my spirits from part of the weight by which they feel at present burthened, by writing to you.

Letter XI.

Mr. Wansey returned one day last week from B—, where I understand he has been on a visit to his friends. He called on us the same evening, and the day after sent me a letter, containing professions of love, and an offer of marriage.

Not willing to add the anxiety of suspense to the pain of disappointment, I sent him my answer on the same day, written as I had previously determined to write, should I receive from him this, I may say expected, address. Mr. Cooper, from whom, as Mr. Wansey had made him a confident, I could not conceal my refusal, has since been both chiding and arguing with me on the subject; and I have been obliged to make use of all the rhetoric of which I am mistress, to reconcile him to my decision, and to convince him that I am not acting a weak and capricious part. In refusing Mr. Wansey, I may be committing an error; but the error, if it is one, proceeds from my heart, rather than from my judgment. I do not think by the conversation which passed between Mr. Cooper and myself on the subject, that he has any suspicion of my attachment to his other, his superior friend, and this is to me some consolation: my love for him is a madness, a folly, which I wish no one but yourself to be acquainted with. To-morrow I leave Berner Street; my next letter to you will be from Sussex.

Letter XII.

Once more I write to you from Mr. Dennet's, whose house I had looked to as an asylum, where, if I did not find happiness, I might at least hope to enjoy retirement and repose; but in this hope I am at present disappointed, as a circumstance is likely to take place which will render my stay here very uncertain. On the morning after I last wrote you, I bade farewell to London, which city perhaps I may never visit again. Mr. Cooper accompanied me to the coach in which I was to travel, and I stepped into it with a heavy heart. How different were the sensations with which I arrived, from those with which I left the metropolis! My journey was a dull one, and I got to the end of it just as the setting sun was gilding with its last rays the spire of the little church which stands near to my uncle's house. He received me very kindly; but when I told him that I did not mean to run away from him again for a long time, I observed an embarrassment in his manner of answering me, which I could not then account for. The next morning I apologised to him for having made my stay in Berner Street rather longer than I had at first proposed. "I assure you," he replied, "I have more than once been tempted during your absence to get me another housekeeper; for I began to think that you never intended to come back." "Why then did you not send for me? Had you written to me to hasten my return, I certainly should have obeyed your summons." "I do not doubt that, but I did not wish you to shorten your visit on my account: to tell you the truth, I had fancied that you would pick up a husband while you were in town. My friend Cooper promised me that he would look out one for you; for he said, that you were too clever for the young men about us." I smiled, and replied that I was much obliged to Mr. Cooper for his intention, but that I was not at present desirous of changing my situation. "All young lasses, while they are disengaged, say the same," returned Mr. Dennet, "but when the right man comes they are ready enough to alter their tone." "But suppose the right man never should come, then you know I shall be obliged to live single." "You remind me of my daughter, who, before Mr. Woodfield offered to [marry] her, used to talk of being an old maid, and all that nonsense, and you see how well she kept her word; and now whenever I go to see her, she tells me she is as happy as the days are long." "I am glad to hear that Mrs. Woodfield is so happy," said I; "but notwithstanding she has set me so good an example, I much doubt whether I shall very soon follow it." "Well, there is no hurry," he replied; "you are young enough yet, and while you continue single, you are welcome to consider my house as your home, even though I should be foolish enough to take another wife myself." "I am not afraid of that, Sir." "Why less likely things have come to pass: since you left us we have a new neighbor, a widow lady, whom I am much pleased with. She appears to be a very clever managing sort of a woman, and I assure you we are already on very good terms with each other: – I must introduce you to her."

I had not, even after this conversation, the least idea that Mr. Dennet had any serious intention of marrying again, and should have thought no more on the subject, if he had not in the evening again resumed it, when he gave me to understand that it was a settled thing, and would very shortly take place; but he again repeated, that I should be still welcome to consider his house as my home; for the lady whom he was going to marry had made no objection to my living with them; "for, to tell you the truth," continued he, "knowing that the interest of the money which is in my hands would not be sufficient for your support, I made that a part of the bargain." I thanked him in suitable terms for his kindness and consideration, but added, that as the lady whom he had chosen and myself were at present perfect strangers, it was impossible for me to say whether or not it might be agreeable to either of us to live together. A short silence succeeded this speech, which I broke, by saying, "that I purposed very shortly paying a visit to his daughter, Mrs. Woodfield, whom I had not seen since her marriage, after which I should most likely return, at least for a time, to his house." "Well, my dear, do whatever will be most agreeable to yourself," was his answer: "but I will to-morrow introduce you to the widow, and when you have seen her, you will better know how to form your future plans: my daughter, I can answer for her, will be very glad to see you."

Letter XIII.

I have seen my uncle's intended bride, and cannot endure her: I am certain he will not add to his comfort by this new connexion. The late Mrs. Dennet was a gentle, quiet, sensible woman, one who, without any pretension to superior abilities, possessed a thousand good and amiable qualities: this lady, if I am not greatly mistaken in my judgment, is of an exactly contrary character. She appears to be about forty years of age; her person large and coarse: her countenance may have been reckoned handsome, but it does not please me. We went yesterday by appointment to spend the day with her. She received me very graciously, and did the honours of her house with that sort of ostentatious politeness, that overstrained civility, which is rather calculated to give disgust, than to gratify a delicate mind. How different is this mere ceremonious complaisance from that which proceeds from an amiable heart, or an obliging disposition, and still more so from that higher species of good breeding, which diffuses by I know not what sort of magic, a grace, a charm, over the various and nameless intercourses of social life! Perhaps my recent journey to London may at present have rendered me a little too fastidious.

Letter XIV.

The knot is tied, and my uncle's wedding, which was celebrated soon after I last wrote to you, has put not only our own house, but the whole town, in a bustle; visiting, feasting, parties of pleasure, in all of which I have been obliged both to assist and partake, have succeeded each other so rapidly, as to leave me scarcely one moment at liberty. There have, in times past, been seasons when such a stir might have afforded me some diversion: but in my present state of mind, the vulgar mirth, idle parade, and domestic confusion, in which we have been, and are indeed still involved, are more irksome and disgusting to me, than I can well express.

Letter XV.

An entire revolution appears likely to take place in our domestic establishment, and Mr. Dennet I suspect is already beginning to regret the liberty which he has lost, and the quiet which he can no longer enjoy. Mrs. Dennet was no sooner brought home, than she found out that the house was too small, the furniture old-fashioned, and the paddock and orchard, which have been hitherto kept for use, she thinks may be converted into pleasure grounds and shrubbery. In short she is every day proposing or projecting some new plan of alteration. My uncle objects both to the trouble and to the expense attending these new schemes, and sometimes opposes them; the lady is then offended; he remonstrates, she replies, I of course am neuter, and when I see an altercation likely to ensue, leave the room. Mrs. Dennet I am persuaded, views me with a suspicious eye, and already considers me as a supernumerary in the family. It is not my intention to trouble her long with my company. Next week I purpose going into Surrey on a visit to Mrs. Woodfield, whom I have not seen for some years. Mr. Woodfield I am entirely unacquainted with: what stay I shall make with them, or what plan I shall next pursue, I cannot at present determine. I am now afloat on the great ocean of life; my happiness I fear has already suffered shipwreck. For,

> "The maid who loves,
> Goes out to sea upon a shatter'd plank,
> And puts her trust in miracles for safety."[60]

My heart thanks you for your kind wishes, and for your earnest entreaties that I would return to the little village where I spent so happily my early youth. I have turned it over in my own mind, but feel[61] that I have not sufficient resolution to return to a spot where every thing would so forcibly remind me of those dear parents, who there lie buried. I am also much obliged for the offer which your mother has kindly made me of residing, at least for a time, at your house; but I am aware that your large family, your mother's ill state of health, added to other circumstances, would render my residence with you for any length of time extremely inconvenient to you all, and I am inclined to think, it is to your friendship alone, that I am indebted for the invitation.

Letter XVI.

On Monday last I exchanged the no longer peaceful habitation of my uncle, for the rural and delightful abode of his daughter, in whose family I behold a pleasing and unaffected picture of domestic felicity. Mr. and Mrs. Woodfield, who gave me a most cordial, and hospitable reception, appear to me to be one of the happiest pairs I have yet met with. Neither of them possess cultivated minds, nor extensive information; but they have excellent hearts, and a considerable share of that useful quality usually termed good sense. He is healthy, active, cheerful, and affectionate: she modest, ingenuous, good humoured and industrious. Attached to each other, and both equally devoted to their children, their hopes, their pleasures, their cares are all centered in the delightful though narrow bounds of their own little circle.

> "Small change of scene, small space his home requires,
> Who leads a life of satisfied desires."[62]

Mr. Woodfield occupies a farm, the management of which affords him a constant and varied employment. My cousin takes care of her children, and superintends her household, which, in a large farm-house, I assure you is no little business. Thus each employed in their proper departments, and mutually necessary the one to the other, they appear to be united on terms of perfect equality; while they leave it to those, who in married life are less happy than themselves to settle the question of on which side the balance of power ought to preponderate.

Letter XVII.

The order, the peace, and the innocent cheerfulness which I daily both witness and partake of, in this amiable and happy family, soothes my mind, while it gives both scope and exercise to my benevolent affections. The children, with whom I am already become a great favourite, are my constant companions: the two elder little girls are proud to call themselves my scholars, and receive with avidity whatever I am disposed to teach them; while I endeavor to improve them by blending instruction with the little tales which I tell them for their amusement, their simple remarks, and artless conversation afford me a new, and interesting entertainment.

My temper, naturally tranquil, has since I have been thus employed, nearly regained its habitual serenity. It is true, my pleasures here are less animated, less intoxicating than those which I sometimes tasted, while staying in Berner Street; but are they not safer, and may I not hope they will prove more permanent? Next week Mrs. Woodfield talks of paying a visit to a sister of Mr. Woodfield's who is married to an attorney; they live at ——. We are to have a post-chaise for the day, and the two little girls, who are my scholars, are to accompany us.

Letter XVIII.

Yesterday was the time fixed on for our excursion to ——. Mrs. Woodfield having promised to spend a long day with her friends, ordered the chaise to be at our door at an early hour in the morning; and before six o'clock we set off. The weather was delightful; some soft showers had fallen in the night, by which all nature seemed refreshed and every passing breeze wafted sweet perfume from the fields, where the new mown hay was lying scattered in rich profusion on either side of the road, while the birds, newly awakened to love, and to happiness, were pouring forth[63] their matin strains in grateful and varied melody! Our minds were in unison with the scene; for myself, if I may so describe my sensations, I felt a sort of voluptuous tranquility, a serene, a heart-felt thankfulness for existence, in a world so happy and so fair. Mrs. Woodfield was in excellent spirits, while those of the children were exhilarated beyond their usual flow: their little hearts, which knew no sorrow, were

"Light as thistle's down floating, that sports on the air."[64]

O happy age! when devoid of passion, devoid of care, every hour presents some new pleasure, some new pursuit. We entered the town of —— as the church-clock struck eight, and a few minutes after alighted at a good old-fashioned house near the market-place, where we were received by Mr. Devenish with great politeness, and entertained by his lady, an agreeable woman, with true country hospitality. In the evening, when we were taking our leave, Mrs. Devenish said to Mrs. Woodfield, "Before you go, sister, can you tell me of any respectable young woman whom you can recommend to take the charge of the house and servants?" "I cannot exactly tell what you mean," replied my cousin. "I will explain my meaning," returned Mrs. Devenish. "A short time ago, Mr. D. was employed as agent to sell a small freehold estate in our vicinity. A gentleman from London purchased it. He does not mean to reside there constantly, but talks of coming down occasionally, and has requested of me as a favor, to hire for him two female servants, and some young person, of a superior description, to act as superintendent or housekeeper; the servants, she added, I have already hired; but have not yet met with any person whom I think sufficiently respectable for the higher department." "Is the gentleman married or single?" asked Mrs. Woodfield.[65] "Single, I believe," said Mrs. Devenish; "but he is so much of the gentleman, and bears, I understand, such an excellent character, that I should not be afraid of trusting my own daughter with him, had I one old enough for the situation." "I assure you," cried Mr. Devenish, who was waiting to see us into the chaise, which was standing at the door, "I never transacted business with any gentleman with whom I was so well pleased, as with Mr. Howard." "Mr. Howard!" I spontaneously repeated, while a variety of confused ideas passed at that instant through my brain. "Do you know any person of that name?" inquired Mr. Devenish. "I met with a person of that name last winter while I was in London, who so exactly answers to the description which you have given of this gentleman, that – "What was his christian name?" "Algernon." "The very same," cried Mr. Devenish. The possibility of myself going into the situation which Mrs. Devenish had been previously talking of, seized my imagination, and I immediately desired her not to engage with any other person until she had heard further from me. The children were already in the chaise; I seated myself by their side but could neither attend to their prattle nor engage in more serious conversation with their mother. The slanting sunbeams yet glittered[66] through the trees, while the advancing twilight threw a softened tint over that landscape, which in the morning I had thought so lovely. My mind was no longer at liberty to enjoy its varied beauties. One subject engrossed all my thoughts, and as soon as we got home I hastened to my own apartment, that I might be more at liberty to revolve over in my own mind all the possible consequences which might result from the rash step I was about taking. Ah! my dear friend, I see, I feel all the difficulties, all the dangers to which I am voluntarily to expose myself.

Do not mistake my meaning, it is neither for my virtue nor my reputation that I am apprehensive; his character and my own are sufficient securities for both; but to be under the same roof, without daring to aspire even to that degree of equality which I apparently enjoyed in my intercourse with him during my stay at Mr. Cooper's; to arrive at perhaps the cruel and mortifying certainty that another has prior greater claims to his affection; these are the trials which I dread, these are the evils which I am about to encounter.

Letter XIX.

The die is cast, I have written my determination to Mrs. Devenish, and have received her answer, and to-morrow Mr. Woodfield is to escort me to the house of his sister, where I am to sleep one night, and the next morning she is to introduce me to my new abode. Already do I begin to repent of the precipitation with which I have acted, and shrink at the idea of my own temerity, in thus wildly rushing into a situation where my pride, my sensibility, may ere I leave it, be exposed to more severe and cruel mortifications than I am at present aware of. If I were not afraid of appearing weak and inconsistent to my friends here, who, ignorant of my feelings, approve of the step which I have taken, I should be tempted even now to recede from an engagement which I much fear I have too rashly entered into. Then the thought of being under the protection of him, whom I own I still love, carries with it such an irresistible fascination, that

I know not how to relinquish the dangerous satisfaction which I promise myself from being domesticated under his roof; while the recollection that I have at present no home; for I can no longer consider the house of Mr. Dennet in that light, tends in some measure to reconcile my judgment to the dictates of my heart. My thoughts are perplexed, bewildered, and doubtful of the path which I would, or ought to pursue. I suffer my imagination to lead me astray, while the dim lamp of reason glimmers but to show me that I am wandering in devious ways, without affording sufficient light to guide me on the road which I almost fear to tread.

Letter XX.

Accept, my dear Eliza, my warmest thanks for your kind, your sensible letter. I have read it again and again, and will endeavor, as far as is in my power, to profit by your good and friendly admonitions. You tell me that I am sporting on the brink of a precipice. I own it, see my danger, and promise to be on my guard. It is from myself only that I have any cause of apprehension; the enemy whom I fear is within. I have been now near a week in the enchanted castle, which you besought me not to enter. I had become an inmate in it before I received your last letter; had I not, highly as I esteem your understanding, and much as I at the time doubted of my own, I will not promise that I should in this instance have been guided by your advice. The spell by which I am bound is too strong to be broken, even by the magic wand of friendship; and it is in vain you tell me, though I own it just, that I am seeking perils and courting misery. The day after that on which I last wrote to you, I bade a tender farewell to my amiable cousin and her interesting children, and with agitated spirits, and a sinking heart, set off with Mr. Woodfield on the road to ——.[67] Mrs. Devenish received us with her usual hospitality, and the next morning, agreeably to her promise, conducted me to the house of which I was now going to take the charge. I will not attempt to describe to you the various emotions which agitated my bosom at setting off. They were too complicated to be traced by the pen. On our way, Mrs. Devenish entertained me with the praises of Mr. Howard. Had she chosen any other theme, I am afraid I should have proved but an inattentive auditor. After walking rather more than two miles, we came in sight of a low white house, before which stood a row of aged elm trees, whose mingling branches and thick foliage, threw over the front a dark, but not unpleasing shade. On one side of the house there was a shrubbery and pleasure grounds, by the other ran the river M—, the green banks of which were adorned with wild flowers of various hues and shaded by willow trees;

"Whose pendant branches swept the stream."[68]

"This is the house," said Mrs. Devenish. We stopped, and for a few moments I gazed in silence on a spot, which imagination had already hallowed. "Do you not think it a sweet romantic place?" cried my companion. I could not answer her question. My mind was full of

>"Struggling images, which less
>Than falling tears, can ne'er express."[69]

She saw that I was affected, and attributed my emotion to lowness of spirits, which, she observed, it was very natural for me to experience on the first coming to a strange place.

As we entered the outer gate, she informed me, that she purposed stopping with me the remainder of the day, which she did; and we employed ourselves in looking over the apartments, giving orders to the servants, with other necessary domestic arrangements. When she left me, which was not till late in the evening, she desired me to consider Mr. Devenish and herself as my friends, and promised to call on me as often as her own family affairs would permit. Wearied by the occupations of the day, I went to bed soon after she left me, where very shortly I fell asleep, and awoke at an early hour in the morning, with renovated spirits, and more tranquility of mind than I had experienced for the last ten days.

Letter XXI.

My days since I have been here, like the murmuring stream which softly glides beneath my window, pass on calm and unruffled. I have no one with whom I can converse, and no books, beside the few which I brought with me, that I can read; but solitude even absolute as the present, has no terrors for me. The situation of the house in which I now preside as mistress, is delightful, and the country around as beautiful. I usually spend the greater part of the day in wandering about the grounds and in the contemplation of nature taste those pure, those exquisite pleasures, which the tumultuous world can never bestow. In the evening I sit alone, in my little parlour, which commands a view of the garden, and sometimes by the open window, till the last ray of the sun is lost in the shadows of night. I love the twilight hour; it is then that the mind, disposed to serious and tender contemplation, ascends to heaven, or, borne on the wings of fancy, takes flight to air-built castles of its own creation,

>"Till nothing is but what is not."[70]

I am interrupted; it was by Mr. Devenish, who called to inform me that he this morning received a letter from Mr. Howard, saying, that he intended coming here to-morrow evening; that his stay would be short, and that he purposed bringing a friend with him. What shall I do? how meet him? why does he bring a friend with him? Alas! every illusion of fancy has fled, and I feel nothing at present but the extreme awkwardness, and, must I add, impropriety of my situation.

Letter XXII.

He is gone; I have again seen him; again beheld him smile, again heard him speak: I feel as one awakening from a dream; his presence has been to me as a beatific vision. In the evening of the day on which I received the intelligence of his expected visit, I went to bed with a mind too fluttered to obtain much repose; and feeling no inclination for sleep, arose in the morning ere the soaring lark had closed her matin strain. As I threw open the window of my apartment, and beheld the smiling landscape still spangled with the early dew, I felt my senses refreshed, and exclaimed in the language, and with all the enthusiasm of Werter,[71] "I shall see him to-day; all, all is comprised in that word." The day appeared to me of more than usual length; every hour seemed an age to my perturbed and agitated heart; I went again and again into every apartment in the house, which, though constantly kept very nice, was now by my orders made still more so. I then sauntered into the garden, and there selected the fairest flowers, the sweetest shrubs, to decorate the rooms destined for the reception of their master. As the evening came on my anxiety increased; I listened to the sound of distant carriages, and examined with curious eye each passenger that passed along the road; till twilight cast her sober mantle over the distant hills, and every object was veiled in mist and obscurity. My spirits were now quite exhausted. Hope's "soft responsive voice"[72] no longer cheered my timid mind; a variety of mortifying reflections presented themselves to my imagination, till "my sinking pulse almost forgot to move, and life almost forsook my languid frame," when the trampling of horses roused me from the painful reverie into which I had fallen. I started, trembled, and flew to my own apartment. A loud ringing at the gate increased my palpitation. I listened, and my ear soon caught the well-remembered accent; though the distance prevented me from distinguishing the words which were spoken. Just dead with emotion, I shut too the door of my room, which I had before held half open, and burst into tears. Fortunately for me I was not inquired for that night; if I had I could not have appeared. The next morning about ten o'clock, Jane, the upper servant, came into the parlour where I was sitting in silent and minutely expectation of being called for. She was delighted with her master, whom she had not seen before last night, and full of his praises. He had spoken to her so kindly, so affably. "Did he ask for me, Jane?" "Yes, ma'am; he asked me about you this morning while I was waiting at breakfast, and noticed the shrubs and the nosegays which you had put into the room; and the gentleman who is with him admired them, and said that the flowers were disposed with a great deal of taste."

"Indeed," she continued, "I never saw such good-natured gentlemen before; they seemed pleased with every thing; and my master said, when he returned from his walk, for they went out as soon as they had breakfasted, he must see you, and thank you for the trouble which you had taken." "Did he ask my name?" "No, ma'am, nor did I think of telling it; but I told him as how I thought you must be very dull, for that you were always alone." When this conversation would have ended I cannot say, had not Jane at this instant espied her master walking up the garden. "O there he is!" she cried; "shall I now ask him into your parlour?" and before I could determine on an answer, ran to the door. In a minute he was in the room. The blood forsook my heart; I felt cold as death. "Miss Southerdon!" he exclaimed in a tone of evident surprise. I could not speak. He sat down, inquired kindly after my health, how long I had left London, whether I had lately heard from Mr. and Mrs. Cooper, neither of whom he had seen for some time, having himself been travelling about the country for the last three or four months. He then with a softened accent, and a look which, though expressive of curiosity, was benevolently kind, asked me "if he might inquire to what circumstance he was indebted for the honor of seeing Miss Southerdon at his country retreat?" The blood, which at first entrance had forsaken my lips and cheeks, now rushed at once into my face and neck. "Various circumstances," I replied, "have induced me – " my embarrassment prevented me from proceeding. "No unpleasant ones, I hope," he answered, and then hesitated as if afraid of wounding my feelings by any further inquiry. Desirous of putting an end as soon as possible to a scene so awkward, and to me so truly distressing; I related to him in as few words as possible, the little history of my past life; mentioned my uncle's late marriage as the cause which had induced me to seek for a change of residence; explained by what means I had heard of my present situation; and implied, contrary to my usual practice of always speaking the truth, that I had accepted of it before I was aware that he was the gentleman who had purchased the estate. Mr. Howard listened to my little narrative with great attention, made no comment, but when he perceived I had done speaking, expressed a fear that I should find too little amusement in his house to render a long stay in it agreeable to me. I answered, "I am fond of retirement, and have been accustomed to a country life." "True," he replied; "but Miss Southerdon has also been in London, and is very capable of enjoying society." I bowed, and we both remained silent for some minutes. He then told me, that his stay at present would be very short, as he was in haste to get back to London, where he had not been for some time, but that he purposed returning here in the month of August, and that in the mean time he would send me down some books, or any thing I would mention, that could contribute to my comfort or entertainment. I thanked him by my eyes, in which I felt a starting tear, better than by my words. He then arose, and as he was leaving the room, said, he hoped I would favour his friend, whom he should be happy to introduce to me, and himself, with my company at dinner. I hesitated. They should expect me, he repeated, as he bade me good morning. This wished-for, yet dreaded interview being thus happily got over, my mind felt relieved from some part of the burden, with which for the last twenty-four hours it had been so cruelly oppressed; but my spirits, though lightened, were not sufficiently composed to suffer me to analyse the complicated sensations which still agitated my bosom. The duties of the toilet were not, on this occasion, you may be sure, forgotten. I arrayed myself with my usual simplicity, but with rather more than my usual attention, and disposed my hair, which was the only ornament I wore on my head, in the manner which I thought the most becoming to my style of countenance, which you used in times past to tell me, resembled that of the Madonna.[73] At the hour appointed for dinner, I repaired with a still fluttering heart to the dining-room. The gentlemen, who had been riding, were just come in. Their politeness, their easy manners, their respectful attentions, and their entertaining conversation, dispelled my fears, and re-animated my spirits, and I had only to regret, that the hours which I spent in their company were so short, and so few. Early the next morning Mr. Howard and his friend set off for London: from the window of my chamber I saw them depart.

Letter XXIII.

I have lately received a large parcel of books from London, and reading is now become my principal occupation. Believe me, my dear friend, when I tell you, that I am happy. The expectation of soon again seeing my soul's idol, the knowledge that I am at present domesticated in his household, with the hope that he sometimes thinks of me; these are the sources of my felicity, and in reading authors of his selection, I find an interest, a pleasure, which books, much as I love them, never before afforded me. The "green-eyed monster, jealousy,"[74] no longer haunts my breast. When (may I not now call him?) my friend was here, there was nothing either in his conversation, or manner, that implied any present intention of altering his situation; and I have already persuaded myself, that the story of his engagement, which I heard told in Berner Street, was void of truth, and without any solid foundation. All his plans appear to be those of a single man; nor did he even look or speak like one whose heart was engaged. The man-servant he brought with him, and who had accompanied him in his late tour, as I afterwards learned from Jane, though he talked of his master in the kitchen, said nothing about his going to be married, nor so much as mentioned the name of the particular lady, to whom it has been reported that he was engaged; so I am convinced that it was all an idle tale. I am not so frantic as to aspire myself to his love, but were he united to another, I feel that I could not long continue in my present situation.

Letter XXIV.

This morning, as I was walking down the rustic pathway which leads through the meadow, at the back of our house, to the next village, I observed passing by me a poor, but decent looking woman; on one arm she carried a child, and on the other hung a number of small wicker baskets. The sun shone bright, and the wind blew strong from the east; both were in our faces; mine was shaded by a large straw bonnet. The child, who was uncovered, whimpered, and sought to hide its little head in its mother's bosom. "Snuggle[75] close, my baby," said the woman, in a mild and affecting tone of voice, while she pressed the infant still closer to her breast. The tenderness of her manner, added to the simple plaintiveness of her speech, interested me; and I spontaneously quickened my pace.

The wind had untied the string which fastened the baskets together, and one of them without her perceiving it, fell to the ground. I picked it up, and calling to the woman to stop, presented it to her. "God bless you, madam," said she, dropping a courtesy, "I need not lose my baskets; for I find it difficult enough to sell them." "I will be a customer to you, good woman," said I, and keeping the one which was still in my hand, pulled out my purse, and without asking her the price, gave her more than the value of the basket. The woman looking at the silver, burst into tears. I don't know when I have been so much affected. "I could have wept for company." As soon as she appeared a little composed, I asked her where she lived. "In the next village," she replied, "and was as happy as heart could wish, till about three months ago;" and she again began to sob. "And what happened three months ago?" "It is now nearly that time since my poor dear husband was murdered on board of a man-of-war." "Murdered!" I exclaimed. "Yes," indeed he was, she cried, and sighed most bitterly. She continued. "He was as good a husband as any in the village, and he worked hard enough, God knows, to maintain decently me and my family; for it was his pride to see us all clean and neat of a Sunday. I have four children, madam, beside this baby in my arms; but, as I was saying, my husband one Saturday night, as he was returning home from his work, with his wages in his pocket, fell in with a press-gang.[76] He attempted to run away; they caught him, and obliged him to go along with them, whether he would or no. Finding that he did not come home at the usual hour, I went out to seek for him, and when I found out with whom he had gone, I thought I should have broken my heart." "But how was he murdered?" "I will tell you, madam. After being on board ship some days, finding that they were going out on a cruize, and that there was no chance of his being cleared, he attempted one night to make his escape, by creeping through one of the port holes. A sailor, who was on watch, discovered his intention; an affray ensued, in which my poor husband lost his life. Well, after all this, to add to my grief, I heard as how they would not give him christian burial, but meant to throw his body into a hole like a dead dog; so I scraped together all the money I could raise, and got my brother to go down to the ship and fetch up my husband's corpse; and never shall I forget the day when it was brought home, so mangled, so bruised. I swooned away at the sight; and if it had not been for my poor little ones, who came crying around me, I believe I should have been tempted to have thrown myself into the river, and so put an end at once to all my troubles. But God be praised. I am still alive, and able to work for my children; and it is some comfort to me to think that my poor dear husband lies buried in christian ground." My heart sympathised with the poor woman, while I listened to this simple but pathetic narrative, and I added a trifling donation to what I had before given for the basket. The woman thanked me with artless gratitude; again caressed her child, and pursued her way with lighter steps. This little adventure afforded me, during the remainder of my walk, a sufficient subject for serious reflection, while I regretted that the scantiness of my purse but too often necessitated me to check the benevolent instigations of my feelings.

Letter XXV.

August is at length arrived, and for these last eight days have Mr. Howard and myself been under the same roof: this thought affords me satisfaction, though as yet I have enjoyed but very little of his society. He spends the greater part of his time in riding, and walking out: when at home, and not engaged with company, he is chiefly in his library. His conduct to me is all that it ought to be. I feel its delicacy, and acknowledge its propriety. The high respect which I have ever entertained for him, is if possible increased; but his look, his manner, though uniformly kind, while it extinguishes every presumptuous wish, forbids the indulgence of an hopeless affection. I still find a delicious pleasure in the idea of being useful to him, but feel less happy now that he is here, than I did while anticipating his coming, and when he goes away; but I will not look forward. He does not, I understand, purpose leaving us before the middle of September, and then talks of going into the north. Did I hear, or do I only fancy, that Miss C— lives in —shire? The pleasantest hour which I have spent in his company since he has been down this time, was one yesterday morning. I had been visiting a poor woman, whose children were sick, and whose husband having met with an accident, was for the present disabled from working in the fields. While returning homeward, with my mind occupied and impressed by the sufferings of these poor people, I was overtaken by Mr. Howard, who had also been walking out. I described to him the scene of distress, which I had been witnessing, and applied to his benevolence for a more substantial relief, than it had been in my power to afford this poor family. He was not displeased with the application: immediately, and liberally complied with my request, and begged that for the future I would at all times consider myself as his almoner. This led us into a conversation on the state of the poor in general, and of the labouring poor in this country in particular, and I observed, that charity on the part "of the rich was not wanting; but that charity, however extensive, was inadequate to relieve the increasing demands of the lower classes of people." He replied, my observation was just, and that the evil required a more radical cure, than incidental charity could perform. But still, he observed, it is the duty of every one, in proportion to their ability, to administer to the wants of others, and even those who cannot bestow pecuniary aid, may sometimes by advice or sympathy, mitigate the sorrows which they have not the power to relieve. "A country village," I answered, "affords better opportunities for the judicious exertion of individual benevolence, than crowded cities; where the variety of objects, and the depravity of the lower classes, render it more difficult to discriminate those to whom little services or trifling donations may be beneficial." Mr. Howard assented to this observation, and said he hoped soon to realise some plans which he was now forming for the assistance and instruction of the poor in his neighborhood. We had by this time reached our own gate. We entered the house together: he then wished me a good morning, and retired to his library.[77]

Letter XXVI.

I have been terrified out of my senses. Thank heaven, the effects of the accident which occasioned my alarm, are not likely to prove serious. If he had been killed on the spot, what would have become of me? as it was, I was half frantic, and have scarcely yet recovered myself sufficiently to write you the particulars. It was yesterday evening that it happened. Mr. Howard was gone out on horseback: the weather was hot, and I, in pensive mood, was strolling by the side of the river to catch the evening breeze, which is so refreshing at the close of a sultry day; when I espied Jane running towards me in breathless haste. "What is the matter?" I exclaimed, "and why do you run so fast this warm weather?" She could only articulate, "My master is killed; I am sure he is." Without stopping for farther information, I flew by her – ran to the house, and rushed into the library, where the first object that met my sight was her master, not dead, but lying on the sopha, pale, languid, and apparently lifeless: a handkerchief which was bound round his forehead, and also the one which he wore round his neck, were stained with blood. In an agony of terror I threw myself on my knees by his side, pressed one of his hands in mine, and committed a thousand other extravagancies which I cannot now recollect. A gentleman standing by, whom I had not before observed, but now found was a surgeon, begged me not to alarm myself. "Mr. Howard," he said, "in consequence of being thrown from his horse, which had fallen with him on his return home, had cut one of the arteries in his forehead with a flint stone. The effusion of blood," he added, "had been very great, but he assured me that no danger need to be apprehended from the wound." "Are you sure there is no danger?" I repeated, in a tone of the utmost solicitude. "Quite sure," he answered. His patient, who was by this time sufficiently recovered from the faintness, which loss of blood had occasioned, to notice my extreme agitation, rewarded me with a look so kind, so heavenly, it more than repaid me for all that I had suffered. I relinquished the hand which I held in mine, and should still have held, had not the gentle pressure of his in some measure restored me to my senses. The surgeon now ordered his patient to bed; desired that he might be kept quiet; and said he would send him a draught, which was to be taken as soon as it came; then took his leave, with the promise of calling again early the next morning. When the medicine came I went with it myself to the chamber of my friend, and finding him awake, presented the draught, which I told him "I feared he would think a nauseous one." "Not from your hands," he replied. I then in the softest, gentlest tone of pity, inquired how he found himself, and whether he suffered much pain from the wound. "His head ached," he said. "But I was too good, too sympathizing." He still looked very pale, and as his hand touched mine in returning the glass which had held the medicine, I thought it felt hot, and feverish. My mind was full of anxiety, and I determined to watch myself by his bed-side the whole of the night. Fearful that if he knew my intention, he would not permit it, I opened the chamber door, as if I were going out, then shut it again, and returned on tip-toe to an easy chair, where I sat down. Towards morning, my patient seeming to be restless and uneasy, I ventured to put back the curtain, and asked him whether he would not like to take some cooling beverage, which I had taken care to provide. He was surprised at finding me still in the room, and expressed concern lest my attention to him should injure my own health, requesting at the same time that I would now retire, and endeavor to gain some repose. I assured him I was not quite so bad a nurse, as to mind the loss of one night's rest, and had I gone to bed, my anxiety on his account would have kept me waking. "My dear Miss Southerdon," he replied, "how can I ever repay you?" and he sighed. On his promising to ring the bell for his servant, should he require any further attendance before the usual hour of rising, I left the room, and went to bed, but not to sleep. "Macbeth has murdered sleep."[78]

Letter XXVII.

My patient is perfectly recovered from the effects of his late accident, and ascribes his speedy cure to my care, rather than to the surgeon's skill. The sensibility which I unwarily evinced, when I thought him in danger, has gained for me a tender interest in his friendship. When we meet, he speaks to me with the kind accent of a brother addressing a beloved and younger sister placed under his protection. He does not seek, neither does he avoid my society. I never obtrude myself on his. The knowledge that one roof covers us, is for me sufficient felicity. I wish he were my brother, I should then be happy.

> "Ah! let me nurse this fond deceit,
> For what! if I must die in sorrow;
> Who would not cherish dreams so sweet,
> Tho' grief and care must come to-morrow!"[79]

Letter XXVIII.

I yesterday, early in the evening, went out alone, with the intention of rambling farther from home than I usually allow myself to do, when Mr. Howard, whether by design or accident I cannot say, overtook me, and asked "which way I meant to bend my steps." I replied, "I have not yet determined; the country all around us is at this season of the year so beautiful, that it is difficult to make a choice." "Have you ever ascended —— Hill?" "I have not." "Then you have a new walk in store: the view from the summit is extremely fine, and very extensive." After a short pause he added, "if you are not afraid of the distance, and would like to go there this evening, I shall be happy to walk with you." My heart bounded with pleasure at the proposition, and I replied, "As it is yet early, the distance will be no objection, and I shall esteem myself honored by your accompanying of me." We had more than two miles to walk; I did not think them long ones: desultory conversation on various subjects beguiled the way. We at length reached the foot of the hill. "This," said Mr. Howard, as we slowly ascended, "is the exact hour for seeing the prospect to the greatest advantage." When we had gained the highest point, we paused; and his attention appeared to be for some minutes wholly absorbed in the delightful and beautiful scenery, by which we were surrounded; mine was divided, bewildered. – Pointing to a distant view, he directed my eye, and bade me observe some interesting object, which I had not before descried. He then asked me if the prospect in general had answered my expectation, while he himself appeared enraptured by its rich and variegated beauties. I looked around me for some time, then said, "I fear you think me either very tasteless, or very stupid." "Why so?" he replied. "Because the consciousness that I am at present incapable of entering into your feelings, so entirely benumbs my own, as to make me in fact the stupid mortal I am afraid of being taken for. If you were not with me" – "Forget then," said he, interrupting me, "that I am with you." "Not for the world." He looked at me with a glance which seemed to penetrate my whole soul. I felt that I had spoken with too much animation. We continued silent for some moments. He then said, "We had better rest for a while before we[80] renew our walk." We sat down on the trunk of a fallen tree. He did not seem inclined to begin a conversation. To relieve myself from the awkwardness of silence; I said, scarcely knowing what I did say, "You are convinced by this time that I have no taste." "Because you prefer my company to enjoying, alone, the beauties of nature:" and he smiled as he spake. "You are at liberty to form what conclusions you please; but without drawing any inferences from my inaccuracies of language, I do not think that I have those fine perceptions of beauty, or that exquisite sensibility and delicacy of taste, which many persons possess." "We do not always properly appreciate our own qualifications. Your taste is very correct, and sufficiently delicate; and the want of sensibility is a fault which I should never attribute to Miss Southerdon." "My moral sensibility, is, I own, sufficiently acute; but to discriminate the nicer touches of beauty in the works of nature or of art, requires perhaps a greater degree of intellectual cultivation, than I have hitherto had the opportunity of attaining." "Sensibility of mind is a higher quality, and one more connected with domestic happiness, than the mere scientific cultivation of the taste." "That I allow; but where both are united, one sheds a lustre, a grace over the other." "True, but there are no graces so touching, so interesting, as those which flow from genuine sensibility, when united with good sense and artless simplicity." He then turned from me to admire the fantastic forms of some passing cloud which the sun had gilded by his last setting ray.

I observed that it grew late, and proposed walking; he assented, immediately arose, and offered me his arm. On our way back, we had very little conversation. He once or twice expressed a fear, lest I should be too much fatigued by our excursion. I thought not of fatigue.

When we got home, he saw me safe into the house, then left me. The gardener was waiting to receive orders concerning some improvements which were making in the pleasure grounds. I went into the supper room, sat down by the window, the sash of which was open. The harvest moon, which was now risen, threw a silvery light on the surrounding landscape. The softened beauty of the scene accorded with the state of my feelings; and after musing some time on the peculiar circumstances of my wayward fate, I sang, in a sort of low and under key; "To the woods, to the winds, to the waves I complain," – and repeated the line of "I dare not worship where I pay my vows,"[81] with genuine, because it was heartfelt, sensibility. A short time after this, Mr. Howard came into the room where I was sitting; and approaching the window, said, "this is a night to attune the soul to harmony." "It is indeed," I replied; and pointing through the opened sash to some rising ground which the moon shine had beautifully illumined, said, in the words of Shakespeare, "How sweet the moon-light sleeps upon that bank." He repeated with an air of real or affected gaiety, "Just such a night did little Jessica accuse her lover falsely, and he forgave her."[82] He then carelessly ran over the keys of a grand piano which stood open in the room, and turning to me enquired "if I played?" "A little." "You sing?" "Sometimes, to amuse myself."

"As I was just now passing under the window, my ear caught the soft sound of your voice." "I was not aware that you were so near me." We then talked of music, both ancient and modern. Mr. Howard, who has been in Italy, treated the subject scientifically. "I confessed, that I knew but little of music as a science, and owned that I had frequently received more pleasure from listening to a Scotch ballad, or simple melody, than to more artificial, and intricate compositions." He then asked me to play to him. I replied, "You are a judge of music, and I have not the courage to play before you." "One tune, one little song; you will oblige me." I hesitated, and was again going to excuse myself, when he repeated, "You will oblige me;" and at the same time placed the music stool before the piano: I could no longer refuse, and sat down. Jackson's Canzonets lay on the instrument; I opened them, and selected the one which begins,

"When absent from my soul's delight."[83]

When I had got through it, I shut the book. "Not yet," he cried. "Jackson's music exactly suits your style of playing, nor did I ever hear that Canzonet sung more sweetly. You must favor me with another." I turned over the leaves of the music book, uncertain which to fix on; then began, "O say, thou dear possessor of my breast." I could not have made a worse choice. The words were too appropriate, my hands trembled, my voice faltered. Incapable of proceeding, I hastily shut the book, and threw it from me, saying, "You must excuse me, I cannot sing to-night, my voice fails me; the exercise which I have taken this evening has exhausted me." He replied in a softened accent, "You stand in need of some refreshment after so long a walk:" then taking my hand, as if to lead me to the table on which the supper tray had been long standing, pressed it to his lips. At this moment the rattling of a post-chaise, as it drove up the road, followed by a loud peal at the outer gate, startled me. I refused taking any refreshment, and immediately left the room. Mr. Howard had for some days past been expecting the gentleman who accompanied him the first time he came down, after I was here; and who, I have since heard him say, is his most particular friend. It was he who had now arrived.

Letter XXIX.

I no longer tread on fairy ground, the enchantment is dissolved, the spell is broken; yet I still linger here, anxious, irresolute, and uncertain as to the future. Mr. Howard, and his friend, who came down on the preceding evening, were out together the whole of the next morning, and did not come home to dinner till a very late hour. In the evening I had occasion to pass the room in which they were sitting. The door was open. Not wishing to be seen, I stood for a few moments in the passage, hesitating whether to proceed, or to return; when my attention was arrested, and my feet riveted to the spot, by hearing Mr. —— say, "I am afraid Miss C—'s disposition is not sufficiently domestic to render you happy in the marriage state." Mr. Howard replied, "I have for some time past been of that opinion; and have more than once repented of an engagement, which a particular circumstance, added to my friendship for her brother, led me to form, I have since thought, rather too hastily. The lady's person, fortune, and connexions, you must own, were unexceptionable." "Certainly, nor do I see how you can recede with honor. Miss C— is not a woman to be trifled with." After a short pause, Mr. Howard in a less serious tone than he had before been speaking with, said, "I wish the lady would herself sign my dismissal; for however mortifying it may be thought to be a discarded lover, it is a mortification which I am at present very well prepared to endure, nor would I long wear the willow." He then added: "I must shortly go into —shire, and that visit will, one way or the other, decide my fate." I had heard enough, and escaped unseen to my own apartment. The next morning both Mr. Howard and his friend set off for London. Before they went, the former came into the room where I was, and said, "particular business had called him to London, where he was now going; that it would be long, perhaps very long, before he should return to this place. In the mean time could he do any thing for me, could he in any way render me any service, had I any letter or commands for Mr. or Mrs. Cooper? I gravely answered, "Not any." My manner was cold and reserved; but my heart was full. "Farewell, then," said he; "and should we never meet again, may Heaven preserve you," and hurried out of the room. I stood for some minutes after he had quitted me, as one stunned or stupefied. "Should we never meet again," I at length repeated to myself, and then burst into tears, which afforded me a seasonable relief. Had I not wept, my heart must have broken. What could be the particular circumstance which led him to form this fatal engagement with Miss C—? Did she also first lose her yielding heart? I thought those of the daughters of fashion had been better guarded. Or is it true, "That women are most wooers, though closest in their carriage."[84]

Letter XXX.

Here I am alone, forlorn, like the owl of the desert, or the pelican of the wilderness. Since the Genius of the palace has flown, all nature has changed her aspect. The bright morning sun no longer gems the early dew. The pale moon with her silver beams no longer illumes the mild evening landscape. Black[85] clouds obscure the ether, chill rains descend, while the cold northern blast sweeps from the aged elms their poor remains of scanty foliage.

For the last six weeks the weather has been so bad, that I have rarely ventured out beyond our own domains, excepting one morning, last week, when a deceitful gleam of sun-shine tempted me to extend my walk. No sooner was I through the gate, than I turned almost involuntarily towards the meadow which leads into the road that takes us to —— Hill, without any fixed design, and vainly fancying, "that, alas! where with him I have strayed, I could wander with pleasure alone;"[86] pursued the path till I arrived at the foot of the Hill, which after a little time I with difficulty ascended. "While to my feet in clods, the moist earth clung,"[87] when I had reached the summit, unheeding cold or wet, I sat down on the same fallen tree, on which I had rested on my former expedition. The gathering clouds at length warned me to depart, but not soon enough to escape the coming shower: I reached home about noon, fatigued, dabbled, and drenched with rain. The consequence was a violent cold, which has since confined me to the fire-side.

Letter XXXI.

Mrs. Devenish has just left me. My uncle Dennet is dangerously ill, and I am requested to go into Sussex immediately, how long I shall stay there, or whether I shall ever again return to this place, I know not. I purpose setting off to-morrow morning. Mr. Devenish and Mr. Woodfield will accompany me. Mrs. Woodfield is at present confined with another little girl, which prevents her being of our party.

Letter XXXII.

Sussex.

We got here just time enough to witness the last scene. Mr. Dennet had the day before been seized with a paralytic stroke and was speechless when we arrived. The next morning at six o'clock he expired: we none of us went to bed, and I sat by his bed-side during the whole of the night, watching every breath which he drew, knowing not but it might be the last. To me it was a night of solemn and awful meditation. Seated by a death-bed, how little appear all earthly passions, all sublunary pursuits; and witnessing the moment of final dissolution, were it not for the bright hope to which religion points beyond the grave, how melancholy would appear the lot of man, passing but a few years on this great globe, struggling with passion, disappointment, sickness and sorrow, then closing the scene with suffering and death! What is death? – Is it, can it be the total extinction of existence? Oh no, Revelation tells us that the various particles of matter, whose combinations make us what we are, will be again revivified with the breath of life, and after resting for a long, long night in the grave, once more reproduce the same conscious, active, thinking being; while our own powers, our faculties, our restless thirstings after immortality and unknown good, convince us, that there is some future world, some purer state, where those powers, those faculties, will properly unfold, and find their true end and full attainment.[88]

Letter XXXIII.

I am no longer in suspense, it is past. He is married to Miss C—. I return no more to ——, and am again a wanderer without a home. The death of my uncle who was my nearest relation, has left me an orphan indeed. No will has yet been found, and I possess no written document of the little property which I intrusted in his hands; and if I had, I know not that it would be, at least at present, of much service. Mrs. Dennet, instead of being, as she represented herself, a woman of property, was, as we now find, deeply involved in debt, and her creditors are already making large claims on the estate of my late uncle. Mr. Devenish, who acts for Mr. Woodfield, talks of throwing the affairs into Chancery; so when they will be settled no one can tell. Mrs. Woodfield begs me now to consider her house as my home. Not wishing to be a burden on my friends, and having at present an insuperable objection to returning into Surrey, I have commissioned Mr. Devenish to look out, and engage for me any situation which he thinks may be eligible for a young woman situated as I am: what it may be, I care not. I have no choice, no hopes, and scarce a wish to gild the gloom.

Letter XXXIV.

I have heard of, and accepted a situation, on which I shall enter in the course of a few days. It is to go as companion or humble friend to an elderly lady of the name of Blount; who resides at —— Hall, a respectable mansion some miles distant from this town. She is a widow, has no family, and bears the character of being a worthy, good kind of a woman. She lives, I understand, quite retired, is of a delicate constitution and nervous habit, keeps very little company, and seldom or never goes abroad.

Letter XXXV.

—— Hall, Sussex.

I yesterday morning took a formal leave of Mrs. Dennet, and accompanied by Mr. Devenish set off for this place, where we arrived about one o'clock. We found the good lady of the house at breakfast, sitting by a large fire, and wrapt up in a great India shawl. Her aspect was mild, but imbecile; she looked sickly, and older than I had expected to find her; and her whole appearance and manner, though not unpleasing, bespoke the valetudinarian. She received us with politeness, and spoke to me with kindness. My heart felt desolate, and my spirits much depressed; but not wishing to appear before Mrs. Blount with a melancholy countenance, I endeavoured to assume a cheerful air: but the endeavour was too painful to be long supported, and I was glad when the hour of repose arrived, that I might be at liberty to indulge the painful emotions which I in vain tried to repress. Every thing which I saw around me served rather to increase, than to diminish the gloomy thoughts which weighed heavily on my mind. The house, which is too large for its present inhabitants, is partly shut up; the rooms in use are capacious, but not elegant; the furniture heavy and old fashioned, the outer buildings in a dilapidated state; and as we yesterday rode up to the house through a long avenue of stately but now leafless trees, the grounds, which are extensive, not being well kept up, appeared to me a wilderness. Our perceptions of things depend much, if not altogether, on the previous state of our minds; mine at present is, I fear, more disposed to receive disagreeable than agreeable impressions, for all is dark within. I feel at times as I can conceive our mother Eve felt, when she looked back to Paradise, and saw it guarded by a flaming sword.[89]

Letter XXXVI.

You complain of my silence: why should I write, when I have nothing to communicate? I have, since I have been here, become a perfect automaton; my mind has lost all its energies; all its powers, nothing amuses, nothing interests me. Yet I do not find fault with Mrs. Blount, nor with my situation; she is very kind and very good, and I am surrounded with all the necessaries and what is generally termed the comforts of life; but my time is not my own, and every day brings with it the same insipid, tiresome routine. I have at present no pursuits, either sedentary or active; Mrs. Blount finds me but little employment, and yet she will not permit me to employ myself. All around me is stagnant, and the stream of life appears to stand still, for nothing marks its course.

Letter XXXVII.

The dull uniformity of our days, of which I complained in my last, has since suffered some interruption by the arrival of a nephew of Mrs. Blount's, who has been stopping with us for the last ten days. He is a young man, and his name is Vernon. His figure is good, his eyes fine, and his complexion dark. His manners those of a man who has seen the Town, rather than the World; easy and assured, but not elegant; his conversation entertaining, but neither intellectual nor refined. He professes to be a great admirer of the ladies, and persecutes me with his gallantry; to repress which, I am obliged to behave to him with a greater degree of reserve than accords with my disposition. His father, who has been dead some years, was, I understand a West India merchant, and his son, to whom, though an only child, he did not leave a very large fortune, has at present some concern in a mercantile house. I write to you of Mr. Vernon, because I have at present no other subject; to-morrow he talks of taking his leave, which, though he has afforded me some slight amusement, I am not sorry for. My spirits are not good, and the gloomy season of the year, the atmosphere cold and misty, conspire to increase my melancholy. Spring will soon return, and restore to nature her beauty; but it will not restore to me the fair enchantress Hope, whose magic wand embellished all around.

Letter XXXVIII.

Mr. Vernon is again our visitor, and the more I see of him, the less I am able to form a judgment of his real character. There is at times a levity in his manner which displeases me. He talks a great deal, and with apparent openness, yet I can scarcely call him frank, or distinguish between his real sentiments and what he means to pass for mere rattle. He this morning gave me great offence, whether intentionally, or not, I cannot say; but I shall take care for the future how I behave to him. The weather was clear, and frosty, and Mrs. Blount observing that I had not taken any exercise for a long time, Mr. Vernon intreated me to walk out with him. I did not wish to go; but on Mrs. Blount's saying, "Do walk with Mr. Vernon," I knew not how to refuse, without the appearance of affectation or prudery; so we set off. When we got on the downs the keen air seemed to brace my nerves, and revive my spirits. My heart, which I had lately thought dead, even to the beauties of nature, expanded, as I viewed her still lovely, though in her wintry garb; and feeling, as I viewed the open country around me, less dependent, less unhappy, than I had done for some time past, I talked to Mr. Vernon with more freedom and vivacity than I had ever done before. He appeared to be in high spirits, and on my refusing to accept his arm, gave the conversation a turn which I was not prepared for, and could not at the time rightly comprehend, but which I have since thought, meant more than met the ear. Not considering what he had said as worthy of serious notice, I made no answer, but proposed shortening our walk. He soon after asked me, if I had ever been in London, and whether I should not prefer a gayer and more cheerful life to the one I at present led. I answered gravely, that I had not the choosing of my own situation, and if I had, should greatly prefer a country life to a town one. He replied with warmth, "You may, and shall choose your own situation;" at the same time seizing my hand, which he pressed so hard, that it was with difficulty I withdrew it from his grasp; in so doing my foot slipped, and I nearly fell. He caught hold of me, and again offering his arm, said, "You find you are not able to stand alone, though you are too proud to accept of my support." I returned, "I hope I shall always be too proud to accept of support improperly or impertinently offered;" and again refused taking hold of him. He appeared checked by the serious manner in which I spoke, and gave me no further cause of offence. I shall, if possible, avoid being alone with him for the future.

Letter XXXIX.

As I was this morning sitting alone, reading, Mr. Vernon, who I thought had been out, came into the room. He walked up to the fire-place without speaking, and stood for some minutes in the true English style, humming a tune. I took no notice of him. At length he said, "Pray may I presume to ask what book you are reading? I must suppose it to be a very interesting one, as it seems at present so deeply to engage your attention." I replied coolly, "that I was reading Dr. Johnson's poem on the Vanity of Human Wishes." "Mere wishes may be vanity; but if we can realise our wishes – " "If – but who does realise them?" "Thousands; but you study too much: why do you not walk out? – it is a sin to stay within doors this fine morning." "Mrs. Blount is indisposed, and will shortly require my attendance." "Mrs. Blount is a very good sort of woman, notwithstanding which you *must* find your present situation intolerably irksome." "When I find any situation irksome I quit it;" and arose with the intention of quitting the room. He saw my design, placed himself between me and the door, and as I endeavored to pass him, rudely threw his arms around me. I felt extremely indignant, and insisted on leaving the room, which, finding I was in earnest, and seriously offended with him, he at length permitted. We did not meet again till dinner, when his behaviour to me was peculiarly attentive, and respectful. To-morrow he goes to London. "Never," he said to me, "had he before left the Hall with the reluctance with which he should at present quit it, for never before had it contained for him so much attraction." – I hope he will not return again very shortly, as his frequent visits here would render my residence with Mrs. Blount both disagreeable and improper.

Letter XL.

I have been exceedingly hurt, and mortified by receiving from Mr. Vernon, a few days after he left us, a most curious and equivocal epistle, full of flaming professions of love, without any direct offer of marriage, though at the same time he declares, that it is impossible for him to live without me, and that himself and his fortune are at my command. Situated as I am at present, I must consider such a letter as an insult, and therefore, without saying any thing to Mrs. Blount on the subject, inclosed it in a blank cover, and sent it back by return of post. My conduct to Mr. Vernon has not been such as to justify his addressing me in the manner he has done; and had I been a young woman of fortune, or under the protection of any relative, he would not have dared to have written me in such a style. But men, who are designed both by nature and society for our protectors, seem to consider us, when unprotected, as their natural and easy prey. I feel every day more and more unhappy, and this unexpected and undeserved insult has not tended to raise my spirits.

Letter XLI.

Since I last wrote to you, I have received several letters from Mr. Vernon, all of which I have returned unopened; and some days having elapsed after the last one, I had begun to flatter myself with the idea of having got rid of his importunity, when, yesterday morning, as I entered the breakfast parlour, who should I find there but the gentleman himself. Surprised, and disconcerted at seeing him, I was instantly for retreating, when he laid hold of my gown to detain me, at the same time intreating me to grant him a few minutes' conversation, which, he said, he had travelled in the night in order to secure, knowing that I was generally down stairs some time before Mrs. Blount arose; and though I had not condescended to open the last letters which he had sent me, he hoped I should not be so cruel as to refuse to listen to what he had now to say. I replied, that after the letter which I had read, he could not be surprised at my not opening any other, and that I must beg that he would permit me to withdraw, as I could not at present, with any propriety, listen to any thing which he had to say. He assured me that he would say nothing which could give me the slightest offence; on the contrary, if, as he perceived was the case, I had conceived that he had not treated me with all the respect which I deserved, he now asked my pardon, and with his heart, which had been mine for some time, he now seriously offered me his hand. He then confessed that, like many other young men of his age, he had entertained some objections to matrimony, but that his passion for me outweighed at present every other consideration, and that his future happiness depended on my answer. I replied that, situated as I was, I did not consider myself at liberty to listen to, much less accept of, any offer of marriage from Mrs. Blount's nephew, without her knowledge. I must therefore intreat him at present, either to change the subject, or permit me to leave the room. He said, it was not, after this morning, his intention to renew the subject without Mrs. Blount's knowledge, whose consent to his honorable addresses to me, he meant to solicit; and as she was partial to me, and had frequently advised him to marry, he had very little fear of not being able to obtain her sanction; and if I would but promise him to abide by Mrs. Blount's decision, he would not importune me any farther, till he had first spoken to his aunt. I told him in answer, that I would make no promises, nor bind myself to abide in affairs of consequence by any person's decision but my own. I also added that I considered marriage as a very serious thing, and not a state to be entered upon lightly; that he confessed he had objections to matrimony. I would not therefore take the advantage of his present predilection in my favor, to force him into forming an engagement, which it was more than possible he might, in a short time after, repent of; the more so as there appeared to me to exist between us a total dissimilarity of taste, sentiments, and principles. He was going to reply, when a servant came into the room and told me, Mrs. Blount wanted me. "Tell Mrs. Blount," said Mr. Vernon to the servant, "that I am here, and wish to pay my respects to her." The servant soon returned, and said, Mrs. Blount would be down stairs in a few minutes. I immediately left the room, which I did not enter again till I was summoned by Mrs. Blount, whom I found alone. She said, she could not prevail on Mr. Vernon to stop at this time, but that he had promised to be down again very shortly. I made no answer, and we soon after went to dinner. In the evening she told me, that she wished to have a little serious conversation with me, and then informed me that Mr. Vernon had asked her consent to his making me his wife. She added, "It has certainly for some time past been my wish to see him married, and there are doubtless many ladies, both of fortune and fashion, to whom he might make pretensions; but as he tells me he has fixed his affections on you, and I have no doubt but that you will make him a good wife, I shall not object to his choice; though perhaps a woman with some fortune might at present have been more desirable, as his own is not large." I sat for some minutes silent, then said, "I have never aspired to the alliance, which you are so good as to consent to; and till now, I assure you, I have never thought of Mr. Vernon, but as your nephew. The partiality which he at present professes for me, I consider as a mere transient inclination, which absence will, in a short time, totally eradicate. I will, therefore, with your leave, pay a visit to my cousins, Mr. and Mrs. Woodfield, where I can stay for any length of time which you may think necessary." "By no means," she replied: "Charles has been gay, and if he should now be prevented marrying the woman on whom he has fixed his affections, may in future be still more so." "You allow that Mr. Vernon is, what is commonly called gay, and on that account I wish to decline the honor of becoming your niece." "I have at times heard from some quarters, anecdotes of my nephew which have not quite pleased me; but I do not upon the whole, think that he has been more dissipated than most other young men of his rank in life. When he is married he will become more steady: you are a prudent and sensible young woman, and will reform him."[90] "I cannot be sure of that, and the experiment is a dangerous one: Mr. Vernon had better look out for a woman of fortune and family." "Your family," said Mrs. Blount, interrupting me, "cannot be objected to, and fortune is of less consequence at present, as I have long promised to leave the greater part of mine, which is at my own disposal, to Mr. Vernon: I have other nephews, but his father was my own brother, and on that account I purpose making him my heir." I attempted to speak, but knew not what to say. Mrs. Blount then complained of being weary, and proposed lying down. "We will not," she said, as I assisted her to the couch, "talk any more on this subject to-day." – And now, my dear friend, how shall I act, and what shall I do? I have no personal objection to Mr. Vernon, but I both fear and feel that he is not the man to make me happy. My decision will soon be called for, and whichever way I decide, it is more than probable that at some future period I may repent of that decision.

Letter XLII.

Mr. Vernon has been again here, and I have consented to become his wife; which I had no sooner done, than my heart misgave me. If, as Mr. Cooper told me at the time, I was guilty of an error in refusing Mr. Wansey, may I not at present be committing a still greater one, in accepting of Mr. Vernon? Yet situated as I am, how could I refuse him? With a clear perception of right and wrong in the abstract, in every important action of my life, circumstances have hitherto led me to act against my better judgment.

Nurtured with extreme tenderness, and educated above my fortunes, the forlorn isolated state in which I have for some time past found myself, has, I confess, for me a thousand terrors. Unused to labour, I know not how to work for my living. Accustomed to liberty, and possessed of an active mind, a state of indolent dependence is to me a state of almost insupportable slavery. With Mrs. Blount I have had no hardships to complain of; but my time and attention she has justly claimed in return for the support and protection which she has afforded me. By changing my situation I may possibly only change my cares; but as a married woman, I shall have that station in society, which I now have not: I shall also have affections to cultivate, and duties to perform, and engaged in scenes of active life, shall cease to cherish that first, that fatal prepossession which it would be a sin, as well as a folly, to indulge.

Letter XLIII.

Every preliminary is arranged; my paraphernalia ready; on Saturday next I have promised to meet Mr. Vernon at the Altar; after which we are to make a tour of a few days round the coast, return to Mrs. Blount, then go to H—, a small sea port not many miles from hence, where Mr. Vernon has taken a house for the remainder of the summer. He tells me he has a very good one in Bedford Square,[91] which, when we leave Sussex, will be our usual place of residence. I have written to Mrs. Woodfield to inform her of my intended marriage, and have received an answer, congratulating me on my future prospects. When married, it is my wish, and it shall be my endeavour, to perform all the duties of a wife; but with a man of Mr. Vernon's disposition and character, may not those duties be more arduous than I am at present aware of? In marriage I could have wished to have found a partner in whose virtues I could have confided, whose understanding I could have respected, and one whom I could at all times consider as my "Protector, guardian, friend." In the connection which I am going to form, the scene will, I fear, be in some measure reversed. Mrs. Blount tells me, "I must take care of her nephew!" Alas! it is he who ought to take care of me. But be that as it may, it is now too late to retract from my engagement, were I inclined so to do; and with worldly prospects such as I have at present before me, to be querulous and discontented, would be ungrateful both to God and man.*

Letter XLIV.

I am just returned from Brighton, where we have been spending the last four days. It was the races, and Mr. Vernon being fond of the sport, talked of going, and proposed my accompanying him. I made no objection, and never having witnessed any thing of the sort, promised myself some pleasure from the excursion. The first morning we were on the race course, where I was much amused

---

* Some letters containing nothing of importance, excepting the celebration of the marriage, are here omitted.

by the gaiety and novelty of the scene, we met with several persons of Mr. Vernon's acquaintance, with some of whom we associated every day while we staid; at night we went to the balls; and in short passed the whole of our time in one continued round of amusement. I was at first entertained by the various succession of objects which presented themselves before me, but soon recoiled with disgust from the scenes of vice and folly, which (more especially during the race week,) a fashionable watering place daily and hourly presents. The jockey, the gambler, the courtesan; in short the idle, the dissipated, and the profligate of every description, appear to be there assembled as in one great focus. I was also more than once rendered somewhat thoughtful, by observing the extreme avidity with which Mr. Vernon seemed to enter into every species of dissipation, fearing lest when we went to London, I should there find him equally thoughtless. At Mrs. Blount's he is under some restraint; and having since our marriage spent the greater part of our time in comparative retirement, I began to think him quite domesticated; and indeed till we went to Brighton, he had not given me any cause of complaint; when there, I was not greatly delighted with the party whom we joined, and not unfrequently felt myself disconcerted at bring introduced to many more persons than I thought it at all necessary that I should be. Mr. Vernon, who at present thinks very highly of my personal charms, on which you know I never myself set any great value, is not satisfied unless other persons do the same. He is therefore anxious to exhibit me to all his acquaintance, and appears gratified by the transient, and indiscriminating admiration, which, being in public what is called a new face, he tells me I have everywhere attracted. Is there not more of vanity than love in all this? and to me there appears to be a great want of delicacy in a man's wishing to make, as it were, a show of his wife's beauty. While I resided in Surrey, I forgot that I had ever been reckoned handsome: there mental, not personal charms, appeared only to be appreciated. But perhaps I refine too much. Mr. Vernon tells me, that I am yet too young to set up for a philosopher. On our return we called on Mrs. Blount, who, since I left her, has had with her as a companion, a Mrs. Morgan, a widow lady of small fortune, distantly related to the late Mr. Blount, whom she offended by marrying beneath herself, and contrary to his advice. Her husband did not live many years, and left her involved in some difficulties: she has two children at school, whom she spoke of in high terms, as being every thing at present which a mother could wish. I suppose most mothers think the same of their offspring. She appeared to pay Mrs. Blount, who has I believe been a good friend to her, great attention, and was very polite both to me, and to Mr. Vernon, with whom nevertheless she is no very great favorite. Her attention to Mrs. Blount he attributes to the hope of being remembered in her will; and notwithstanding her politeness to himself, he says, he knows she hates him in her heart, and has frequently done him ill offices with his aunt, of whose predilection in his favor she is extremely jealous. This may be the case. I recollect Mrs. Blount once saying, that she had heard from some quarter anecdotes of Mr. Vernon which had not pleased her; perhaps this was the quarter to which she alluded.

Letter XLV.

On Wednesday last Mr. Vernon went to London; and on the Friday morning, about two o'clock, I was suddenly awakened from a sound sleep, by a most violent ringing at the gate, – I instantly jumped out of bed, and on inquiry heard that Mr. Vernon, whom I had not expected till the next day, was arrived. Finding that he did not come up stairs, and impressed by the idea that something more than ordinary might have occurred, to occasion his returning home at such an unseasonable hour, I hastily slipped on my clothes, and wrapping a loose dressing-gown around me, went down to inquire what was the matter. On opening the door of the dining-room, I found Mr. Vernon seated at the table, and with him a gentleman whom I had never before seen; disconcerted at appearing before a stranger in little more than my night-clothes, I was going to retreat as precipitately as I had entered, but was prevented by Mr. Vernon, who immediately arose, insisted on my stopping, and taking my hand led me to his companion, whom he introduced to me as Mr. Malvern, a gentleman, of whom I had often heard him speak as his particular friend, and most intimate associate. He then told me, they were going to supper, and that I should take some with them; I wished to retire, and intreated, but in vain, to be excused. Mr. Vernon had been dining in company, and though not absolutely intoxicated, was, I could perceive, sufficiently flushed with the wine which he had been drinking to render him arbitrary and captious if contradicted; so I judged it most prudent to humor him by complying with his whim; and without any further resistance, or apology to Mr. Malvern for my undress, made the best of an awkward situation, and took my place at the table. Mr. Malvern begged my pardon for having intruded on my hospitality at such an improper hour; and very politely expressed his concern at my rest having been disturbed by their arrival. After a very hasty supper he refused taking any thing to drink, and reminded Mr. Vernon, who did not seem inclined to go to bed, that they were robbing me of my repose. We soon after retired, when Mr. Vernon informed me that he had invited a large party of gentleman to breakfast on the ensuing morning, with whom he had promised, should the weather permit, to go a sailing; and that I must be ready to receive them by eight o'clock. The hour and the gentlemen soon arrived, and I had the honor, or rather the trouble, of making tea for a dozen men, most of whom I had never seen before. The weather had for some days been very sultry, the morning was dark and cloudy, and before we had finished our repast there came on a most tremendous thunder storm, accompanied by unceasing torrents of rain; the gentlemen having, in consequence of the unfavorable weather, postponed their aquatic excursion to some future opportunity, Mr. Vernon proposed their spending the remainder of the day with him, which, after some little hesitation, and many apologies to me for the trouble they were giving me, was unanimously agreed to. Mr. Malvern, who though not exactly to my taste, was certainly the superior man of the party, made a number of fine speeches on the occasion, and concluded them with pronouncing his friend Vernon a very happy man. I soon withdrew to give the necessary orders for the entertainment of so many unexpected guests; and before

I returned to the breakfast room, exchanged my simple morning dress, for one rather more elegant and ornamental. On re-entering the room, I found the gentlemen amusing themselves with cards and dice. Mr. Malvern, who has before looked at me rather more than I thought quite well bred, now surveyed me from top to toe with an attention that embarrassed and disconcerted me. To avoid his scrutinizing gaze, I seated myself near a window, behind the table where he was playing whist with Mr. Vernon. In a few minutes he was by my side. He had lost the rubber, declared that he hated cards by day-light, and would play no more unless he could prevail on me to be his partner. This, of course, I declined; he then sat down by the window, observed on the fine marine view which it commanded, asked me if I had ever been on the sea, talked of sailing, parties of pleasure, and I don't know what beside, with the obvious view of drawing me into conversation. Finding me not quite so easily led to talk to him, as he perhaps, at first imagined I should be, he, Proteus-like, shifted his ground, and varied his subjects, till he found what topics were best suited to my taste. Amused by his unremitting endeavors to please, I at length found the reserve which I had intended keeping up, by degrees give way to the natural frankness of my disposition. Dinner was now announced. Mr. Malvern seated himself at my right hand, and assisted, or rather took from me all the trouble of the table; while he observed to the other gentlemen, that they ought to consider themselves as greatly indebted to the thunder-storm, as it had given them not only the opportunity of benefiting by my hospitality, but of admiring the ease and urbanity with which I had entertained so many intruding guests. This polite speech produced from the other gentlemen answers equally gallant. In short, being the only female of the party, I was so overwhelmed with civilities, that I was glad to make my escape, as soon after the cloth was removed, as etiquette, being the mistress of the house, would permit me to leave the room. In the evening, Mr. Malvern was the only person who accompanied Mr. Vernon into the drawing room; the other gentleman, having some distance to ride, had taken their leave. While I was making tea, an elegant pair of pearl bracelets which Mr. Vernon had presented me with, and which out of compliment to him I had that day put on, attracted the attention of Mr. Malvern, and afforded him an opportunity, which he did not let slip, of admiring the delicacy of my hands and arms. Mr. Vernon appeared to be highly gratified by the profusion of compliments which I had this day received from his gay companions; the admiration which they had in the morning bestowed on a favorite mare, which he had lately purchased, did not, I dare say afford him, much greater satisfaction. For myself, I was sick of compliments; women are accused of being fond of flattery, and I do not pretend to be entirely free from this foible of my sex, but I have lately been satiated with it; beside which, flattery to please me must be delicate, discriminate, and bestowed by those whose taste and judgment I consider as superior to my own. Since my marriage, I feel as if I had entered into a new world; but it is not a world of my own creation. I have been introduced into a quite new society, but it is not the society which I should have chosen; but I must not follow this train of thought, lest it should carry me too far. The boasted influence which our sex are sometimes said to possess over the other, from my own short experience of the marriage state, I already believe to be nugatory. A vain or weak woman may lead her husband into vanities and follies, for which he might possibly possess, though not called into action, the previous inclination; but can a woman of sense guide a man into the paths of truth and virtue, who has never before attempted the road? I fear not, and may not she herself stumble by the way, as a punishment for her temerity in venturing on so bold and hopeless an undertaking? Mr. Malvern left us the next day, and when he was gone, Mr. Vernon asked me my opinion of him, and appeared both surprised and disappointed at finding that it did not entirely correspond with his own. Mr. Malvern has had a superior education to Mr. Vernon, is a few years older, he also possesses a large and independent fortune, which gives to him a sort of consequence in society which men engaged in commerce do not always possess. Mr. Vernon, therefore, though the handsomer man of the two, and no ways deficient in self-approbation, is ready at all times to yield the palm of fashion and elegance, to his more gentlemanly and accomplished friend. We shall soon be going to London; I shall not therefore write to you again from hence. Mrs. Blount is not very well at present; Mrs. Morgan is still with her.

Letter XLVI.

Bedford Square.

Till this morning I have not been able to dedicate one hour to friendship; engagements abroad, company at home, added to a variety of petty domestic occurrences, having, since my arrival in town, occupied the greater part of my time. Mr. Vernon has been accustomed to an amused, not to say, dissipated life, and considers an evening past without some engagement either at home or abroad, as an evening lost. I endeavour, but in vain, to inspire him with a taste for more refined and domestic pleasures, but for conversation our ideas are too little in unison to afford many subjects; reading he detests, and music he is not fond of. Despairing of ever making him what I could wish him to be, I sometimes, perhaps, but too often, sacrifice my own inclination to his. Were it but for one month, one winter, I would not complain; but alas! a whole life is before me, and there is no end to sacrifices; I find that already. – But enough of this. Mr. Malvern is our frequent visitor; he rather improves on acquaintance; and sometimes assists me in detaining Mr. Vernon at home, when I believe he would rather be spending his time at the card table, to which, I am sorry to say, I find he is but too much attached. You ask me if I am happy; it is a question which I dare not ask myself. I had yesterday morning an unexpected, and may say an unwished-for, visitor – it was Mrs. Cooper. When the servant announced her name, I felt extremely agitated, but recovering myself as well as I could, went forward with a smiling countenance to receive her. She embraced me, and kindly congratulated me on my marriage, of which she said she had only been informed by the public papers; and was, till very lately, ignorant of my being in town, or should have waited on me sooner. She then said, that both Mr. Cooper and herself had felt hurt by neglecting for so long a time to write them, as they thought on the score of friendship they had some little claim to my correspondence; and it would have given them pleasure to have heard from myself of the changes which had taken place in my situation since I left their house. I felt confused while I stammered out some poor and frivolous excuses for my seeming ingratitude, and neglect of persons from whom I had received so many civilities. We then talked of indifferent subjects, and among other things she informed me, that Mr. Wansey, my old sweetheart, as she called him, was lately married to a lady of large fortune. She said nothing of the marriage of their other friend, and I had not the courage to mention his name, though I felt a wish to make some inquiries concerning him. I wonder if she ever heard of my imprudent residence in his house. I believe, and now hope, it is a thing which but a few persons are acquainted with. I have once or twice thought, and indeed wished, to mention it to Mr. Vernon, but have never yet found resolution. His disposition and manners do not invite confidence; and after all it is a circumstance of which, perhaps, it would be as well he should never be informed. I see now in the strongest light of all the errors of which I have been guilty. In solitude, and in the world, how different are our ideas of the same subject, and how different the standard by which we judge of the same action! In the former, the enthusiasm of our sentiments, the rectitude of our hearts are our only guides; in the latter, opinion, the voice of the multitude, and "the dread laugh, which scarce the stern philosopher can bear,"[92] is all in all.

Before Mrs. Cooper left me, she said "Mr. Cooper much wished to see me, and would have accompanied her this morning had he not been particularly engaged." I replied, "that I should have been very happy to have seen Mr. Cooper, and that I would take the earliest opportunity of returning her call." "We shall not let you off so," she cried, "you must introduce us to Mr. Vernon, and while in town I hope we shall be good neighbours." She soon after took her leave. When Mr. Vernon came home to dinner, I mentioned to him who had called on me; he said, "he had no acquaintance with the Coopers, but if they were my friends he had no objection to visiting of them: he supposed they gave good dinners." Mr. Vernon had an engagement for the evening; I spent the remainder of it at home and alone, and endeavored to amuse myself with a book, but could not read. I then sat down to the piano, but could neither play nor sing. I wish Mrs. Cooper had not called on me, as I have many objections at present to visiting in Berner[93] Street. It would be better, much better that my acquaintance with Mr. and Mrs. Cooper should not be renewed, but how am I now to avoid the renewal? I must at least return her call.

Letter XLVII.

Why did Mrs. Cooper call on me, and why did I suffer myself to be prevailed on to dine at their house? better to have appeared rude, ungrateful, anything, rather than have exposed myself to the risk of a trial, to which I proved so unequal. If when I last wrote to you I was far from happy, I am now completely miserable. Berner Street is doomed to be fatal to my peace; I deferred from day to day returning Mrs. Cooper's morning call, but at length took courage to wait on her; she was not at home, so I only left my card. A short time afterwards, we received a note of invitation from Mr. and Mrs. Cooper to dine with them [on][94] yesterday, which Mr. Vernon happening to be disengaged, immediately accepted. I was sorry that he did – I did not wish to go; I did not like the thought of introducing him to my old friends; their parties would not suit him, our parties would not suit them. I was no longer the same being that I was when I first entered their hospitable dwelling; and I did not wish to enter it again. The dreaded day at length arrived; we set off at the appointed hour, and were received with great cordiality both by Mr. and Mrs. Cooper, to whom, with some trepidation, I introduced Mr. Vernon. There were at dinner some persons whom I recollected having seen before, and several strangers. At the table I began to feel myself rather more at ease, than when I first entered the house, though every well known object reminded me of the parties which I had formerly made one of in that room. In the evening we sat down to cards. I played with Mr. Vernon. We had nearly finished our rubber when a servant came into the room, and announced the name of Howard. – I started, and hastily and involuntarily turned my head toward the door; at that moment a gentleman entered the drawing-room; it was he himself; my eyes met his; the blood in one instant ran to and from my heart, a sudden faintness came over me, and the cards fell from my hands; what followed I know not, till I found myself in Mrs. Cooper's dressing room, with her and Mr. Vernon standing by me. When I was sufficiently recovered to speak, I begged Mr. Vernon to order the carriage, as I still found myself too much indisposed to venture again into the drawing-room. Mrs. Cooper kindly attributed my fainting to the heat of the room. Our coach was soon at the door, and, accompanied by Mr. Vernon, I stepped into it with the feeling of a culprit going to the bar. Mr. Howard was, I believe, an unexpected guest; and I was fearful, lest the unguarded emotion which I had betrayed at his sudden entrance, should give rise to some suspicions in the breast of Mr. Vernon, which it would be difficult for me to remove, and lead to some questions on his part, which it might be painful to me to answer. We neither of us spoke during the ride home, but as soon as we entered the house, Mr. Vernon threw himself on a sopha near which I had sat down, and in an ironical, though angry tone, said "I think we have acted a pretty sort of tragi-comical farce this evening, in which it would be difficult to say, whether you or I have made the most ridiculous figure." I attempted to reply, but the words which I would have spoken died away on my lips. "I am sorry, very sorry," was all I could articulate. In the same bitter tone of irony he continued – "If I may be allowed to ask the question, pray who is the gentleman, whose sudden entrance produced such a wonderful effect on your fine feelings, and delicate nervous system." I replied with some degree of firmness, "The name of the gentleman whom I suppose you allude to, is Howard" – "Howard, when, and where, were you acquainted with him?" "He is a particular friend of Mr. and Mrs. Cooper's, and was a frequent visitor at their house, while I was their guest." "Have you never seen him since that time, till this evening?" "Yes, I met with him again in Surry, but never saw him after I returned into Sussex; and before I went to reside with Mrs. Blount, I heard of a marriage with a Miss C——, so let us, at least for the present, talk no more of Mr. Howard." I then offered Mr. Vernon my hand which he took, but soon relinquished. He shortly after took up his hat and went out, saying I had better not sit up for him, as it was uncertain at what hour he should return. – I went to bed, but with a mind too much discomposed to admit of repose. The night was far spent before Mr. Vernon came home. In the morning at breakfast he appeared sullen, and disinclined to speak, though I made several ineffectual efforts towards conversation. When we had finished our unsocial meal, he went out as usual, but without, as is his general custom, wishing me good morning. At the dinner hour he returned home, but apparently in a no better humor than he had left it. We dined alone, and as soon as the servant who waited on us had quitted the room, I said to Mr. Vernon, in a conciliatory accent, "I fear you are not well, or are you still angry with me? If I offended you yesterday evening by breaking up the rubber, which I believe we were on the point of winning, be assured my offence was involuntary, and those who are bound together for life, must learn to forget and to forgive." "My memory, Madam," he replied, "is not quite so accommodating as yours[95] appears to be; for as you never yourself informed me of your having resided for nearly six months with this Mr. Howard, whose accidental appearance yesterday evening at Mr. Cooper's occasioned you such evident and unaccountable emotion, I suppose I am to conclude that it is a circumstance which when you married me had entirely escaped your memory." Indignant at the unjust, and unworthy suspicions, which his manner of speaking, still more than the words themselves, seemed to imply, I answered, with some degree of warmth, "that though I had not forgotten, nor had any reason to wish to forget, my six months residence in the house of Mr. Howard, I was not, when I married Mr. Vernon, aware that I was bound by any law either human or divine to make him acquainted with every circumstance of my former life." He replied: but it would be vain to attempt to tell you what he said, or all that past between us on this painful subject. As soon as I found him sufficiently cool to listen to reason, I endeavoured by a simple recital of facts to remove from his mind every cause for suspicion, or distrust of my conduct while I was my own mistress; after which a sort of reconciliation took place between us, notwithstanding which, I am by no means certain of having reinstated myself in his good opinion. Mr. Vernon is not the man who can appreciate properly, either my character, or that of Mr. Howard.

Letter XLVIII.

The little, and it was but little influence which I could ever boast of possessing over Mr. Vernon, is since our visit to Berner Street entirely at an end. By his altered manner, and the distant hints which he occasionally throws out, I perceive that he is not satisfied with the account which I the next day gave him of my situation in the house of Mr. Howard; and if he is not, what can I now say that will satisfy him? If he chooses to make any further enquiries concerning it, he is welcome so to do; otherwise, it is a subject which I shall never again mention to him, conscious of the innocence and purity of my own conduct. I must leave the event to time and accident. Mr. Vernon, at present, is very little at home; and Mr. Malvern, who is still our frequent visitor, occasionally chides him for spending so much of his time abroad, when he has so charming and interesting a companion as myself, by his own fire-side. He also very often proposes our going to the theatres, or some other place of public amusement, where I can be of the party; with the view, as he tells me, of breaking Mr. Vernon off the pernicious habit, which he fears he has formed, of passing his evenings at the gaming table.

I have a curiosity to know who it was that informed Mr. Vernon of my six months' residence, as he invidiously called it, in the house of Mr. Howard. I recollect that Mr. Malvern once asked me if I knew a gentleman of the name of ——. I answered that I remembered the name, but could not at that moment tell where I had seen the person. Nothing more passed between us on the subject; but some time after, I recollected that a gentleman of that name once dined with Mr. Howard while I was in his house; but as I only saw the gentleman for a minute, and that by accident, the circumstance had entirely slipt my memory, till Mr. Malvern, by his question, brought it to my mind. But, surely, Mr. Malvern is too much of the gentleman, and, I trust, too much the friend both of Mr. Vernon and myself, to repeat to him any anecdote to my disadvantage, that is, supposing that he had heard any from this Mr. ——; which I cannot think at all probable he should, for no friend of Mr. Howard's could be so despicable, or so ignorant of his character, as to form any improper conclusions from merely seeing me at his house: but conjectures are vain, so I will no longer perplex myself on the subject. Mr. Vernon this morning received a letter from Mrs. Blount's steward, informing him that his mistress had for some days past been extremely ill, and requesting him to come down as soon as possible. In consequence of this information, Mr. Vernon immediately set off post for the Hall. I offered to accompany him, but he did not think my going necessary, unless his aunt particularly wished to see me. He promised to send me a line to-morrow, to inform me how he found her. I shall, on various accounts, be very anxious till I hear from him.

Letter XLIX.

Poor Mrs. Blount is no more; and Mr. Vernon, who came home yesterday evening, did not get down time enough to see the last of her. She had expired, he was informed, about an hour before he arrived. The next morning Mrs. Morgan produced a will, which, she said, had been properly executed during Mrs. Blount's late illness, and which she wished might be opened in Mr. Vernon's presence. It accordingly was, when to his great mortification he found that, a few trifling legacies excepted, Mrs. Blount had left the whole of her disposable property to Mrs. Morgan and her children. Finding that his presence was no longer necessary, or wished for at the Hall, he immediately took his leave. His speedy and unexpected return home, added to his appearance, which was gloomy and fearful, led me, the moment he entered the house, to suspect that all was not right; and my suspicions were soon confirmed. After briefly informing me of what had passed, he raved like a madman, and seemed for a while almost beside himself. When the violence of his passion began to subside, I endeavoured to soothe him, and tried by every argument my reason could suggest, to reconcile his mind to the disappointment he had suffered; but nothing which I could urge had the least effect. He said he had been both deceived and ill used, Mrs. Blount having from his earliest childhood promised to make him her heir; "and that promise," he exclaimed, "has been my ruin." In short, from what he said, I gathered, that on the strength of the property which he expected to inherit, he had at different times borrowed large sums of money, which he now knew not how to repay. He also informed me that he had this winter entered into some large mercantile speculations, which he had reason to fear would not turn out well. He then began to execrate women in general, and Mrs. Morgan in particular, and ended by swearing, that if it were in the power of the law to set the will aside, it should be done. But this is mere vapor; wills are solemn things, and, when properly executed, not easily set aside.

Letter L.

How difficult is the science of self-knowledge! I never thought myself either mercenary or ambitious, yet now that our golden dreams are over, I feel that I never should have married Mr. Vernon, had I not considered him as the promised heir of Mrs. Blount's very ample fortune. Yet, notwithstanding this confession, could I but indulge the hope that the change which her will has made in our prospects, would in the end produce a favorable change in the habits and character of Mr. Vernon, I should not think his reformation too dearly purchased, though at the expense of a good estate; but of this, alas! I have no expectation. Instead of exerting himself to retrieve, if possible, his affairs, which are at present, I fear, much involved, his chief study appears to be either to avoid, or to banish reflection. To gambling, which used to be his predominant foible, he has, since the death of Mrs. Blount, added the still more disgusting, and not less pernicious habit, of drinking wine to excess; a vice, of which I had never before any great reason to accuse him. Mr. Malvern, who appears to interest himself in our affairs, frequently reproves him for his want of sobriety; and would, were I to give him the opportunity, speak to me very freely on the subject of our present embarrassments; but this I endeavour to avoid. Situated as I am, I cannot be too scrupulous, too guarded in my conduct. To you, and to you alone, I at present confide my domestic troubles; and were I disposed to seek for another confidant, Mr. Malvern, certainly, would not be the person.

Letter LI.

My mind is at present greatly agitated; our affairs appear to be drawing towards a crisis; and God knows what will be the result. This morning Mr. Vernon, who had been out, and whose return I did not expect till the usual dinner hour, entered abruptly into the room where I was sitting. He appeared much discomposed; and in a hurried manner asked me, what cash I had by me; I answered, and that truly, "Very little." He made no reply, but walked up and down the room apparently in a state of great perturbation. His brow was contracted, his eye wild, and his complexion, which is naturally ruddy, changed to a deadly yellow. His manner and appearance united, struck me forcibly. I gazed on him with undefinable apprehension, and then said, "Mr. Vernon, you alarm me; has any thing new occurred?" He answered, "I am going out of town; should I not return this evening, to-morrow I will send you a line; but be sure that you do not quit the house till you hear from me." With these words he was going away. I felt terrified, and grasped hold of his coat with the intention of detaining him; but he broke from me, and rushed out of the room. I sat for some time like one thunderstruck; then rang the bell, and enquired if Mr. Vernon had left home. On being answered in the affirmative, I gave orders to be denied to every one who might call during his absence; and retired to my own room, which I do not mean to quit, till I hear from Mr. Vernon; for as to his returning home this evening, of that I have not the least expectation. I conjecture that the mercantile house in which he is a partner, and which I am afraid he has injured by his imprudence, has stopped payment. What I am to do, or where I am to go, I know not: but I am no longer my own mistress, or at liberty to act for myself. My fate is united to that of Mr. Vernon, let his be what it will; and by the line which I hope to receive from him to-morrow, I must regulate my actions. I look forward with patience for its arrival, as no state of mind is so unpleasant as that of suspense. I will write to you again when I hear from Mr. Vernon.

Letter LII.

Dover.

Two whole days elapsed without my hearing from Mr. Vernon. On the morning of the third, I received a note from Mr. Malvern, saying that he wished to speak to me alone, and would call on me in less than half an hour. Conjecturing that he had something of importance to communicate, I gave orders that he might be admitted. He soon came; I went down stairs to receive him. He looked grave when we met, and addressed me in a tender yet respectful tone. I judged by his voice and manner, that he was the bearer of unpleasant tidings, and without waiting to hear what he had to say, eagerly enquired whether he had received any intelligence of Mr. Vernon. "I have," he answered; "and I have also a letter from him to yourself;" which he, at the same time, put into my hand. I instantly broke the seal. It contained the following words, written apparently in haste, and with an unsteady hand: "The embarrassed state of my affairs obliges me to absent myself from home for a time. In a few hours I hope to embark for the continent, where it is my wish that you should follow me. As it would be improper for you to travel alone, Mr. Malvern, who has promised to join me at Paris, and who will settle every thing relative to your journey, will escort you. He is my friend; so you need not scruple to accept of his protection. You cannot remain where you are, as I expect an execution in the house." When I finished reading the letter, I sat for some minutes with it in my hands without speaking. Mr. Malvern, who had been the whole of the time attentively watching my countenance, was the first to break silence. "I am," said he, "apprised of the contents of your letter, and do not, my dear Mrs. Vernon, ask you how you mean to act in this dilemma, for, I am sorry to say, the case at present admits of no alternative. Mr. Vernon's affairs are I fear very bad, and the sooner you quit this house I believe the better. I only therefore wait to receive your commands." "I have no commands," I cried; "Mr. Vernon has left me in a cruel situation. He ought to have apprised me of his intentions before he went away, or if he wished me to accompany him in his flight, have taken me with him." "Very true, he ought so to have done, but when he left you he had no time to spare; and the hurry and perplexity which his mind was in at that moment, might possibly prevent his doing, what he certainly ought not in any situation to have neglected. On my care and attention to your accommodation till we join Mr. Vernon, I think you can rely; and were not the circumstances of an unpleasant nature to which I shall be indebted for the honor of attending you, I should consider myself but too happy." – "This, Mr. Malvern," I cried, interrupting him, "is no time for compliments; I respect you as the friend of Mr. Vernon; but if I must leave England, I should certainly have preferred doing so under his protection." "That is now impossible, and a very few days will take us to Paris; with your leave therefore I will bring a post-chaise to your door at an early hour to-morrow morning." He then took his leave. My head was all of a whirl; and I passed the remainder of the day in a state of extreme perturbation. I was far from satisfied with the arrangement which had been made, but if I refused to follow Mr. Vernon, where could I go? and I had too many things to do, preparatory to my leaving the house, to allow of much time for deliberation. By daybreak in the morning Mr. Malvern was true to his appointment. I was ready, and he handed me into the chaise with an air of respectful, yet visible satisfaction. We quickly rattled over the stones; and lost sight of London before the busy crowd has begun their daily toils. Mr. Malvern, who was in a gayer humour than I was, exerted his utmost powers of conversation to entertain me on our journey; but my mind was too full of anxiety to permit me to be easily amused. The varied prospects and fine views with which the high Kent road (which we travelled) so particularly abounds, had a happier effect on my feelings than all his studied rhetoric; and while I exhaled the pure country air, which I had not breathed for some months, my spirits, naturally elastic, but which for the last few days had been greatly agitated, began to revive. We reached Dover before it was dark; where, after taking some slight refreshment, I soon retired for the night; and, fatigued in body and in mind, enjoyed a few hours' sound sleep. Awaking refreshed, I arose early in the morning, that I might have an opportunity of writing to you once more before I leave England. Mr. Malvern has summoned me to breakfast; he has secured us a passage to Calais, in a packet which is to sail in less than an hour. It may be long, perhaps very long, before you hear from me again; till then farewell.*

Mr. Cooper to Miss F—.

Madam,

Being no stranger to the friendship which for many years has subsisted between yourself and the amiable, though unfortunate Mrs. Vernon, I think it incumbent on me to send you the following particulars. Last Monday se'en-night I accompanied my friend Mr. Howard, a gentleman with whose name I presume you are not unacquainted, to a masquerade. In the course of the evening a female masque, in a black domino, attracted our notice by the singularity of her manner and appearance. She passed and repassed us several times with quick and hurried steps, and seemingly too much absorbed by her own feelings to be conscious of the attention which she attracted. In her hand she held or rather grasped a something, but we could not discover what. In a scene devoted to pleasure, a human being entirely abstracted from all outward objects, and apparently agitated by strong mental emotion, presented too striking a contrast to the gaiety and dissipation by which we were surrounded, to be viewed with indifference. Our sympathy was excited, our curiosity awakened, and as she was pacing the room backward and forward, we at last ventured to accost her, with the intention of offering her our protection or assistance. She seemed terrified at our attempting to stop her, and broke from us with a wild and fearful precipitation. Her manner interested us; our sympathy, our curiosity was increased. After this we saw no more of her till we entered the supper-room; there, while Mr. Howard was engaged with some ladies of his acquaintance, I again beheld her. She was sitting on a bench in one corner of the room, still alone, but more composed in her appearance than when we had first observed her. I seated myself beside her, and again ventured to speak to her. She remained silent, but seemed to listen to what I was saying. I was going to repeat my offers of service, when my friend Howard joined us, and addressed her in those kind and soothing tones, which he so well knows how to command. She started at the sound of his voice, and raised her eyes, which were before fixed on the ground. On seeing his face, for he had taken off his mask, she hastily rose from her seat, and would have run from us, but she had not the power. She uttered a piercing shriek, and fell lifeless into the arms of my friend, as he

---

* Twelve months had now nearly elapsed without any correct intelligence of Mrs. Vernon, whose elopement with Mr. Malvern had, for a time, given rise to various reports and much scandal; while Mr. Vernon's bankruptcy afforded an equally interesting subject of animadversion to the circle in which they had moved. But these topics for conversation had been long superseded by new elopements in the fashionable, and new failures in the mercantile world, when Miss F—, whose anxiety about her friend had been every day increasing, received a packet from Berner Street inclosed in a letter from Mr. Cooper.

attempted to prevent her from again escaping us. I thought her dead, so entirely was she deprived both of sense and motion. We carried her in this state into a private room, and were there going to leave her a while to the care of some women, when, on removing her mask, we recognized the lovely features of Mrs. Vernon. "Good God!" exclaimed Mr. Howard, "can it be possible?" I was myself much affected by the discovery, but my friend appeared still more concerned. We stood by her for some time in a state of agitated and anxious suspense, watching in vain for symptoms of returning life. She at length heaved a deep sigh, and once more opened those fine eyes, which I feared were closed forever. She looked wildly around her, and on seeing Mr. Howard, exclaimed, "Leave me, leave me forever!" and immediately went into strong fits, in which she remained for some hours. When she began to revive, I requested Mr. Howard to withdraw, as I feared his presence might occasion another relapse. He therefore left us; and when I thought her sufficiently recovered to bear being removed, I asked her, "whether she had any objection to my taking her to my own house, where I could answer for Mrs. Cooper's receiving her kindly, and paying her proper attention; or if she had any home to which she would rather I see her conveyed?" "I have no home" – was her answer. She appeared too much exhausted to add any more. So without waiting for any further assent, I procured a couple of chairs, and ordered the men to carry us to Berner Street.

When we got home she again fainted, and it was some time before Mrs. Cooper, whom I briefly informed of our adventure, assisted by the servant, could put her to bed, where she lay all the next day in a state of apparent insensibility; her hands clenched, her eyes fixed. Dr. S—, whom we sent for, ordered us to keep her perfectly quiet, and to supply her with as much wine and cordial medicine as we could possibly force her to swallow. For three days we thought her life in extreme danger, on the fourth she began to revive, and by the end of the week entirely recovered her senses, though she still continued very weak and low. On the Monday morning following, she expressed a wish to see me. I went immediately to her bed-side, and taking her hand, which she held out to me, told her I was glad to find her so much better. – "You are very good," she answered, "to interest yourself about one, whom all have abandoned;" and her eyes filled with tears as she spoke. "We will talk about this," I replied, "another time; you are yet too weak to bear much conversation." She said, she could not boast of her strength, but that she meant to arise in the afternoon, which she purposed devoting to writing. "I have not many friends," she added, "but I wish to make one whom I have ever loved as a sister, acquainted with every circumstance which has happened to me, since I left the house of Mr. Vernon. You, also," she continued, "have a right to my confidence. I may be thought even more faulty than I have been." I told her I was not apt to condemn my friends unheard, but I could not at present permit her to fatigue herself by entering into any particulars of her story; that I had always entertained a very high opinion of her, and doubted not that she had been more unfortunate than guilty. "I have indeed been unfortunate," she replied, and sighed deeply. I soon after left her chamber, being engaged out to dinner with a friend, who resides some miles distant from town. It was late in the evening before I returned home, where I soon heard that Mrs. Vernon was no more. She arose, I found, soon after I had quitted her, and had been engaged in writing the whole of the afternoon. Towards evening she complained of her head, and about seven o'clock was seized with a return of the faintings, followed by convulsion fits, in one of which she had expired. I was much distressed by this account, and asked Dr. S—, whom Mr. Cooper had sent for, and who was still in the house, what could have occasioned this relapse. He answered, that he imagined too great mental exertion (for he heard she had been writing the greater part of the day,) had again produced that extreme nervous irritation, to which he had from the first attributed her disorder. The papers in which I inclose, and which, though not directed, were, I take for granted, intended for yourself, will explain to you the circumstances which have produced this fatal and melancholy catastrophe.

"After a long silence, and to me an eventful period, I once more, my dear Eliza, take up my pen to address you, while I soothe my weary soul with the thought that there is yet one human being who is interested in my fate. It is true I have experienced kindness and humanity from persons on whom I had but little claim; but those who ought to have protected me – who were bound by every tie both human and divine – it is they who have betrayed and destroyed me. But it will not be long. Let me then, while I have strength remaining sufficient for the task, relate to you, though briefly, all that I have done and suffered since you last heard from me. I was then at Dover, about to embark for Calais with Mr. Malvern. The morning was rough and stormy: we nevertheless went on board the vessel in which he had taken our passage. Being the only female passenger on board, I remained on deck till a hasty shower of rain obliged me to seek shelter in the cabin, where, being much indisposed, I was prevailed on by Mr. Malvern to lie down. Exhausted by the sea-sickness, I fell asleep; but was soon awakened by a distracting noise over my head, and one not much less violent below, which proceeded from the boxes, portemanteaux, and other lumber which was in the cabin, tumbling from side to side in utter confusion. The rolling of the vessel was so great, that I could scarcely preserve myself from falling out of the little bed on which I had reposed. A squall of wind had arisen, which to me, who had never before been at sea, appeared a tremendous gale; and while I heard the waves dash over the sides of our little bark, I thought we were going to the bottom. The idea afforded me no terror. Life had for me but few charms; and without a fear or a murmur I could at that moment have resigned myself and my misfortunes to a watery grave. In a minute Mr. Malvern was by my side. He appeared much more alarmed than I had been, though he came down, he informed me, to assure me that there was no danger. The wind being now fair, and the storm abated, a few hours brought us to Calais, from which place we travelled with the utmost expedition to Paris, where I hoped to meet with Mr. Vernon; but in that hope I was disappointed. We drove to the —— Hotel, where Mr. Malvern told me he expected to find him. He was not there; nor could we gain any information concerning him. I was extremely mortified by this disappointment, and expressed to Mr. Malvern the surprise and vexation which I experienced at not meeting with Mr. Vernon at the place which he himself had appointed. Mr. Malvern appeared to partake of my chagrin, and endeavoured to relieve the anxiety of my mind, which was every hour increasing, by urging a variety of causes which might have prevented Mr. Vernon from coming immediately to Paris; adding that he had no doubt but that we should very shortly either see him in person or receive intelligence where to find him. I was myself inclined to be of this opinion; and agreeably to Mr. Malvern's advice consented to remain at the hotel where we then were, till we either saw or heard from Mr. Vernon. Day after day passed, but no letter came – no Mr. Vernon appeared. A variety of apprehensions, mingled with some distrust of Mr. Malvern's honor, now entered into my mind, and I felt strongly the impropriety of remaining much longer under the protection of a gay and single young man; one, too, who from the first of our acquaintance had professed himself my devoted friend and warm admirer. My situation was delicate, and from the tender and gallant attention which I received from Mr. Malvern, became every hour more and more distressing. I at length determined to speak to Mr. Malvern without reserve, and frankly demand of him an explanation of his conduct. He at first endeavoured to evade my questions and elude my suspicions; but finding, by the solemnity of my manner, and the pointed force of my interrogations, that I was not to be deceived, he at last gave me to understand that my husband had betrayed and abandoned me – nay more, had bartered for a sum of money the honor of his wife. Indignation swelled my bosom, and in the bitterness of despair I exclaimed, 'It is you who have betrayed me; Mr. Vernon, thoughtless and dissipated as he is, could not have acted thus.' He besought me to be calm, and endeavoured to soothe me, but I would not listen to any thing which he had to say. 'Tell me,' I cried, 'the truth – and nothing but the truth.' 'I have,' he replied, 'told you the truth, but not all the truth. I have this morning received intelligence of Mr. Vernon; but I am afraid it is of a nature which you are not at present equal to bear.' 'Whatever be its nature,' I replied haughtily, 'I must bear it, and I solemnly demand it of you.' He sighed and hesitated. I repeated, 'I demand it of you, and will not be deceived.' 'Mr. Vernon,' he then said, 'did not leave England. He was arrested on his road to Harwich; he travelled with pistols, and was determined not to be brought back to London. I need not tell you the rest; I am at present your only protector.' Horror chilled my blood, which indignation had but a few moments before set a boiling. Nature could support no more, and I fell lifeless on the floor. Mr. Malvern, much alarmed, called the women of the house to my assistance. As soon as I recovered my senses, I hastened to my own apartment, where I threw myself on the bed in an agony of mind not to be described. Every evil of Pandora's box now appeared to me to be poured on my devoted head. I wept, I sighed, and raved alternately; till, quite exhausted, I at last sunk into a sort of slumber, from which I soon started, in a state of terror and extreme agitation: frightful images presented themselves before me, my temples throbbed, my pulse beat; in short, I was in a high fever, attended with delirium. I attempted to arise, but found myself unequal to the exertion. When Mr. Malvern, who sent early the next morning to inquire how I was, heard of the state which I was in, he immediately procured the best medical assistance, provided me a nurse, and in short omitted nothing which he thought could contribute to my comfort or facilitate my recovery. After fourteen days and nights of acute suffering, my fever subsided: I felt as one awakened from a frightful dream; and it was some time before I could fully recollect the various circumstances which had reduced me to the state in which I found myself. An extreme languor pervaded my whole frame; my nerves had lost their tone, my mind its vigor. I was unequal to the least exertion, and incapable of forming, much less executing, any plan by which to regulate my future conduct.

"As soon as I was able to bear being removed, Mr. Malvern, by the advice of the physician, took apartments for me a few miles out of Paris, to which I was, through extreme weakness, with some difficulty conveyed. This change of air and scene was beneficial to my health: and I began, though slowly, to recover from the effects of my disorder. My bodily frame was daily regaining strength, but my mind still continued in a state of extreme anxiety and dejection. I wished to return to England; but, as I had no money, knew not how to get there without the assistance of Mr. Malvern, who, whenever I mentioned the subject to him, either pleaded my delicate state of health, or some other excuse, as a motive for continuing longer where I was. And should I return to England, I had when there, no home, no husband, no friend to receive me. I was also aware that long ere this my reputation must have been blasted. My voluntary elopement with Mr. Malvern could in the opinion of the world bear but one construction; and I recollected with a sigh the sentiments which I once heard Mr. Howard express, respecting the force of opinion as it regarded the character of women, and, though conscious of no deviation from virtue, I felt degraded; I had sunk in the opinion of the world, and was already lowered in my own. Had I been in full health, I should most probably have risen superior to this prejudice. My own heart did not upbraid me; and it is rectitude, and not opinion, which ought to be the support of our virtue, and the standard by which we should try our conduct. But my nerves were weakened by illness, and my mind, depressed by misfortune, had lost all its native energy.

"In the mean time, Mr. Malvern paid me the most respectful and unremitting attention; and though in the vicinity of a city famed for gaiety and pleasure, would, had I permitted it, have devoted the greater part of his time to me; while the fervency and tenderness of the attachment which he professed for me, though it failed to touch my heart, softened in some measure the resentment which I had previously been inclined to cherish. Conscious that I could not with any degree of prudence remain much longer under his protection, I was one morning sitting ruminating on my strange destiny, and revolving in my mind a variety of plans, in the hope of fixing on some one which might extricate me from the delicate and difficult situation in which I found myself placed, and had nearly determined on throwing myself into a convent, where, though my religion would prevent my taking the veil, I thought I might remain for some time secluded from society, at least till I had made some one of the few friends whom I had in England, acquainted with my situation; when Mr. Malvern, accompanied by a young man in a clerical habit, entered my apartment. Seeing me look surprised at the intrusion of a stranger, Mr. Malvern approached me and said, 'Will you pardon me for introducing this gentleman, without having first obtained your permission? There are times and circumstances, when perhaps our friends can judge for us better than we can judge for ourselves. Your health is still too delicate to admit of your departure from this country, where you are only known by name, to which this gentleman, who is my friend, comes prepared, with your permission, to give you a legal title. I have settled with him every necessary preliminary, and there are persons in waiting who will witness the ceremony.' Being entirely unprepared for such a proposal, I was perfectly astounded, and remonstrated with vehemence against this hasty proceeding. Mr. Malvern would listen to nothing which I had to say, but entreated, nay almost insisted in my immediately receiving from him a legal right to the protection, which he said both his heart and his honor impelled him to afford me. I urged the indelicacy of forming a second connexion, before I had even put on weeds for the dissolution of a first; and begged at least for time to consider of his proposal; but he would hear of no delay; and seizing my reluctant hand, held it fast in his, while the priest read over the marriage ceremony, to which I was too much agitated to pay the proper or needful attention. When it was finished Mr. Malvern saluted me as his bride. I shrunk, as it were instinctively, from his embrace. He now endeavoured by every means in his power to soothe and cheer my spirits; and finding that I was by no means satisfied with this strange marriage, assured me again and again that the ceremony which had just passed was binding, but if I was not satisfied of its validity, he offered to take me to England whenever I chose to go, and there wed me again according to the rites of our own church; otherwise he had proposed taking a house, or apartments, in Paris, where he meant to stay for some time, as thinking it might be more agreeable to me to reside for a few years on the Continent than to return immediately to my native country. He then pleaded his passion – a passion which, he said, I had inspired him with the first moment that he beheld me, but which he should for ever have concealed in his own breast, had I been happy in my former marriage. My heart was not softened by his professions of love; but my reason and my senses were alike bewildered by the argument which he afterwards made use of, to convince me that I ought on every account to reconcile myself to the thought of being his wife. I felt that I was ensnared; but, like the silly bird when caught by the fowler, I vainly fluttered about, without being able to effect my escape.

"Mr. Malvern after this seldom left me; and day after day passed on, till I gradually relinquished the idea of returning to England. I had not yet completed my twenty-second year, and cold indeed must be the heart which at that early period of life can remain long insensible to love and to hope. My health was now perfectly re-established, and my spirits, though occasionally depressed, had in some measure recovered their usual tone. When I thought of Mr. Vernon, whose remembrance I endeavoured to banish from my mind, it was with a mingled sentiment of pity and disgust. I had never loved him, and the late baseness of his conduct towards myself counteracted those feelings of sorrow and regret, which his shocking and untimely end might otherwise have occasioned. We now removed into elegantly furnished apartments in one of the best situations in Paris, where Mr. Malvern did every thing in his power both to gratify and to amuse me. He at times introduced me into some of the first circles which that great city, celebrated for its brilliant society, afforded; where, being received with the respect due to the wife of an English gentleman, I soon ceased to question the validity of a marriage, which had hitherto been productive of nothing but happiness, and which love, at least on one side, had apparently sanctioned. Alas! how short-sighted are mortals! how delusive, and too often evanescent, the dazzling sunbeams of prosperity!

'Delights, those beautiful illusions,
Play around us; when grasped, they glide away:
They show themselves, but will not with us dwell,
But, like hot gleams, approaching storms foretell.'[96]

"One morning, after returning from our usual promenade, I went into the library, where I saw, lying on the table, a letter for Mr. Malvern, which the servant told me had been delivered during our absence. I took it up, and carelessly casting my eye over the direction, recognised the hand-writing of Mr. Vernon. I gazed on it for a moment in stupid amazement, then examined the seal, which bore the signature of his initials. I tore it open with trembling hand, but could not read a word; a mist swam before my eyes, a deadly sickness pervaded my whole frame. At that instant Mr. Malvern came into the room. He remarked my pallid cheek, and hastened towards me. I gave him the letter, saying, 'You have deceived me; what can this mean?' 'I have not,' he replied, 'deceived you intentionally. I heard that Mr. Vernon had shot himself, nor did I know that he had recovered of the wound, which I was told was mortal, till it would have been useless to have made you acquainted with the truth.' I shook my head, and sighed bitterly. 'But why,' he continued, 'need you distress yourself? Mr. Vernon has not written to me to demand you back; on the contrary he relinquishes to me all claims on your person; my heart, and my fortune, are still at your disposal, and if they are not sufficient to your happiness, when we return to England you can procure a divorce from Mr. Vernon, which may be easily obtained, after which I will marry you in any church you please.' 'This speech afforded me but little consolation. Mr. Malvern had now entirely lost my confidence, and I felt displeased at the seeming levity with which he treated a subject to me so serious; but either reproach or recrimination would now have been equally vain and useless; so with a full heart I retired in silence to my own chamber, where, sending Mr. Malvern word that I was indisposed, and wished to be alone, I shut myself up for the remainder of the day. When we again met, which was not till the next morning, he appeared very gay; and after inquiring after my health, he gently braided me for my absenting myself from his society on the proceeding day, then affected to rally me on my old-fashioned English notions of morality, which he told me but ill suited with the light atmosphere of Paris. I was offended by this conversation, and declared that I would no more appear in society as Mrs. Malvern, now that I was conscious I had no real title to the name, and peremptorily refused to grant Mr. Malvern those privileges, to which he could no longer urge a legal claim. He chid me for what he chose to term my perverseness, and endeavored to overcome my scruples, first by flattery and blandishments, and then by upbraiding me with a coldness and insensibility, which he said an attachment so ardent, and so constant as his had been, but ill deserved.

"A deep melancholy now seized my spirits. I felt as one lost both to virtue and to happiness. To add to my distress, I was pregnant. I had never been so before, and now – what a situation! I had from my infancy been taught to entertain the highest, I might almost say reverential respect for the maternal character. I considered children, of whom I was extremely fond, as a precious and solemn charge entrusted to us by the Almighty, and for whose well-being, both as it respected this world and that which is to come, a parent would be in some degree accountable; and the thought of becoming a mother under my present circumstances agitated my bosom with various and painful emotions. I felt that all the strongest affections of my soul would center in my offspring, while the bare idea of involving my innocent babe in the consequences of my errors was agony. I acquainted Mr. Malvern with my situation. He appeared affected by it, and proposed our immediate return to England, where he said he would endeavour to procure for me, as soon as possible, a divorce from Mr. Vernon, that my marriage with himself might be properly solemnized before the birth of our child. I consented to this arrangement. It is true, I felt at present the greatest repugnance to going back to London, where nothing but disgrace awaited me, and my heart sickened, while my delicacy at times shrunk from the thought of my name being bandied about in newspapers and public courts of justice. But for my child I was willing to encounter every thing; and with the hope and anticipation of future comfort I endeavoured to overcome the feeling of present misery. The preparations for our departure were soon made, and the day fixed on which we were to leave Paris. When the morning arrived I found myself very far from well; but being now bent on going to England, I said nothing to Mr. Malvern of my indisposition till the carriage which he had provided for our journey came to the door. I was then taken so extremely ill, that to have attempted setting off would have been madness. Mr. Malvern then proposed postponing our departure till I was better. I assured him that my present indisposition merely proceeded from extreme agitation of spirits; but, as it might be some time before I could venture to travel, I entreated him to return to England without me, and when he had put the affair which I had now most at heart in a proper train, come back to Paris, where I would remain during his absence, which I hoped would not be many weeks; and by that time I doubted not but I should be sufficiently recovered to accompany him to London. He made many objections to the leaving of me behind him, but I urged it so strongly, that he at last consented; and after making some arrangements for my accommodation till he should return, set off. I shortly after received from him a few lines acquainting me with his safe arrival in England, and requesting that I would send him by return of post a particular account of the state of my health. My indisposition had increased, and ended in a miscarriage. I thought it proper to inform Mr. Malvern of this circumstance, and wrote to him immediately. He answered my letter, but neither in the style nor manner which I had expected from him. He complained of not having yet found Mr. Vernon, who, he had been told, embarked a short time since for the West Indies, but added that he was by no means satisfied with the truth of this report, and should not return to Paris till he had made some further inquiries concerning him. I knew not what to think of this epistle, and in the hope of receiving more satisfaction from the next, soon wrote to him again. Weeks elapsed before I had another letter from him, and when it arrived, it afforded me no satisfaction. The style was evidently cold and constrained. He apologised for his long silence, without giving any sufficient reason for it, fixed no time for returning to Paris, neither did he urge me to follow him to England, where he said business of his own would probably detain him for some time. I felt myself both piqued and perplexed at the receipt of this unlover-like epistle. My residence in Paris, after Mr. Malvern's departure, had become very disagreeable to me, and indeed the state of public affairs in France, at that time, was such as to have rendered a longer stay in that country nether safe nor pleasant. The revolution had already commenced, and as the English began to be looked on by many with a jealous eye, I felt myself in a very disagreeable predicament. A young English nobleman then resident at Paris, who had, while Mr. Malvern was with me, once or twice distinguished me in public by some polite attentions, now sent me a letter, which, though respectfully and cautiously worded, and containing nothing more than general offers of service, I thought proper to return in a blank cover. At a loss what other course to pursue, I at length determined on going back to England; and having previously informed Mr. Malvern by letter of my intention, set off for Calais, accompanied only by a female servant. We there embarked for Dover, where I found Mr. Malvern waiting for our arrival. Our meeting was on both sides formal, rather than tender. My affections, so frequently repelled, had recoiled on my own heart, and my feelings, so often tried, so often excruciated, were at this time under command. In losing the prospect of becoming a mother, I seemed to myself to have lost all my sensibility. Mr. Malvern's cold and altered mein affected me not, and the opinion of the world no longer appeared to me of any importance; my senses were benumbed: I called it fortitude, but it was a fortitude which had arisen from despair. I was sensible that Mr. Malvern's attachment to me had, since he had left Paris, suffered some diminution, but always gentlemanly, always polite, his manner at present, though very different from what it had been, left me no room for reproaches, had I been disposed to make any:

>'When love begins to sicken and decay,
>It useth an enforced ceremony.'[97]

"We staid but one night at Dover, and early the next morning set off post for London, where Mr. Malvern told me he had engaged a lodging for me in

—— Street. On the road, he informed me that he had not as yet been able to trace Mr. Vernon, but as he was convinced, by many circumstances, that he was still in England, he hoped it would not now be very long before he should find out where he had concealed himself. No other conversation of any importance passed between us during the journey; and it being late in the evening before we got to the apartments which had been previously prepared for my reception, Mr. Malvern soon took his leave with the promise of calling on me again early in the next day. I had never been what is usually termed in love with Mr. Malvern, yet his ardent and devoted attachment to me had, while I considered myself his wife, gained for him a tender interest in my affections. It was also by his means alone that I could now ever hope to regain that station in society, to which I proudly felt I had still a rightful claim. From these circumstances, the stability of his attachment to myself had become a question to me of the first importance. No sooner then had he left me than all my fancied fortitude entirely forsook me. Alone, and in a strange place, I almost repented of having returned to England, where I felt as an alien in my native-land – nay worse, an outcast from society, deceived, disgraced, perhaps to be soon abandoned by him in whom I had so lately trusted. All the horrors of my forlorn situation now passed in dread array before me. On the review of them, I experienced for a moment the terrors of guilt, without being conscious of any crime. In the agony and bitterness of my spirit, I wished for death, and more than once determined to end my misfortunes with my life. Religious principle, which had been early and deeply implanted in my mind, soon checked these rash resolves, while Piety, devoid of superstition, now shed her divine and balmy influence over my wounded heart, and on bended knees I raised my eyes, filled with penitential tears to that Being 'who seeth not as man seeth, who judgeth not as man judgeth.'[98]

"The next morning Mr. Malvern called on me, agreeably to his promise. His countenance was cheerful, his manner kind, his conversation animated; and indeed so different did he appear altogether to what I had found him when we first met at Dover, that I taxed myself with being guilty of injustice in harbouring those doubts of his love and honor, which had on the preceding evening taken entire possession of my breast. Some weeks now passed away, during which I formed a thousand contradictory plans, and experienced a variety of opposite and painful emotions. Mr. Malvern continued to visit me daily, but his visits, though frequent, were short. He still talked of finding Mr. Vernon, and endeavouring to obtain the long-wished-for divorce; but the manner in which he mentioned the subject was to me far from satisfactory. One morning when he called on me, he appeared to be in a gayer humor than I had lately seen him, and presenting me with a ticket, said he was going on the Monday following to a masquerade, to which, as a favor, he requested me to accompany him. I returned the ticket, telling him at the same time that he knew I had determined to seclude myself from the world, till I could return to society in my proper character. He answered me, 'You have already too long secluded yourself from the world, whose censures on young and beautiful women are less to be dreaded than you apprehend. But at a masquerade,' he continued, 'and in a domino,[99] you will be perfectly incognito, and may amuse yourself with observing others, without any danger of being known yourself, even should you meet with your nearest acquaintance.' I had never been fond of public places, and at this time felt but little inclination for amusements of any description; but Mr. Malvern pressed me so much, and so earnestly, to accompany him on Monday evening, that I at last suffered myself to be prevailed on to give him my promise to go with him, under the condition of his engaging to see me safe back to my lodging whenever I should become weary of a scene, to which, notwithstanding he endeavoured to paint it in gay and lively colors, I felt in my own mind an extreme aversion. Monday evening soon came. While I was dressing for this hated masquerade, the servant girl who attended me, and whom I had brought with me from Paris, after some hesitation and various attempts at conversation which I did not encourage, said that she had heard a piece of news in the morning, from the lady in whose house we lodged, which she hoped was not true. My curiosity being now awakened, I replied, 'What news is that?' 'O! dear me, ma'am,' she answered, 'I dare say it is not true; and I am afraid you will be angry with me for repeating it; but Mrs. —— told me she had been informed that my master keeps a lady in his own house, a French woman, whom he met with in the packet in which he came over, when he left you so ill in Paris, and she supposes that is the reason why you do not now live with him.' I chid her for listening to idle tales; and under the pretence of no longer requiring her assistance, dismissed her from my dressing-room. Her words had struck like ice upon my heart; while the mortifying anecdote which she had related was a clue which unraveled to me, in an instant, the whole mystery of Mr. Malvern's late vacillating, and till now inexplicable conduct. He had formed, I doubted not, a new connection, which, though most probably of the lightest kind, (such is the inconstancy of men,) had superseded his attachment to myself, and made him no longer desirous of uniting me to him by sacred and indissoluble ties.[100] All that now remained for me was to determine on what line of conduct I ought, in justice to myself, and in prudence toward him, to pursue. I was aware that reproaches never yet reclaimed a wandering heart; beside which, now that he had lowered himself in my esteem, I felt too proud, too deeply injured, to upbraid him with his infidelity. Before I could come to any fixed resolution how to act, Mr. Malvern was with me. It was too late for me to recede from my promise of accompanying him to the masquerade; so without saying any thing concerning what I had heard from the servant, I put on my mask, gave him my hand, and he led me to the chair which was waiting at the door to receive me.

"On entering the place of entertainment, I was for a moment dazzled by the splendor, and amused by the novelty of the scene, but my bosom was too full of thorns, to admit of more than a temporary forgetfulness of my own sorrows; and in the midst of dissipation I sighed for privacy and leisure to unburden my mind of that weight of anxiety by which it was so cruelly oppressed. Mr. Malvern, observing that I did not partake of the general gaiety, endeavoured, by ludicrous remarks on the motley crowd, to excite my vivacity, and solicited me to drink a glass of champaigne in order, as he said, to raise my spirits; but all would not do. I felt wretched, and could not exert myself and irritated almost to madness by his unaccountable and unpardonable conduct, I at length determined on endeavouring to get back to my lodgings in the best manner I could, when I was arrested by a tall masque, who forcibly put my arm through his, and addressed me in the language of gallantry. It was the figure, the manner, the accent of Mr. Vernon. I called him by his name; he recognized my voice, and instantly turned from me. I seized hold of him, and to convince myself that I was not mistaken, tore off his mask. He disentangled himself from my grasp, and broke from me, leaving his mask in my hand. Phrenzy and despair now fired my brain, and, insensible to all outward objects, I continued to pace the rooms backwards without knowing where I was, or whom I was seeking, till quite exhausted I sat down at the lower end of a room, in which several parties were at supper. A gentleman, who I believe had before noticed me, came up to me, sat down by my side, and spoke to me in tones of pity and humanity. His manner, which was that of a friend, roused me, and in some measure recalled my scattered senses. I was going to throw myself on his protection, when my attention was suddenly arrested by one whose accents vibrated to my inmost soul. I raised my eyes, – Mr. Howard himself was standing before me; his countenance beaming with sympathy and compassion. I gazed on him for a moment with a complicated and agonizing recollection, then started from my seat with the intention of flying from his presence, though, desolate as I was, I knew not where to go, or in what place to hide my aching head. A sudden pain pieced like a dagger through my temples, an icy coldness shivered in every vein; I felt it as the period of my existence. I can write no longer. My web of life is spun, the thread is broken:

'I come, ye ghosts, prepare your roseate bowers.'[101]

When I am no more you will lament my Fatal though involuntary Errors, while you shed a tear to the memory of your once beloved, once admired, but now POOR MARY-ANNE!"

Concluding Note by the Editor

Should any of my readers be sufficiently interested by this little Tale, to inquire why Mr. Malvern urged Poor Mary-Anne to go to the masquerade, and why when there he deserted her, I am sorry to say that the correspondence here ending, it is not in my power fully to answer these inquiries. A note in the margin of one of the last sheets intimates, that Mr. Malvern, desirous of freeing himself from an engagement which he no longer wished to fulfill, Lord ——, who had seen Mrs. Vernon at Paris, and was enamored of her beauty, had proposed to him, the taking of her by stratagem from the masquerade, and conveying her to his country seat, in a remote part of the north of England; but that in consequence of some mistake in the agreement, or error in the arrangements, Lord —— had failed in the execution of this plan, which Mr. Malvern had left the rooms in order to facilitate. The consequence was, Mrs. Vernon's being left as she describes.

Another note also says, that a few days after the death of Mrs. Vernon, a paragraph appeared in the public papers, stating that a duel had been fought in Hyde Park between two gentlemen, both of whom were mortally wounded; whether each by the ball of his antagonist, or whether, as is more probable, that one party, after firing at the other, had lodged the contents of his remaining pistol in his own brain, could not, as there were no seconds, be ascertained. These gentlemen were Mr. Vernon, and Mr. Malvern.

Having heard much of the beauty of my heroine, should any of my fair readers be desirous of knowing whether she was tall, or short, fair or brown, or, in one word, whether she most resembled themselves, or any of their acquaintances; to gratify their innocent, and natural curiosity I inform them, that she measured exactly five feet four inches and a half; that her figure was light and elegant, while her form, exquisitely proportioned, appeared to be cast in nature's finest mould. Her complexion though not decidedly fair, was clear, delicate, and animated:

"The pure and eloquent blood,
Spoke in her cheeks, and so distinctly wrought,
That one night might almost say her body thought."[102]

Her hair, which was very luxuriant, was of the chestnut brown. Her brow was that of Raphael's Madonna. Her nose neither exactly Grecian nor Roman, but something between the two. Her eyes shaded by long, dark eye-lashes, and beaming with intelligence and sensibility, were at once both soft and brilliant; their color blue – by candle light they were sometimes mistaken for black, sometimes thought to be a dark purple. I never but once knew eyes that resembled them, and they were closed in earliest youth by the cold hand of death.

Finis

APPENDICES

Appendix A

TWO TALES BY ELIZABETH HAYS, IN *LETTERS AND ESSAYS, MORAL AND MISCELLANEOUS*, BY MARY HAYS (1793)

No. X.[1]

Cleora, or the Misery Attending Unsuitable Connections

Among the various sources of infelicity in human life, no cause has been more productive of complicated wretchedness, than the union of persons whose minds and dispositions are dissimilar: "sympathy is the charm of life:" – and no exterior circumstance, or adventitious advantage can procure happiness, where domestic harmony is wanting.

Frances and Cleora experienced the misfortune of losing a very excellent father during their early childhood. Mrs. L. their mother, an amiable and accomplished woman, when the first transports of grief had subsided into calm resignation, though still young, and peculiarly qualified to appear with advantage in public life, retired on the small fortune left her by her husband; and in a village many miles from London, devoted her time and faculties to the education of her beloved daughters. The improvement of the young ladies, both in person, and mind, was answerable to a mother's fondest wishes: – health glowed in their cheeks, and vivacity sparkled in their eyes, while natural good sense, directed by virtuous principle, added dignity to the graces which youth and innocence bestow.

At twenty years of age, Frances became acquainted with Hilario, the son of a neighbouring farmer. This young man was possessed of a noble and ingenuous mind, heightened by a good, though not a learned education, situated far from the temptations which great cities present, his heart was uncorrupted by vice, and his notions unsophisticated by prejudice, or fashion: – the hours that could be spared from agriculture, he devoted to books; and blessed with health, virtue, and competence, he wanted only a female friend to participate, and complete his happiness. In Frances L. he found this friend: – the sympathy was mutual: – for congeniality of taste and sentiment soon produced, on both sides, a sincere and animated attachment: – no obstacle intervened to obstruct their union. Frances had no fortune: – but Hilario, whose soul disdained all sordid, and mercenary considerations, and whose choice was dictated by nobler views, esteemed her a fortune of herself: her heart was to him a more valuable treasure than millions of gold. Time, instead of weakening, gave strength to their reciprocal affection, for their love was founded on the firm basis of reason and virtue; and a family of fine children cemented their esteem by still dearer ties.

Cleora, who was some years younger than her sister, contemplated their felicity with the most heart-felt satisfaction. – But while her fancy strayed to future periods, in which she hoped to realize the same domestic scenes of happiness, the tear of sensibility would glisten in her eye, while fearful doubt, and soft anxiety, agitated her youthful bosom, and obscured for a moment, the sun-shine of hilarity, with which her countenance was generally illumined. – Thus time rolled on, and Cleora attained her five and twentieth year, but met not with another Hilario. About this period a gentleman from London came on a visit to the house of her brother-in-law. Mercutio, for so I shall call him, had acquired a considerable fortune on the stock-exchange; – his general character was fair; – for he had ever punctually fulfilled his engagements in the alley, and had neither decreased his wealth, nor impaired his constitution, by any of those vices, and follies, by which so many young men, consume, and shorten their days. But riches had not liberalized the heart, that early associations had rendered narrow; and beyond himself, he never knew a generous care. – His person was tall, and thin, he might be reckoned handsome, at least he thought so, and when adjusting his cravat to the nicest minutia of fashion, would frequently contemplate his own figure with no small degree of self-complacency.

The rural scenery, the effect of which was heightened by novelty, – the innocent cheerfulness of Hilario's family, – and above all, the animated features, unaffected manners, and modest dignity of Cleora, (so unlike the town ladies, whom he had had the honour of gallanting to a play, or dancing with at a city ball) awakened in his soul all the little energy, and native sensibility, that for many years had lain dormant, or had been absorbed in the grand pursuit of acquiring money: these new and tender sensations, made him for a while forget even his compting-house, and venture to trust his business to the management of his clerks; these days of vacation, he devoted to the fair nymph, whom from the first hour in which he beheld her, he determined to make his wife.

Cleora, though possessed of an excellent understanding, and enthusiastic love of virtue, – was not devoid of vanity. Mercutio's obsequious attentions gratified this foible. It is true, her first impressions were not of the most favourable cast; but when she heard the public testimony of his good character, and in conversation found him assent to every observation that she made, and echo back the sentiments which she uttered, she willingly retracted her too hasty judgment. Accustomed to observation, and priding herself on her penetration, she determined to scrutinize his disposition attentively. But, alas! the man was disguised in the lover, and self-love threw a veil before *her sight*; her own temper frank, and unguarded, the friends with whom she had been accustomed to converse, the same, she could form no proper estimate of the artificial manners, acquired by an intercourse with the world. – That the man had taste she was convinced: he had shown it, by

APPENDIX A

distinguishing *her*; – and in offering to marry her without a fortune, he proved the disinterestedness, and sincerity of his attachment.

In short, after a few journeys, and a few letters, the style of which (though much studied) did not entirely meet with her approbation, Cleora became the wife of Mercutio. Various were the sensations, that agitated her mind, as she bade farewell to the beloved shades of F. and the still dearer friends, and companions of her youth. But when her mother bestowed the maternal blessing, and parting embrace, her emotions were too violent to be restrained. Mercutio, the fond bridegroom, though unused to the melting mood, could not behold the tender scene unmoved, and when in the postchaise, endeavoured with unremitting attention, to soothe her grief, and restore her cheerfulness. Cleora, whose feelings were regulated by principle, and whose heart was ever awake to kindness and gratitude, smiled upon her husband, and in accents softened by sensibility, assured him of her affection. But, though she endeavoured to conceal, she could not entirely dissipate the gloom, that hung over her mind, and which their entrance into London, on a sultry evening in the month of August, by no means tended to remove.

Cleora, though a child of nature, accommodated herself to her new situation: she had no relish for the pleasures of the town: but she loved society, the want of which (when in the country) she had often regretted, and which she now flattered herself she should be able to enjoy. She employed herself also in the regulation of her household, and her leisure hours, as had ever been her custom, she intended to devote to reading. Romantic in her ideas of conjugal felicity, in her husband she expected to find a faithful, and affectionate friend: but, alas! these sound expectations were succeeded by cruel, and mortifying disappointment, and her schemes of rational happiness, "melted into thin air."

Mercutio unfortunately had no ideas of a wife, beyond a mistress, and a housekeeper; and even as such his notions were sordid, and degrading. The superior talents, and cultivated understanding of his lady, created in his mind a narrow jealousy, while the elevation of her sentiments, and the fervent piety of her heart, he now treated with derision, or looked on with contempt: and though she studiously endeavoured to conceal the disgust, which this behaviour excited, and tried to regulate her conduct by motives of duty and virtue, he yet felt that she did not love him. For he was conscious that he did not deserve her affection, and this consciousness joined to some disappointments in considerable speculations, gave additional acrimony to a temper, which before was far from placid. He knew, that Cleora took pleasure in the conversation of sensible, and liberal minded people. With such therefore he was determined to break off all acquaintance, and keep no company, but what his business absolutely required. In her domestic concerns, though conducted with prudence, and economy, he was ever interfering: never satisfied, and always suspecting himself to be defrauded, he was continually obliging her to change her servants, and was constantly ringing in her ears little groveling maxims, that her soul abhorred, and rose superior to. Nor would he even permit her to enjoy her literary pursuits unmolested, but seized every opportunity of uttering sarcasms against reading ladies, and insinuating that his interest was neglected, while she sat wasting her hours in the library.

Dejected, mortified, and wretched, she proposed visiting the loved retreat, in which she had passed her youthful days of happiness, and innocence, and wished to spend a part of the ensuing summer with her mother, and sister. To this Mercutio at first reluctantly consented, but afterwards peremptorily refused his consent, urging, that he had no idea of his wife's spending money, and taking her pleasure, while he was confined in London, and fatiguing himself to maintain her in luxury, and idleness.

Perhaps the truth was, he had not forgotten the tears she shed at bidding them adieu; and though he was convinced that her affections were not his, he could not bear the thought, that she should love any one better. For, notwithstanding the various methods which he made use of, to render her life miserable, he was still at times, what is commonly termed fond of her. To invite her friends to London, was a proposition, which she dared not make. He already thought too high of the favour he had conferred, in marrying her without a fortune. She wished not therefore to increase the stock of obligation. Beside a mingled sensation of pride and duty, made her willing to conceal the horrors of her situation from those friends who believed her happy, and rejoiced in her prosperity.

Cleora, in becoming a mother, found for a while some mitigation of her sorrow: her affections had now an object, on which to rest. To her nursery, therefore, she devoted her whole attention: and while she saw Mercutio delighted with his son and heir caress the smiling infant, she felt emotions of pleasure, to which her heart had been for a long time a stranger. Awakened from the fond dreams of youthful enthusiasm, and habituated to the capricious humour of her husband, her understanding exerted its force. The little happiness, which it might still be in her power to obtain, she determined to secure, and as the fairy vision vanished from her sight, she gradually accommodated herself to the situation, in which, however uncongenial, there was no alternative.

The bloom faded from her cheeks, and vivacity no longer sparkled in her eye. But her countenance still shone with intelligence; her features were often illumined by maternal tenderness, and the serene smile of conscious virtue; her increasing family enlarged her occupations, and engrossed her cares, and all concern for herself was quickly absorbed in the welfare of her beloved children: but new sources of disquiet soon arose. Cleora and Mercutio, whose ideas on almost every subject were entirely unlike, differed materially in their notions concerning education. Of course, in all their operations they were constantly counteracting each other. The faults, which Cleora thought deserving of punishment, Mercutio would encourage, and the precepts that she inculcated with the most earnest seriousness, with him were frequently the subjects of derision. On the other hand, when out of humour, which was too often the case, he would vent his passion on the children, and for trifling misdemeanors threaten chastisements, which he never intended to inflict. The master, to whose care Cleora wished to intrust the instruction of her boys, Mercutio capriciously objected to; though he could assign no rational cause for so doing, and placed them under a pedagogue of narrow abilities, and superficial learning. The girls, whom she intended educating herself, he insisted on being sent to a cheap boarding-school, many miles distant from the metropolis, kept by a relation of his own, of whose talents and economy he entertained a very high opinion.

Cleora, disappointed in all her favourite plans, enervated by confinement, and long languishing in an unfriendly soil, had not sufficient spirit to dispute his authority; indeed her declining health in a measure incapacitated her for the task that lay nearest her heart, the education of her daughters. She attended her children, therefore, to their respective seminaries, and, while she gave them lessons for their future conduct, endeavoured to conceal the deep melancholy, which in secret preyed upon her heart. On her return, the malady with which she had been long struggling became more violent; a nervous fever shook her whole frame; advice was called in, the air changed, and every art made use of, but all in vain; perpetual conflict had exhausted the vital powers, and Cleora expired in the arms of her mother, recommending to her care the dear children, for whose sake alone she could have wished to have lived a few years longer.

Let this simple narrative be a caution to women, respecting the connections they form for life. As society is at present organized, the most sensible and best educated, if they have not fortunes, can scarcely form a plan for a future advancement, nay, maintenance, unconnected with matrimony. This, joined to the various tender images which float in the youthful fancy, is the cause why we see many women, who deserve a better fate, united to men unworthy of their affections, through a desire of securing an establishment. The first man who pays them serious attentions, they are willing to believe possest of all the good qualities and virtues, which they deem necessary in a companion for life. Misled by the flattery of the lover, and deceived still more by their own hearts, they find not their mistake, till experience convinces them when too late, that neither riches, beauty, nor talents, can secure happiness, when suitability is wanting, which alone can give permanency to friendship, and prove the source of domestic felicity and social bliss.

E. H.

No. XI.[2]

Josepha, or the Pernicious Effects of Early Indulgence

Nekayah, Princess of Abyssinia, casting her eyes upon the Nile that flowed before her, "Answer," said she, "great father of waters, thou that rollest thy floods through eighty nations, to the invocation of the daughter of thy native king. Tell me, if thou waterest through all thy course a single habitation from which thou dost not hear the murmurs of complaint!"[3]

Melancholy are the pictures which Dr. Johnson draws of human life: But after making every allowance for the dark medium, through which his natural temper might lead him to view the world, we are obliged to confess, though oft-times with reluctance, that his observations are, generally, too much founded upon truth. In the house of mourning, the chamber of sickness, within the gloomy walls of a prison, or in the cheerless hut of poverty, we allow of sorrow, and expect complaint; but the murmurs of discontent are not confined to these. The palaces of the great, the mansions of the rich, the abodes of the apparently healthy and prosperous, are too frequently inhabited by mortals bending beneath a load of real, or imaginary afflictions, and many a gilded coach contains an aching heart. What are the causes of this comparatively universal uneasiness, in a world where so much beauty is displayed, and so much bounty distributed? The benevolent Creator of men gave us existence, that we might be happy; he rejoices in the felicity of his children, and we never more properly enter into his "everlasting plan," than when our hearts are expanding with gratitude, and exulting with virtuous and pleasurable emotions. To answer the question philosophically, the limited capacities of human beings might be alledged, as the primary cause of all our woes. Ignorance produces error, and every deviation from truth and virtue, however small, may be considered as a deviation from happiness in a moral sense. The discontent so prevalent, may be attributed also to factitious refinement, our slavery to fashion, and wrong education. The wants of nature are few, but we are for ever increasing our desires, and disturbing our repose in search of ideal good, and artificial luxury. By false delicacy we enervate our minds, relax our nerves, and render our sensibility so unpleasingly acute, that the lighting of a grass-hopper becomes a burden, and the most trivial disappointment a serious calamity. In conforming to fashion, we frequently are obliged to sacrifice our own inclinations, and submit to a bondage more arbitrary and intolerable, than the heaviest chains. By wrong education these evils are perpetuated, which may therefore be mentioned both as a cause and an effect. The wrong education of youth produces weakness and impropriety of character in more advanced life; and this effect is again the cause of improper tuition to posterity.

Mr. B. a man of amiable disposition and unblemished moral character, but possessed of a weak and uncultivated mind, lost his wife, a very valuable woman, at an early period of life, who left behind her an infant daughter. Deprived of his beloved companion, and not choosing to enter into other connections, he devoted his whole attention to this child; to enrich her, he pursued his trade with indefatigable industry, and no moments appeared to him so sweet, as those, in which he caressed his little darling; he thought no expence too great, which might contribute to adorn her person, and improve her mind. Conscious of the defects of his own education, he prized learning in others, and endeavoured to procure the best masters the town afforded, to instruct his young Josepha in the various branches of polite knowledge supposed to be necessary for ladies in genteel life. Some of his friends advised him to send her to boarding-school; but Josepha wept, and remonstrated; he immediately therefore gave up the plan, and, in the stead, invited to his house a young lady in the joint capacity of governess and companion.

APPENDIX A

Josepha was agreeable in her exterior, and engaging in her manners. Nature had also endowed her with warm affections, and some share of good sense; but indulgence rendered her impatient of disappointment, and the delicacy and tenderness with which she was brought up, increased her natural sensibility to a degree bordering on weakness. It was her father's wish, to see and make her happy; his intentions were good, but he mistook the way. His fondness led him to anticipate her desires: he watched her very looks; and the least cloud on her brow overwhelmed him with anxiety. The young lady her companion, accustomed to dependance, and naturally blessed with a mild and gentle disposition, instead of counteracting, increased the evil, by uniformly giving way to all her little whims and caprices. Being thus never contradicted, and gratified in all her wishes as soon as formed, Josepha grew restless and languid, for want of sufficient motives to awaken her energy and exert her faculties: she was both too timid and too delicate to be fond of public amusements, and the indulgence she met with at home, rendered her too fastidious to cultivate much acquaintance. What then was to be done? She painted, she drew, amused herself with musick, read novels and poetry, and repeatedly changed the fancy of her clothes; but all proved insufficient to employ her time, and occupy her thoughts: she felt herself discontented and unhappy, though she knew not why. Thus passed the first nineteen years of her life, when she was one day aroused from the torpor of vacuity, by Mr. B——'s informing her, that he expected a large party of gentlemen to dinner. They came, and among them was a young man of the name of Clermont: he appeared to be about twenty-eight; he was not handsome, but his person was graceful and his conversation intelligent; while equally devoid of fulsome flattery and coxcomical self-sufficiency, his easy ingenuous manners gave the promise of an amiable and benevolent heart.

When dinner was ended, and the dessert gave place to the wine, Josepha and Miss —— retired to the drawing-room. Clermont allured by the sound of the harpsichord, and preferring the company of the ladies to the noisy toast, and bacchanalian song, soon followed them. Josepha played and sung with more than usual pathos, and when at the tea-table, entered into conversation on the topic of the day, the last new publication, &c. &c. in a manner uncommonly animated, though somewhat embarrassed: the company were no sooner gone, than Josepha asked a thousand questions concerning the gentleman, whom she had taken so much pains to entertain: and learned that he was young man of good character, genteel family, but small fortune; and her father added, that he believed he loved books better than business. She expressed her approbation of his polite and elegant conversation, and intimated a wish that he might be again invited to the house: this wish the old gentleman took the earliest opportunity of complying with, in consequence of which an intimacy ensued. Clermont was now a constant visitor: he lent her books, and brought her music; listened with pleasure while she sung, and admired the landscapes that she drew; but "he never talked of love," nor was there any peculiarity in his manner, by which she could judge of the state of his heart. Josepha's partiality increased, and every repeated interview served but to cement her attachment, and involve her in greater anxiety. Harassed by suspense, and tortured by the possibility of mortification and disappointment, she indulged the most cruel inquietude: sleep forsook her pillow; and her complexion, in which the lily was before rather too predominant, acquired a still paler hue.

Mr. B. fondest of parents, saw her droop, and suspected the cause; when one morning surprising her in tears, he besought her with the most soothing tenderness, to make known to him the occasion of her sorrow. Unable to resist his paternal endearments, she hid her face in his bosom; and confessed without reserve the soft cause of her present infelicity. He affectionately embraced her, smiled at her embarrassment, and bade her dry her tears: Mr. C. he said, could not remain insensible to her attractions, (for, who could behold his beloved Josepha with indifference?) the attachment, he had no doubt, was reciprocal, and it was inferiority of fortune that kept him silent: but, what was fortune, when put in competition with her happiness? He had gold enough for them both, and if she would give him leave, he would that day make Clermont acquainted with his good fortune. Complicated were the emotions, which at that moment changed the faint tints of Josepha's cheek, to the liveliest crimson; nor would she suffer her father to depart, till he had promised to relinquish his scheme for the present, and take no future step without her knowledge and approbation. Yet the consolation, that he had administered, sank deep into her heart. If Clermont really loved her, (which she now persuaded herself was the fact) how delicate, how disinterested his conduct.[4] Gay hope once more gilded the fairy prospect, and the fond illusions were too enchanting to be soon resigned; after indulging for a while these romantic reveries, she formed the resolution of making him acquainted with the favourable sentiments, which he had inspired; but, how was this to be done? Her father, it is true, had offered his interference; and, perhaps, he was the properest person to act in an affair so delicate: but she was fearful of the manner, in which he would execute his commission. Clermont possessed a mind refined and elevated, and she shuddered at the idea of the blunt and mercantile style, that Mr. B. might probably address him in, and her pride prevented her confiding in any other friend. After a thousand projects, one moment embraced, and the next rejected, she determined to write to him herself; and the very same evening returned to him a pamphlet, within the leaves of which he found the following epistle.

"After much anxiety and mature deliberation, I sit down to write what some persons would term romantic, and others deem ridiculous and inconsistent with propriety. Mr. Clermont I am convinced is possessed of a mind, that rises superior to vulgar notions and debasing prejudices; and under this conviction I venture to confess even to him, that his character, understanding, and the sentiments which at various times I have heard him utter, (on many subjects so similar, and congenial with my own) have made an impression on my mind, more deep and interesting, than I was myself at first aware of. This sympathy is not the effect of youthful levity, or the wayward child of yesterday. It is now many months since you was first introduced to my acquaintance, and time, instead of obliterating, has added strength to a partiality, which a first interview began: I think I have no reason to be ashamed of a sensibility founded on nature and awakened by reason.

Why then should I blush at declaring sentiments, the basis of which is virtue? Yet at this moment a crimson glow suffuses my cheek, – whilst an hesitating doubt suspends for a while the motion of my pen, and bids me burn what I have written, and endeavor to subdue, or continue to conceal within my own bosom a preference which ought not to be given unasked for. In return for this frank, and perhaps unguarded avowal of my sentiments, I ask an answer equally open and ingenuous. If your heart is already occupied by any prior attachment, tell me so: should this not be the case, and yet you love me not, attempt not to deceive me. I am persuaded you are above being actuated by interested considerations; and be assured I am too proud to wish to owe your attentions to any other motive than that of affection."[5]

No sooner was this important letter out of her own power, then her spirits failed, and her heart misgave her; the most torturing agitation racked her bosom. One moment she repented the rash step, and would have given the whole world to have recalled the lines which she had so precipitately written: the next she endeavoured to calm her mind, by the recollection of what her father had said in the morning. Thus passed the night. The next day she was in some measure relieved from this cruel sate of anxiety, by receiving an answer full of gratitude, respect, and professions of attachment. Clermont, though not absolutely in love with Josepha, was not engaged to any one else: her letter awakened his sensibility, and excited his astonishment: for notwithstanding she had ever received him with smiles, and distinguished him by many marks of favour, his vanity had never flattered him with having made so strong an impression on her heart.

Josepha, though secure of her lover, was still far from being happy; fear and jealousy continually haunted her sickly imagination, and a word or look less animated, created a thousand doubtful suspicions. Clermont feeling himself both hurt and perplexed by her distrust of his sincerity, entreated, that an early day might unite them for ever. She consented, and he soon after met her at the altar; where smiling, yet weeping, she appeared like an April sun, faintly beaming through a watery cloud. In becoming his wife, she changed her situation, but not her disposition. Of Clermont's behaviour she had no just cause of complaint: for in him she found the kind, the affectionate husband, and the sensible and worthy friend; but Josepha was too much spoiled by indulgence, and enervated by prosperity, to enjoy the blessings with which she was surrounded: the most trivial occurrence, if it happened contrary to her wishes, was considered as a real misfortune; and, if she was indisposed, the whole house must be employed for her relief. Three years passing after their marriage without children, were the source of much disquiet! – a son at the end of the fourth, removed this cause of discontent. But the care attending the delicate constitution and precarious life of an infant, involved her in new and perpetual anxiety. Their family was soon increased by the birth of another son: but this was a terrible disappointment; for she had set her heart upon a daughter. The next child proved a girl, and all her wishes now seemed gratified; for Providence had never yet denied her any blessing: but, alas! the little Josepha, whose opening beauties the mother beheld with fond delight, was seized with the small-pox. The child after fourteen days of suffering, began to recover her health, but the charms of her face, and the delicacy of her complexion, were gone for ever: this was a cruel mortification; and all the good sense and persuasive eloquence of Clermont proved ineffectual to reconcile his lady to this irremediable misfortune: from her weak and useless lamentation she was roused by a stroke heavy and severe indeed. She had hitherto been groaning under the weight of imaginary evils; misery too real now awaited her; the sun-shine was past, though past without enjoyment, and the gathering storm burst with horror on her devoted head.

Clermont returning rather late one evening to their country retreat, was attacked by two highwaymen. He surrendered his purse; but one of the villains not content with the booty, and suspecting himself to be known, fired a pistol at his head; the ball pierced his temple: – he fell. – The hour passed over, in which he was accustomed to return; the children inquired for their father, and went to bed with reluctance. – Josepha stood gazing with anxious solicitude at a window, which commanded the prospect of the London road. Their house was situated at the foot of a bridge, through the arches of which the river M— fell with a murmuring noise. The wind whistled hollow among the bending willows that hung over the stream, and the pale moon beamed a shadowy light on the surrounding prospect. She looked with wild uncertainty on every object, and mistook the mingled sounds for distant carriages; every moment increased her terror. At last the clock struck twelve, when a post-chaise came rolling slowly along the dreary road; breathless with agitation, she ran with an almost phrensied impatience to the outward gate; when, what were her sensations at beholding! – but I forbear to paint the soul-harrowing scene. Suffice it to say, that Josepha was for a while deprived of reason; time restored her senses and bitter anguish was succeeded by dark and languid melancholy: undisciplined by early adversity, and unfortified by education, – she struggled not with her feelings, but remained in all the lassitude of unavailing sorrow. A prey to ungoverned sensibility and childish caprice, unsteady in her conduct, and peevish in her temper, she neither gained the affections, nor secured the respect of her family and dependants. Her constitution originally delicate, grew still more sickly: she seldom now quitted her chamber, and yet seldomer the house: her children whom she had neither spirits to instruct, nor resolution to control, lived in a state of continual discord. The sons wild and impetuous, gave way to all the levity of youth, and entered with avidity into every species of extravagant dissipation which the town afforded: her daughter, a girl of high spirit and violent passions, weary of the dull life she passed at home, eloped at sixteen with a young officer of profligate character, who allured by the report of a large fortune, contrived secretly to pay his addresses to her. – Such were the fatal effects of wrong, or neglected education. – May it be a lesson to those whose talk it is

> —— "To rear the tender thought,
> And teach the young idea how to shoot,
> To pour the fresh instruction o'er the mind,

APPENDIX A

> To breathe th' enlivening spirit, and to fix
> The generous purpose in the glowing breast."[6]

Though we cannot by the utmost care and diligence bestow talents, where nature has denied capacity, the mind may be always in some measure improved by cultivation; and the moral character depends much, if not altogether, on early associations. It has been urged as an argument against the power of education, that many brought up under the same roof, with equal advantages both of precept and example, have proved very opposite characters on the stage of life. But, may not this objection be in a measure obviated, by replying, that as some individuals differ materially from others in point of capacity, natural temperament, &c. so they of course require a contrary treatment? and likewise by observing the negligence and inattention of parents in general with regard to the culture of the mind! – If a father provide for the fortune, and a mother takes care of the health, and exterior of their offspring, they are supposed to have done their duty; boarding-school it is falsely imagined will supply the rest: thus sent into the world to take their chance, on adventitious circumstances their future fate entirely depends.

For young women this tale and these observations are principally intended: many, my contemporaries, have been the times, and various the ways, in which you have been addressed: the grave divine, the sober matron, and the anxious parent have alternately taken up the pen for your instruction. May I flatter myself that, for once, you will attend to the words of advice which come from your equal, your friend? I am young like yourselves, and the sentiments which I write, are neither dictated by spleen, nor rendered gloomy by misfortune. I mean not to satirize your foibles, I wish not to restrain your vivacity; it is not ill humour; it is not affected singularity: no! it is benevolence, – it is virtue, that stimulate me to take up my pen. I blush for the folly, the frivolity in which we have consumed so many of our best days; too long have we been slaves to vanity and giddy flutterers of the hour: it is fit we should now rise superior to this empty trifling. Poor is the praise and ignoble the ambition which aspires no higher than to be first in a new fashion, or most admired in a circle of petit maitres (whose very flattery is satire). In this age of light and liberty, may our bosoms be fired with a more worthy emulation! and in the reformation of manners so much talked about, and so loudly called for, let us catch the glorious enthusiasm, and take the lead! – If we would but unite in intention, great would be our power, and extensive our influence; the character of one sex has ever been found to affect that of the other: for the confirmation of this we need not refer to the days of chivalry, we need but observe on the present times. Ask an impertinent coxcomb, Why he dresses, dances, and, in short, loses the man in the monkey? He will tell you, to please the ladies. And, are we pleased with this foolery? I leave the question unresolved; I dare not answer it: but this I will venture to affirm, – if there were no fine ladies, we should not long be offended by fine speeches, and fine gentlemen, both equally useless and insipid.

With us also are intrusted the morals of the rising generation: many of you, my young friends, may one day become mothers: think of the importance of the character: reflect likewise on the day of final retribution, which every passing moment hastens on. Will it avail us in that solemn hour, that we have not been guilty of any intentional evil? Alas! I fear not. We shall surely be called to account both for *what we have done*, and what *we have left undone*, "and even ignorance when voluntary is criminal."[7] – Let us then while we are in possession of health, of youth, of life, those precarious blessings which to-morrow may deprive us of, exert our faculties, and awake to virtue. "Be watchful, be diligent;"[8] my country women! forego the empty gewgaw and ignoble praise, and aspire after rationality here, and immortality hereafter; leave it to fops and beaux to determine who is the fairest, and the best drest; let our subject of debate be who have most improved their understandings, best performed their active duties, and appeared with the greatest advantage in the respective capacities of daughter, sister, friend, &c. &c.

E. H.

Appendix B

SELECTIONS FROM ELIZABETH HAYS LANFEAR'S *LETTERS TO YOUNG LADIES ON THEIR ENTRANCE INTO THE WORLD; TO WHICH ARE ADDED SKETCHES FROM REAL LIFE* (1824)

Letters to Young Ladies[1]
on their
Entrance into the World;
to which are added
Sketches from Real Life.

By Mrs. Lanfear,
Author of 'Fatal Errors,' &c.

Seek to be good, but aim not to be great:
A woman's noblest station is retreat;
Her fairest virtues fly from public sight –
Domestic worth, – that shuns too strong a light.[2]
Lyttleton.

London:
Published by J. Robins and Co. Ivy Lane,
Paternoster Row.
1824.

APPENDIX B

Introductory Letter[3]

School education finished, or the more fashionable home-governess and attendant masters dismissed, the accomplished and inexperienced maiden anticipates with hope and eager expectation her introduction into those circles which, to her ideas, constitutes the world; and where, having as yet seen only the external surface, she thinks to find pleasure unalloyed with pain. Flattered and caressed by all around her, the thoughtless and innocent girl knows no care, and fears no evil; happy under the protection of respectable parents, blessed with kind and partial relatives, her affections expand, and her heart dilates while she contemplates with joy and hilarity the gay scenes and fairy prospects by which, while all is novelty, she appears to be surrounded.

Lovely and interesting females, before you enter on the great theatre of the world – even now, while you are standing tip-toe on its threshold – pause for a moment, and at this important period of your existence permit a friend – one who has travelled far in the journey of life – to address you in the kind but warning voice of reason, experience, and truth. Yet fear not, while reading the didactic page, to meet with harsh rules, formal precepts, or crabbed censures, from one who, though herself no longer young, has not unfrequently been the confidential friend and the chosen companion of youth[4] – one who still loves the artless maiden, and views with a lenient and indulgent eye those errors and foibles which originate in simplicity, and may necessarily be expected in the inexperienced, before time has corrected the judgment, adversity the heart.

Young women, in the early periods of life, resemble the flowers in our gardens in the spring of the year: like them they bloom and fade in beautiful and quick succession. The white snow-drop, the yellow crocus, the purple violet, the gaudy and variegated tulip, by turns attract the eye and charm the sense; but soon, too soon, they droop, they fade, are cast aside, forgotten: the rose only fragrant even in death, retains her power to please when her withering leaves have lost their living bloom. The fresh colouring, delicate forms, and airy graces of early youth, are evanescent as the vernal flowers; but virtue and intellect, more valuable and more permanent than personal beauty or external accomplishments, will continue to attract regard when these are fled; and will shed a rich perfume, and adorn the possessor with unfading charms, when the radiant lustre of youth and health no longer bloom in the cheek nor sparkle in the eye.

Education is a word of serious import; often talked of, but little understood. In the proper and enlarged sense of the term the education of human beings may be said to commence with their birth, and finish but with their existence: we may even stretch the idea still further, and suppose that, in the world to come, our education will be progressive through an infinite series of ages: for the great plan of Providence, which includes and comprehends all rational as well as all physical nature, is ever going on link by link of an everlasting chain.[5]

But, waving at present entering into that divine and moral education of our species, over which the most prudent, the most circumspect, can have, if any, but limited power, education, in the more popular and confined view of the subject, must, to be effective, be prolonged beyond the time usually allotted for youthful studies. During childhood and their period of adolescence little more than the rudiments of any art, science, or particular branch of knowledge, can be taught by the ablest tutor, or acquired by the quickest and most docile pupil; much less can any degree of perfection be attained or expected in that variety of elegant accomplishments which it is now the fashion to crowd too indiscriminately into female education, whatever may be the talents, fortune, or rank in life, of the young ladies.[6]

But few persons are possessed of what may be termed an universal genius. By attempting too many things at one time, we sometimes fail of attaining excellence in any; therefore, setting aside useful knowledge, which should never be sacrificed to what is merely ornamental, it surely would be more judicious and more meritorious in a young person to aspire after perfection in one or a few things, than to be content with humble mediocrity in many. On leaving school, young ladies should endeavor to cultivate that particular art, science, or accomplishment, which natural taste, talent, or accidental circumstances, may lead them to make choice of in preference to others equally fashionable; and, for that purpose, it would be desirable that they should appropriate a certain portion of every day to their favorite pursuits, and, beside practicing what they have already learned, endeavor to acquire a greater proficiency by availing themselves of every assistance which their stations or opportunities for improvement may afford.

To please the other sex has been proposed by some writers as the grand desideratum to which female education should ever tend; but, as females are not always young, for their own sakes, as well as for the benefit of society at large, they had better find stimulus for improvement in some more noble and more permanent motive. Woman has been, and still is, too much considered as the mere toy to amuse the leisure hours of man, rather than as his friend and companion for life. Young ladies, therefore, who have been educated agreeably to the present mode, while they cultivate those graces and accomplishments which serve both to soften and to embellish society, should remember that there are lessons to be learned, and duties to be practiced, more serious, and of more intrinsic value, than the mere art of pleasing, which, though it should not in female education be entirely overlooked, can at best be considered but as of secondary importance.

Both men and women are travellers in the great journey of life: as a species, their origin, their final destinies, their moral duties, are the same. Women, equally with men, to prepare themselves for the as yet unknown paths which they may be called to tread, should, while young, endeavor to acquire some store of useful knowledge, and daily and hourly try to regulate their hearts, their understandings, their tempers, and their duties, by fixed and steady principles of religion and morality.

For the purpose of gaining pure, true, and unsophisticated notions of religion, no better method can either be recommended or pursued than the attentive and

APPENDIX B

diligent study of the scriptures of the Old and the New Testament: in the former is recorded some account of the various revelations which it pleased the Almighty Father of the universe to make of himself and of his will to the early inhabitants of this globe; also a summary description of the creation of the world, and of the persons by whom it was at first peopled, with the subsequent progress of society and civilization among men, who, from cultivators of the earth, became builders of cities – from shepherds and husbandmen, warriors and princes. The scriptures of the Old Testament are also particularly valuable and instructive from their containing a circumstantial history of the Jews – a people chosen and set apart by God, not for any peculiar deserts of their own, but to preserve the knowledge of the Divine Unity[7] in times of great ignorance: and, when the surrounding nations were sunk into darkness, idolatry, and vice, to the Jews were committed the oracles of God; to them, at different times, he made known by promise his benevolent designs to all mankind – designs which were in after-ages more fully revealed and confirmed by his son Jesus Christ, the Messiah, whose message of grace and favour was not confined to any particular people or nation, but was sent to the whole human race without exception, among whom it is to spread and be received, without distinction of kindred or tongue, ere time shall be no more.

The scriptures of the New Testament contain the history of Jesus Christ, his mission, his crucifixion, his resurrection from the dead, and his ascension into heaven, with an interesting and simple account of the first promulgation of Christianity by the immediate disciples and followers of our Lord; to which are added epistles sent by the apostles to the various infant churches which they had formed in different parts of the Roman empire. These epistles, being written under peculiar circumstances, addressed to new converts, most of whom had been heathen idolaters, and adapted for the times and the people for whose instruction and edification they were principally intended, are necessarily at present more obscure and less calculated for the perusal of young persons than the Gospels and the Acts of the Apostles: nevertheless, they may at times be read with advantage.

In most of the epistles are to be found, richly scattered in every page, excellent principles of morality, with safe and good advice, and many a golden rule by which to regulate the conduct in all the changing scenes and various circumstances of human life. The epistles of the different apostles may also be considered valuable in other points of view, as literary relics of the age in which they were penned, and as throwing light and confirmation on the Gospels and the Acts, in the same manner as the letters of Pliny, Cicero, and other illustrious Romans, elucidate circumstances and confirm facts related by the historians Livy, Tacitus, &c. The apostles of Jesus Christ being after his ascension inspired and illumined by the Holy Spirit, their epistles may be received as unquestionable authority on many points of doctrine; and in no other part of scripture is the end of the world and the resurrection of the dead so fully or so grandly described as in the First Epistle of St. Paul to the Corinthians.

Having seriously and attentively studied the scriptures of the Old and the New Testament, some of the most celebrated divines, both in and out of the establishment, may be occasionally read by young persons; those authors, in particular, who have written on the general principles of religion, both natural and revealed, and on the evidences of Christianity.

Of the various and numerous sects into which the Christian world is at present fallen it is scarcely possible, and not absolutely necessary, for very young women to form any decided judgment: it is to be hoped that every sect, whether its creed be simple and rational or metaphysical and redundant, retains all that is fundamental in religion, or, in other words, all that is essential to salvation.

When the world is divided by party spirit on any subject of importance, we are all of us, old as well as young, liable to be influenced in our judgments of that subject by accidental circumstances; such as connexions, friendships, &c. It is the privilege and the felicity of strong minds only, to detect the mistakes of others, and emancipate themselves from the errors and prejudices of education. It is certainly the duty of all persons, in matters of conscience or religion, to inquire for themselves, and, divested of prejudice, form their own conclusions; but how few, even among the best and the wisest, can guard their minds from being influenced by the persuasions and representations of those to whom they are attached, or their conduct from being in some degree regulated by the example or to suit the convenience of those whom they respect, and by whom they are daily surrounded!

After the scriptures, profane history and the belles lettres should be attended to. Poetry and novels may be read occasionally, but not indiscriminately or too frequently. Indulging too often in works of fancy, or what is commonly called light reading, vitiates the taste, promotes indolence, and deters young persons from pursuing graver and more important studies.

Letter II.

On the Motives for Female Improvement[8]

Having acquired fixed and steady principles of religion and morality, rectitude of judgment on every subject connected with social life will necessarily follow. From the neglecting to form clear ideas and determinate principles on important subjects in early youth arise that vacillation of sentiment, that inconsistency of conduct, and that feebleness of character in riper years, which are conspicuous in but too many individuals, who, in other respects, are sufficiently amiable.

In science a few simple axioms form the foundation on which is erected the whole superstructure of mathematics and mechanics; so, in morals, a few simple principles, constantly resorted to, may be made to embrace the whole circle of human duties. An enumeration of those minor virtues and more particular duties which the female sex are called to practise in their various and relative situations

APPENDIX B

in life shall be reserved for the subject of some future letter: in this I shall confine myself to enforcing the advice already given by such motives as observation and experience may furnish.

The first and grand motive to improvement, and which ought to operate on both sexes as a stimulus to the attainment of both moral and intellectual excellence, is the hope that, by improving the talents intrusted to us in this life, we shall be rendered more meet, and fitter subjects, for that higher, purer, state of existence, which is promised in the Gospel to the good and faithful servant.

Though all that this life can either give or promise is less than nothing, and vanity, when compared with those joys which await the good and the virtuous realms beyond the grave, motives arising out of the present state of things may have a better chance of gaining the attention of the young than those which originate in the expectation of things to come. In the imagination of youth, the world, with all its fascinating charms, stands gaudily portrayed; while death and futurity, placed in the back ground of the picture, are but scarcely perceived, and seldom dwelt on with a steady or willing eye.

Mental acquirements and moral excellence, even were this life the whole of existence, would enhance the attractions of youth, give respectability to age, and afford resources and consolation amid disappointment, affliction, and adversity. Mere personal charms, though not without their value, are too common, and in this country, famed for female beauty, too frequently exhibited to public view, to excite any very strong or permanent sensation in the beholder. Regular features, a delicate complexion, or a fine figure, adorned by the hand of fashion, may attract the transient gaze and gain the prize of vulgar admiration; but to please the man of taste, to charm the sense and touch the soul, the features must be illumined by intelligence, the complexion varied by sensibility, and the fine figure rendered interesting by unaffected simplicity and grace.

In a large or mixed party, it is not the most beautiful, the most fashionable, or the richest-dressed female, who will be generally found to attract the greatest share of homage and attention from the other sex, but she whose manners and conversation are the most elegant and agreeable. It is true that, for the mere purpose of being admired in company, very superficial acquirements will frequently suffice; but the fair maiden whose higher ambition and better feeling may lead her to wish to gain more solid esteem, more permanent admiration, than that of the passing hour, must lay the foundation of her fame a little deeper, and store her mind with useful knowledge, as well as embellish her fancy with ornamental literature.

Novels, poetry, reviews, and the publications or pamphlets of the day, with which book-clubs at present amply supply the reading world, may afford sufficient materials for the purposes of entertainment and conversation; but those who wish to improve their minds must not permit light reading to interfere with, much less to supersede, graver pursuits and more important studies, such as theology, history, philosophy, &c.

There are in every library authors whose fame and value time has sanctioned: with these every person who makes any pretension to literature ought to be acquainted; and perhaps the earlier many of them are read the better. Young persons, who put off reading what may be called the English classics from the common and idle excuse of want of time, very seldom read them at all. If youth will not afford leisure, can we expect or hope to obtain it in riper years? The fact is, those who complain of want of time are, generally speaking, those who do the least. It is not want of time, but want of inclination – want of vigour of mind, of order and arrangement in our pursuits and occupations, added to a trifling or indolent disposition – which gives rise to this excuse: one or two hours every day, stolen from the pillow or the toilette, would be sufficient for the acquisition of much useful knowledge and real learning.

The youthful female whose heart beats but for vanity, and whose first or only wish is to shine, sometimes mistakes the road, and, by too much effort to please, too elaborate a display of her own accomplishments, and too frequent demands on the attention and flattery of her associates, defeats her own purpose. On the contrary, she who is more careful to be well informed than anxious to be thought learned, more desirous of gaining instruction from others than solicitous to show off her own acquirements, thoughtless of pleasing, often pleases the most: well grounded in those accomplishments which are wont to be exhibited in genteel society, and not ignorant of those topics which are usually and frequently discussed by the intelligent and the polite, she feels perfectly at ease, prepared either to speak or to listen, as occasion shall demand. No affectation, no flutter, no undue anxiety concerning the place she shall claim in the circle, the impression she shall make on her hearers is apparent: modest, sensible, attentive to others, occupied by what is going on, she forgets that too-often obtrusive and important individual – self: absorbed in the subject discussed, all that she feels is real, all that she says natural and spontaneous: when no impression is made on her imagination, no enthusiasm excited in her feelings, she attempts not to supply their places by affected sensibility, artificial phrases, or silly and unmeaning exclamations.

Venus, the goddess of beauty, is represented by the poets as possessed of a cestus, by which she effected[9] and secured her conquests over gods and men; intimating by this that beauty, though perfect and divine, requires something beyond mere external show to render it truly fascinating and irresistible. Juno, the fabled queen of Heaven, having a boon to ask of her husband, Jupiter, borrowed of Venus this alluring cestus before she ventured to offer her petition. This fiction shows that, even in the earliest periods of society, men looked for and expected to find in women other and more seductive attractions than those which belong to mere personal charms.

Having urged the necessity and the advantage of adding mental cultivation to external graces for the purpose of attracting[10] the other sex and being distinguished in society, with equal truth, though probably with less chance of being attended to, might be portrayed the necessity of improving the mind, in order to enable women to support, with resignation and dignity, disappointment and solitude. The gay spring of youth gone by, the world and all its intoxicating vanities shut out from us perhaps for ever, no brilliant circle to dazzle the imagination, no social party to cheer the drooping spirits, no obsequious admirers to flatter and adore, no partial friend to sustain or sooth the sinking heart: it is then, in that lone hour, unsupported by extraneous or external objects, the mind recoils on itself, learns to estimate its powers, appreciate its resources, and either rejoice in its own strength, or, benumbed, and wanting courage to exert its energies, sinks into lassitude, imbecility, and wretchedness.

Letter III.

On the Motives for Female Improvement[11] (continued)

Having endeavoured to gain over vanity to the side of improvement by representing intellectual beauty as the handmaid or auxiliary to personal charms, I shall not in this letter address my fair readers merely as young ladies, but as rational beings, citizens of the world, in which, whatever may be their future destinies, they are each called to act their own individual parts, whether with propriety or impropriety. Though fair their prospects, their success or propriety in life must depend in great measure on the rectitude of their judgments, the soundness of their understandings, and the steadiness of their principles.

Happiness, even such as this can bestow, is not a thing to be defined: it has neither a local habitation nor a name. Happiness, under the title of the supreme good, was the theme of the ancient philosophers, and it is still sought for by mortals in various ways and under various names: many place it in riches, a few in fame, numbers in sensual pleasures, and not a few in the gratification of vanity: some have sought for it in the palaces of the great, while others have idly pronounced that it is only to be found in the cottages of the poor: all are equally mistaken; it is neither the gifts of fortune nor of nature, the luxury of the court, nor the simplicity of the hamlet, which constitutes happiness. The portion of felicity which may be attained, even in this life, must depend on the mind and the disposition of the individuals, rather than on the station in which they are placed, or on the eminence on which they stand.

It would be a folly to deny that some situations are less favorable to morality, and consequently to happiness, than others; indeed, both extremes of society – that is, the very high and the very low – are more inimical to the attainment of virtue and intellect, without which there can be no real enjoyment, than the middle rank: yet the great Creator and Governor of all mankind is not a partial being, and is more equal in the distribution of the blessings which his providence bestows on all his creatures than, on a slight and superficial view of civilized society, some few persons are disposed to admit. That a certain degree of felicity is the consequent attendant on virtue, while even the slightest deviation from moral rectitude is sooner or later, in one way or other, followed by pain even in this life, is a fact which might easily be proved in theory, and which experience and observation daily confirm. This incipient retribution is in proof of the moral government of God, which, begun below, will reach beyond the grave. 'Angels are happier than men because they are better;'[12] and one human being is happier than another in proportion as he more resembles that great Being who is the source and fountain of all good.

Arrived at that period of life when the maturity of womanhood is added to the bloom of youth, when vanity gives place to sentiment, and puerile amusements or trifling occupations cease to charm, it is the natural wish and laudable desire of every virtuous and amiable female to form those ties which shall increase the objects of her affection, while they enlarge the sphere of her pleasures and her duties. Friends more experienced and more advanced in life may tell them, and tell them truly, that every state has its mixture of good and evil, and that marriage, instead of being the end of care, is but too frequently the beginning of sorrow. This will not avail; youth listens with distrust to the trite maxims and chilling advice of declining years: when love and matrimony are in one scale, prudence and celibacy in the other, they stop not to decide on which side lies the balance of comfort; or, if for a moment they hesitate, hope, thrown into the favorite scale, soon makes the other ascend to the beam.

The maiden transformed into the wife, the mother, and the mistress of a family, what but the previous cultivation of her mind can enable her to perform aright the various and serious duties which these important relations demand and involve? Should she be united to a man of sense, will not her partner expect to find in her a friend in whom he can confide, a companion with whom he can communicate in his graver as in his lighter hours? Should it, on the contrary, be her unfortunate lot to be bound to a man of weak and scanty intellect, an improved understanding on her part will be still more indispensable, as she may not unfrequently be called to supply by her better judgment the defects of his; and, on many occasions, to rectify by her prudence the errors and mistakes which his weakness or vanity may lead him to commit. Many men with abilities below mediocrity have, when united to women of good sense, who have known how to lead without appearing to govern, passed through life respectably.

As mothers, if young women wish to act with propriety or appear to advantage in that important and interesting character, a variety of useful knowledge is necessary. Maternal love is an instinct, or, to make use of a more elegant term, a sentiment so strongly implanted in the female breast as to require the control of reason to prevent it from overstepping these limits by which even our best and purest affections require to be bounded.

In a silly or ignorant woman maternal love will sometimes become a selfish passion, which, degenerating into weakness instead of promoting the benefit of her offspring, may produce effects injurious [to] the object it was fondly designed to cherish.

When riches and prosperity are the lot in marriage of the fortunate fair one, an enlightened and cultivated understanding will enlarge her capacity for happiness, and give a higher zest to all those pleasures which wealth or power can command; while, at the same time, it will lead her to moderation in enjoyment, and teach her how to make the proper use of those goods which Providence has so plentifully bestowed. Avoiding ostentatious profusion on the one hand, and a parsimonious meanness on the other, she will settle her establishment and regulate her domestic economy with equal propriety and prudence. Partaking with cheerfulness and dispensing with liberality all that is necessary for the comfort of her household, or for respectability in the situation of life in which she is placed, she will still reserve a surplus ready at command to be applied to the purposes of private benevolence or public utility.

If an enlarged and improved intellect is requisite in order to enhance the value of, and give stability to, the blessings of prosperity, in the dark and trying time of adversity mental advantages are still more important and still more necessary. In the gay morning of life, in the bright noon of prosperity, beauty, fashion, taste, accomplishments, are all-sufficient; but when sorrow dims the eye and strikes the heart, when the relentless hand of Death tears from the affectionate wife the beloved husband, or suddenly snatches from the tender mother the infant she had fondly cherished, or by slow and wasting disease bereaves her of the child of her heart – the one on whom her best, her brightest, hopes had centered – can aught this world affords, much less its vanities, suffice to strengthen and support the hapless mourner?[13] Tell the afflicted widow, tell the distracted mother, whose bosoms are pierced with sorrow's keenest dart, that they still possess riches, beauty, external accomplishments, with all the world calls good and fair – they listen not; the ear of grief is deaf to the voice of flattery, and the tear-filled eye of sorrow sees nothing but its own woes. Even the mild voice of friendship fails of pouring balm into the deeply-wounded spirit. In the language of Job may it be said, 'Wretched comforters are ye all.'[14] But, when all external help fails, the well-stored mind is a tower of strength: it is like the house built upon a rock, which, when the rain descended and the floods came, and the winds blew and beat upon that house, it fell not, for it was founded on a rock.[15]

So she whose mind has been exalted and imbued with religious principles, whose memory is filled with wisdom's lore and virtue's precepts, while she sheds the tear which nature prompts, and which religion does not forbid,

'Adores the storm which wrecks her earthly joys.'[16]

Piercing with the eye of faith the dark cloud which envelops humanity, she perceives behind it the bright beams of heavenly love, till at length, calm and resigned, she follows cheerfully the path marked out for her by her God, as did the children of Israel the pillar of cloud and fire which guided them through the wilderness to the promised land.

Should early disappointment blight the fair blossoms of hope, or blast in evil hour the fruit of enjoyment but scarcely tasted – should misfortune, sudden and destructive as the storm in harvest, destroy in one fatal hour present comfort and future prospects – should sickness, and

"Poverty, to fill the band
Which numbs the soul with icy hand" – [17]

should dependence be the lot of declining age – what can preserve the hapless female, who lived only to vanity, from wretchedness and contempt? Stripped of the gaudy trappings of prosperity, deprived one by one of those artificial elegancies and real comforts by which she had in her better days been accustomed to be surrounded, shunned or neglected by hollow friends and summer acquaintances, she sinks under the iron hand of adversity, or dwindles by degrees into meanness and nonentity.

True dignity depends not on extraneous circumstances: friends, connexions, fashion, style, may for a while throw a dazzling lustre around the minion of Fortune; but it is mind, and mind only, which can confer real and permanent respectability, and constitute the only essential difference between one human being and another. The lowliest female whose head is trained to knowledge, and whose heart is formed to virtue, is more truly great than she whose brows are bound with a diadem, if that diadem be not adorned with those fairest jewels in the female crown – religion, virtue, and good sense.

Letter VII.

On the Single Life[18]

During the long and glorious reign of Queen Elizabeth, women in England occupied a lofty station in society, and both demanded and obtained from their lovers a respectful homage and a chivalrous fidelity. Ladies of rank received an education similar, if not equal, to that of their male relations, and, like them, were instructed in the learned languages, and in all the different branches of knowledge and science which were at that time the fashion of the day. In the subsequent period of monarchical tyranny and civil commotion, the female sex lost much of that respect and many of those advantages which they had enjoyed during the brilliant and fortunate reign of the virgin queen. At the restoration of Charles the Second, of licentious memory, a laxity of principle, and a corresponding dissoluteness of manners, succeeded to the rigid morality and formal exterior of the old puritans: the ladies of England no longer retained that sanctity of manner and elevation of character which had distinguished not only many individuals among them, such as Lady Jane Grey, Lady Rachel Russell, &c. but British females in general.

In the court of a gay, luxurious, and dissipated monarch, women sank from the high pinnacle on which they had been placed, and soon came to be considered merely as beings, or rather as slaves, who, by their charms, their graces, and their allurements, were to adorn society, and give zest to pleasure. Too many, flattered by the mock homage of gallantry, submitted without murmuring to the tyranny and sexual gratification of their depraved and voluptuous masters.

The female character thus degraded, women soon lost that elevated station in society which they had previously occupied, but which they have never since entirely regained.

The evil consequences of this humiliation have been, and perhaps still are, in a degree, felt more severely, after a certain age, by unmarried than by married females. The matron has sufficient occupation and amusement in her own family to prevent her, as she advances in life, from regretting the flight of time and the decay of beauty, or from vainly attempting to prolong, beyond the time prescribed by nature, the pursuits, the follies, or the charms of youth. If she has performed the important duties of domestic life with any tolerable degree of propriety, she is sure of being rewarded by the affection of her family and the respect of the world: satisfied with the protection and the esteem of her husband, interested and gratified by the love and the attention of her children and grandchildren, her cares, her pleasures, her hopes, and her wishes, all centre in the home circle.

The elderly unmarried female is differently, and, generally speaking, less fortunately, situated. The season of youth and of beauty, of flattery and of juvenile amusements, passed and gone for ever, she gradually awakes as from a morning dream, and reluctantly exchanges the gay, the delusive, visions of her early years, for the more sober and dull realities of mature age. Her parents are, perhaps, no more, or, if still in existence, declining in health and years, and fast sinking into the gaping tomb: the home circle is broken; brothers and sisters, companions of childhood, dispersed and scattered abroad; partial and admiring friends no longer surround her – by some she has been deserted, by others forgotten; till, at length, no longer sheltered by the paternal roof, she feels alone in the world, destined to travel the remainder of life's dull journey solitary and unregarded. A limited, too often a very limited, income adds to the difficulties with which she has to struggle: depressed in spirits, and sometimes, from a feeling of mortification and disappointment, peevish in temper, she vainly seeks for sympathy or friendship: instead of that attention and consolation which her forlorn situation demands, the finger of scorn is, by the frivolous and the gay, ever ready to be pointed at the antiquated virgin; while the silly youth and giddy girl find amusement in ridiculing those little foibles and harmless singularities which not unfrequently mark the character of the single woman.[19]

The dread of encountering these evils, which the generality of females, from education and other circumstances, are but little calculated to sustain, has induced many an amiable, though, in this respect, feeble-minded girl, to accept the first offer of marriage which may be made to her, rather than risk the remaining single while her young associates are marrying around her, or till a new generation of youthful damsels spring up to occupy her place, and to demand that homage which a maiden turned of forty must no longer flatter herself with the expectation of receiving from the other sex. Some of these inconveniences attached to celibacy in general; but peculiarly felt and feared by the delicate and sensitive female, are, though not entirely removed, we will hope, in this enlightened age, gradually wearing away: the greater part of them has arisen out of the circumscribed sphere which custom has allowed to women, and from the prejudices which many have entertained, and some persons of both sexes still continue to entertain, against the rational cultivation of the female understanding, lest such cultivation should take from the feminine graces of woman, interfere with the pride, or encroach on the privileges and boasted superiority of man.

Learned ladies and female authors have long ceased to be regarded either as objects of curiosity or aversion; and the epithet *blue-stocking* lady, as a term of reproach or ridicule, is no longer applied to any but the affected, superficial, and half-witted female, whose pretensions to learning or science are not justified by her attainments.

The progress of civilization, which is daily advancing both in the old world and in the new; the more general diffusion of literature both in town and country, by the means of libraries, book-clubs, reading-societies, &c.; the greater attention paid to female education than formerly; and, above all, the splendid talents which, of late years, have been displayed, and the lofty energies which, in various ways, have been exerted by women, have redeemed their character as a sex from the charges of imbecility and frivolity – charges by which they have been too often and too long both cruelly and unjustly insulted by those who are incompetent to judge of female ability, and who, from mistaken notions of its real value, still wish to debar woman from free access to the tree of knowledge.

The single woman of the present day is chiefly distinguished from her married sisters by possessing more literary acquirements, more elegant accomplishments, or higher attainments in some particular art or science, than the numerous avocations of domestic life have allowed the matron either time or opportunity of attending to.

In the present day, various causes, which it would be unnecessary in this place either to inquire into or enumerate, have operated, and continue to operate, as a check on early marriages; consequently, spinsters of a certain age being more abundant, the unmarried female is no longer considered as an anomaly in society; and the ancient virgin, such as we find her depictured by the dramatist and the novel-writer of the last century, is at present a character but seldom seen, and which will soon become nearly, if not entirely, extinct.

The greatest evil at present attending celibacy is that it tends both to engender and to promote a spirit of selfishness among its votaries: but this is an evil by no means confined to the weaker sex; single men are generally found to be equally, if not more, selfish than single women. Self-love is a passion inherent in human nature; it has by some philosophers been said to be the master-spring by which every other passion is impelled and called into action: be that as it may, self-love will, on inquiry, be found to take its various modifications of character in individuals from the situations in which they are placed, and from the many adventitious circumstances by which they are surrounded.

The infant, stimulated by the desire of food, clings to the nurse from whom it receives its first and natural supply of nourishment; the pleasure afforded to the child by the gratification of its only desire mingling and associating itself, as its faculties expand, with the idea of its nurse, produces in its breast the sentiment of affection to her person, and thus, by degrees, transforms the at-first mere selfish into a social passion. As the child advances in months and in years, other objects and more persons contributing to its happiness and amusement, the sphere of its attachments becomes enlarged. In process of time, if engaged in domestic life, the circle grows wider and wider, till, at length, the selfish passions being all associated with or transferred to other objects, self-love is forgotten, or totally absorbed in the social affections.

The unmarried female, cut off from all the tenderest charities of human life, looks around her in vain for an object on which to fix her affections: none appearing, her sensibility, deprived of the proper channels in which it ought to flow, recoils on her own heart; till, at length, self becomes the central point to which her cares, her anxieties, all tend, and in which, at last, her pains and her pleasures alike terminate.

To counteract, and, as much as possible, keep within due bounds, this fond encroacher, inordinate self-love, the staid maiden should mix, as much as her circumstances will justify or her situation allow, with liberal and general society; she should also, wherever she is situated, endeavour to take an interest in all that is passing around her: by so doing she will learn to abstract her ideas, and prevent her thoughts from recurring too frequently to her own particular circumstances or sensations. She may likewise cultivate individual friendships with females, either married or unmarried, whose pursuits and dispositions accord with her own.

Has she sisters or early friends settled in her vicinity, let her not, because they have no longer undivided affections or unappropriated time to bestow, fancy herself slighted or neglected, and, in consequence of that suspicion, give up their society: on the contrary, she should endeavour to secure their friendship, and evince the sincerity of her own, by taking a kind and affectionate interest in their concerns, being ready at all times to offer them assistance when needful, to visit them in sickness or affliction, to sooth them in the hour of nature's sorrow, to share with them, in a degree, the care and the attention due to their offspring. By persevering in this conduct, she will gradually lose the sense of her own loneliness, secure the respect and esteem of all rational persons, and gain the affections of the rising generation.

Young people are always gratified and flattered by the notice of persons older than themselves; more especially so when such persons are held in high estimation by their parents. When elderly persons complain of the want of deference and attention in the young, the faults alleged most frequently originate with themselves. When women somewhat advanced in life affect the gaiety and folly of youth, or, having themselves passed the joyous season of juvenile amusements, commence censor, and sternly rebuke or indiscriminately blame the levity of childhood, and the innocent but unavoidable mistakes of inexperienced youth, what claims have they to the respect or gratitude of those whom they offend rather than favour?

To those single women who have no very near relatives or connexions, charity, both public and private, offers a never-failing source of praiseworthy and interesting occupation. There are in the present day (to the honour of the ladies of Great Britain be it recorded) so many benevolent institutions of various kinds, both patronised and managed entirely by the female sex, that not one of them who wishes to exert her talents or undraw her purse-strings for the benefit of her fellow-creatures can justly excuse herself on the plea of having no opportunity to render herself useful, or complain of want of coadjutors in the great work of charity. To those who are fond of children, and find pleasure in attending to them, schools of various descriptions and denominations present a substitute for children of their own. Attending in all weathers, and in public, and perhaps mean apartments, teaching over and over again the simple elements of learning to little awkward mean-clad urchins, may be a less elegant, though not a less useful, employment than sitting in the drawing-room with the genteel and accomplished young ladies while they practise their musical lessons, or con over their French and Italian exercises. None, whatever be their fortunes or situations in life, are born merely for themselves: surrounded on every side by our fellow-creatures – united to them, as mortals, by similar wants, similar necessities, and by mutual sympathies – who shall dare avow their right to be idle, or show their charter for being born merely to consume the fruits of the earth? Nature and religion alike forbid the empty boast.

Those, of either sex, who make their own personal comfort and individual gratification their primary object and sole study, seldom, if ever, obtain the end proposed. The less we think of ourselves the more we enjoy existence, which can never be barren of felicity to those whose time and talents are engaged in any laudable pursuit; and, after all we can either hope for or imagine of good in this sublunary world, the greatest portion of real happiness will ever be found in a steady course of virtuous actions, and in the habitual exercise of the benevolent affections.

Sketches from Real Life

Sketch I[20]

Louisa the Indulged

Mr. Randall was a native of Leeds, in Yorkshire. At sixteen years of age, being an active, shrewd, and industrious lad, his father, who was not wealthy, sent him to London to seek his own fortune: here, after overcoming some difficulties, he at length succeeded so well as to establish himself in a lucrative and wholesale business, in which, by prudence and economy, he in a few years realized a handsome and independent capital.

At thirty-five years of age he married a lady of suitable years, agreeable in her person, amiable in her manners, who had been genteelly educated, and who brought him a pretty fortune. Two children were the fruits of this marriage: the first, a boy, a strong and healthy child, whom his father sent into Yorkshire at a very early period, for the purpose of education; the second, a girl, born soon after little James left home, reconciled Mrs. Randall to the absence, which she had before bewailed, of her son. Louisa, the name chosen by her mother for the infant, was a delicate babe, both in frame and constitution: Mrs. Randall nursed and attended to her, during the period of a feeble infancy, with unwearied and unremitting care. These circumstances endeared the interesting and beautiful little Louisa to her mother, and Mrs. Randall herself acknowledged that her affection for this child exceeded even what she had felt for James, her first-born. Sickly children, from being more dependent on their mothers than the healthy, are, generally speaking, the greater favorites. It has also been remarked, perhaps with truth, that women who do not marry very young are more devoted to their offspring than those who at an early period of life enter into the conjugal state. Be that as it may, this darling child excited the sensibility, and called forth all the tenderness, of her mother. Mr. Randall, though a worthy man and a good husband, did not quite satisfy the heart of his more refined and more susceptible partner: her son had been early taken from his mother, in whose affections her daughter now reigned without a rival.

The servant who, after she was weaned, was kept to attend on the little Louisa, was charged, at the risk of losing her place, never to leave the child alone for a single moment, awake or asleep, by night or by day; she was also ordered never to take her out in the air unless the sun shone, and then she was to be wrapped up in shawls and cloaks from head to feet; as, during the first six months, she had never been carried even from room to room without being completely enveloped in coverlids and mantles. The consequence of this over-care was, as might have been expected it should, the least breath of air gave the child cold; and, though she survived the perils of infancy, her constitution every day became more and more delicate.

Enfeebled by excessive and injudicious tenderness, her mind was not less weak than was her frame; and, from being indulged in every whim, her temper, though not a bad one, became too sensitive and too impatient of opposition to afford happiness or comfort to herself or to those around her.

Mrs. Randall, thinking that an airing every day would amuse Louisa, and at the same time benefit her health, but fearful of putting her into a hackney-coach, lest she should take cold or be exposed to the infection of a contagious disorder, prevailed on her husband, who could very well afford it, to set up his carriage. Mrs. Randall and her daughter now regularly took their morning's ride in the new chariot; but, as the glasses were but seldom allowed to be put down, lest Louisa should take cold, her health was not greatly amended by these excursions.

Mr. Randall, who wanted the greater part of the house in Watling Street,[21] where they resided, for the purposes of business, was persuaded by Mrs. Randall that a better air would be of service to Louisa, and at length took a house for his wife and daughter in the neighbourhood of Clapham, to which Mrs. Randall gladly removed: Mr. Randall, it was agreed between them, was to come down every evening, and return to town every morning, Sundays excepted, which he promised to pass at Clapham.[22] This arrangement left Mrs. Randall at full liberty to attend to her darling little girl, whose health began to amend, and who now, being six years of age, and very pretty, was pronounced, by the ladies who paid their respects to her mamma, to be one of the sweetest and most elegant little creatures they had ever beheld.

These common-place and unmeaning compliments, frequently repeated in the presence of Louisa, made her soon begin to think herself a personage of some importance. Being the chief, if not the sole object of the attention of her mother, who omitted nothing which she imagined would either amuse, gratify, or set off her little girl to advantage, and having a servant always at command to dress and wait on her, Louisa was early prepared to become one of those helpless useless beings termed fine ladies, and grew every day more and more capricious, fanciful, and affected. Mr. Randall, though not much at home, perceiving that his daughter was in great danger of being spoiled by the excessive tenderness and over-indulgence of her mother, proposed the sending of her to a boarding-school for education: to this Mrs. Randall would not consent, and urged so many objections to the plan, that Mr. Randall, who was less qualified to descant on the merits and demerits of boarding-schools than his lady, gave up the point; and, as he had taken the management of his son's education entirely into his own hands, conceded to his wife, as her right, the sole superintendence of their daughter's.

Mrs. Randall now engaged a young lady as a domestic governess, while masters of the first celebrity were procured to instruct the little Louisa in every fashionable accomplishment: by so doing, she purposed giving her what she called every advantage of education, without reflecting on the real import of the term; or forgetting that a young lady may be highly educated, and yet remain destitute of all those virtues which raise and ornament the female character.

Louisa, whose figure, though small, was exquisitely proportioned, soon became an elegant dancer: she also made some proficiency in music; learned to paint flowers, and sketch a landscape; and, after a few years of instruction, gained some slight knowledge of the French and Italian languages: that is, sufficient of the former to read or to translate easy French, and of the latter to understand the sentiment, if there be any, in the airs of an opera. For studies which required much or serious application Louisa had no great taste; but, as her mother made it a point that she should read with her for the best part of an hour every day, she gradually became acquainted with some of the lighter productions of modern literature – such as new plays, novels, poems, &c. with now and then a review or a magazine.

Thus passed the early youth of Louisa Randall: she was now sixteen, possessed of a delicate form, regular features, and a fair complexion – nurtured, caressed, and indulged by a fond mother, from whom she had never been separated for more than a few hours at a time – flattered by casual visitors, treated with respect by her governess, attended to with servility by her maid, and enjoying with present luxuries the future expectation of a large fortune – she thought herself a being of a superior description to the vulgar herd, and born for no other purpose but to be admired, waited upon, and attended to, by the rest of the world.

The governess dismissed, Mrs. Randall now deemed it time for her daughter to *come out*, as it is termed, and for that purpose subscribed, which she had not done before, to the Clapham assembly, where Miss Randall was the next season to be introduced. At the first ball, accompanied by her mother, Louisa, elegantly and tastefully attired, made her *debut*: the young men gazed at her – inquired who she was – and happy was the youth who could obtain the honour of dancing with her. While the male part of the assembly were thus paying all proper and expected homage to her charms, the younger females, who could not view these attentions without some little sparks of jealousy, were not quite so civil in their behaviour or flattering in their remarks: one thought her too short to be elegant; another too pale to be beautiful; a third pronounced her features too regular to be engaging; most of them found some faults in her dress; while they all agreed that, as her father was in trade, she ought not to stand above the Misses B—— and ——, whose fortunes were independent.

While the young ladies were thus amusing themselves, some of their mammas were complimenting Mrs. Randall on the dancing and other attractions of her daughter. Mrs. Randall listened to these eulogiums with unmixed delight; and, as her eyes, glistening with tears of pleasure and maternal pride, followed Louisa in the mazy dance, she took care to inform the ladies who sat near her that her daughter was educated at home, and entirely under her own direction.

Mrs. and Miss Randall returned home at a late hour; the latter fatigued, but, on the whole, pretty well pleased with her evening; and the former highly gratified by the notice and admiration which her daughter had excited.

A young lady possessed of so many attractions, among which the report of a large fortune might not be reckoned one of the least, could not be expected to remain long without suitors; and, before the winter was over, Louisa received several love-letters, and more than one serious offer of marriage: but, though her temper was sensitive, her heart was not particularly susceptible to love; and, as she was only seventeen, and her parents in no great hurry to dispose of her, the *billet-doux* were returned in a blank cover; while the more serious offers of marriage were rejected, on the plea of Miss Randall's being yet too young to think of changing her situation.

James Randall, who, on his return from Yorkshire, had been taken into his father's warehouse, and was now become the man of business, spent his Sundays at Clapham. Independent of this addition on that day to their family circle, no domestic event occurred to relieve the monotony of Miss Randall's life, and time glided on as usual till she had nearly completed her twenty-first year. She now began to grow weary of her maidenly amusements: the assembly, in which, being no longer new, she ceased to excite any particular sensation, had lost its attractions; dancing fatigued her; drawing and painting she had given up; music, when she had no one but her mother to hear her, soon palled; reading she was not fond of; and needle-work was entirely out of the question.

Without any strong passion or interesting pursuit to engage her mind, and devoid of daily occupation, that best remedy for the vapours, Louisa became a prey to *ennui*, and began to fancy that a change of situation, though not desired at seventeen, might, at twenty-one, relieve her from the lassitude and tedium under which she at present suffered. Mrs. Randall, whose maternal solicitude about her daughter was unabated, divined this change in Louisa's inclinations, and, without speaking to her on the subject, hinted to her father that their daughter was no longer averse to matrimony, and that it was now high time to think seriously about settling her in life: Mr. Randall took the hint, and, shortly after, brought down with him a gentleman whom he had often thought he should like for a son-in-law. Mr. Batson (for that was his name) was a young man of respectable character and good property, who had been, for some time, his father being dead, considered as the head partner in a substantial and money-getting business. He was, moreover, a countryman of Mr. Randall's, a circumstance which, to him, was no little recommendation.

Mr. Batson, who had more than once asked Mr. Randall to introduce him to his daughter, embraced the opportunity afforded him of paying particular attention both to Miss Randall and her mamma, who, on his departure, pronounced him to be a very civil well-behaved young man. Mr. Randall, pleased with the approbation which his wife expressed of his young friend, proposed bringing him down again very shortly: Louisa remained silent, but her looks testified that she understood their plan, and would not object to a further acquaintance. Mr. Batson was again and again invited, and again and again endeavoured, not unsuccessfully, to render himself agreeable to the ladies, by whom he was treated with all due civility. Secure of Mr. Randall's consent, who had frankly told him he would give his daughter, on her wedding-day, ten thousand pounds, and encouraged by the smiles of the ladies to believe that an offer of marriage from him to Louisa would be acceptable to all parties, he made up his mind to proceed in due form, and bring the affair to a conclusion, as soon as etiquette and circumstances would admit.

In the meantime the Randalls were invited to a grand entertainment given in the town by A— B—, Esq. to a select party of friends. At this *fête* Miss Randall experienced the mortification, both at table and in the dance, of seeing several misses, inferior to herself in point of fortune, dress, and personal accomplishments, placed above her, for no other reason but that her father was in trade, while theirs were either professional men or gentlemen of independent fortunes.

"What great events from little causes spring!"[23]

From that evening Louisa determined on not marrying a tradesman: Mr. Batson, who was unacquainted with these circumstances, made his offer at this crisis, and, to his utter astonishment and great mortification, met with a decided refusal. Mr. Randall was at first, equally with Mr. Batson, disappointed by the unexpected rejection of the latter by his daughter, but consoled himself with the recollection that a young lady who was pretty, had ten thousand pounds for her fortune, beside future expectations, might be allowed to be a little difficult in her choice of a husband, as there was no fear of her dying an old maid; while Mr. Batson as shrewdly suspected that a young man who could maintain a wife need not despair of getting one: while there were so many young women on the market, it would be a folly in him to waste much time in idle regrets, or the vain pursuit of any one individual capricious fair one. Mrs. Randall, who, with her daughter, had been obliged to give precedence to ladies less splendidly attired, justified Louisa in her refusal of Mr. Batson.

At the entertainment where the mortification which Mrs. Randall and her daughter had received subsequently decided the fate of Mr. Batson, Mr. Frederic Irving, a young barrister, who was one of the party, distinguished Louisa from the other young ladies by many little civilities and compliments usual on such occasions: shortly after, she again met him at an evening party in the neighbourhood, and was again the object of his particular attention. Mrs. Randall, who was always on the alert where Louisa was concerned, remarked these circumstances, while she at the same time perceived that her daughter was not displeased with the gentleman. In consequence, she sent him a card of invitation to her next home party, which was readily accepted. Frederic, when he first saw Louisa, was smitten by her personal charms: on hearing that she had a good fortune, he thought her still more lovely, and gladly availed himself of the opportunity which Mrs. Randall afforded him to cultivate their acquaintance, and ingratiate himself with her daughter.

After the usual time of probation had passed over, Mr. Irving offered to Miss Randall in form, and was, in like form, referred by her to her father for an answer. Mr. Randall, who did not quite approve the idea of this match for his daughter, was not at first inclined to give his consent: Frederic's paternal fortune was small, and he had not as yet, being young, reaped much pecuniary advantage from his profession. These were Mr. Randall's objections; but they were soon overruled by his lady, who considered a genteel profession as preferable to wealth: beside which, she told her husband that she was sure Louisa was attached to Mr. Irving, and her happiness was of essential importance, and ought to outweigh every other consideration. Frederic Irving, superior both in education and manners to any of her former suitors, had certainly taken Louisa's fancy; but she was not a young woman to fall desperately in love, notwithstanding that she had been frequently complimented with possessing a great deal of *sensibility*: the truth was, excessive indulgence, acting on a delicate constitution, had rendered her too sensitive and too fastidious to be capable of feeling any very strong passion, or of yielding up her soul to the influence of warm individual affection. Disappointment, to which she had never been accustomed, might, for a time, have rendered her irritable and uneasy, but would not have made any lasting impression on her mind; neither would it have broken her heart.

Mr. Randall having at length consented to the union, and every preliminary to marriage being finally settled to the apparent satisfaction of all parties, Mr. Irving led Miss Randall to the hymeneal altar. When the honey-moon, which was passed by the sea-side, was over, Frederic took his fair bride home to a small but genteel house, which, for the convenience of his profession, he had taken in one of the squares in the vicinity of the courts of law. It being now the winter season, the first few months of Louisa's residence in town passed over agreeably enough; but, as the spring advanced, she began to complain of her situation, find a thousand faults in her house, and daily express her dissatisfaction at being obliged to live in London. Mrs. Randall, who was a frequent visitor to her daughter, also fancied that Louisa did not look well, and endeavoured to persuade Mr. Irving that his wife's constitution was too delicate to permit her to reside in town all the year round; and as, at present, it might not be quite prudent or convenient to him to take a house in the country, he must permit Louisa to spend the greater part of the ensuing summer with her at Clapham, where he might come down every evening, and pass as much time with them as the duties of his profession would admit. Mr. Irving, in reply, said, "I have no objection to Louisa's spending a few months with her mother;" then added smilingly, "If I could but prevail on her to rise a little earlier in the morning, take more exercise – for instance, walk two or three miles every day – I have no doubt but that she would be quite as well here as at Clapham: our situation is very airy." Louisa, piqued by this remark, replied tartly, "How am I to take exercise? I have been accustomed to a carriage; hackney-coaches are detestable: as for walking about London, that is entirely out of the question." Frederic, now offended in his turn, answered in a serious tone, "When fortune puts it in my power I shall be happy to keep for you both a country-house and a carriage; in the mean time you must endeavour to accommodate yourself to my situation and circumstances."

The greater part of the summer was passed by Mr. and Mrs. Irving at Clapham: when the winter approached, and Louisa was again settled in —— Square, she felt the loss of the carriage, and regretted the many indulgences to which she had been but too much and too early accustomed; and she confessed to her mother, that though she had no reason to complain of Frederic, who was very attentive to her, yet she found that his being a professional man did not quite compensate for the want of those luxuries which money only can procure. When he one day told her, though in a jesting and playful tone, that it was her duty, as a barrister's wife, to study economy, make a genteel appearance at a small expense, and visit in a certain routine for the purpose of keeping up a connexion rather than for the sake of amusement, she burst into tears, reproached him with want of tenderness, and complained bitterly that she had, since her marriage, met with nothing but disappointment and mortification.

Frederic, who was very amiable, and really loved his wife, was much hurt by these weak repinings; but, knowing that she had been a spoiled child, he made every possible allowance for her foibles, though he could not at times help feeling that he should have been happier with a woman who had been differently educated, even though her fortune had been less, and her personal charms inferior to those of Louisa. In point of prudence as well as of happiness, it might in the end have proved more advantageous; for, though ten thousand pounds was certainly an acceptable present to a young man just setting out in life, yet if, on the strength of that sum, or of future expectations, he was to be led into expenses which his present situation did not justify, he had better have been without the fortune, and trusted solely to his own talents and exertions for improving his condition.

In the course of a few years Louisa's constitution, never very strong, became, in consequence of her indolent habits and fine-lady whimsies, more and more debilitated. Not having any family, never having been accustomed to much occupation, and being deficient in that energy of mind which everywhere finds or makes employment, she had no pursuit, and, in consequence, became fretful, and every day more and more dissatisfied with her situation, though, in reality, she had no real evil to complain of.

To please his wife, and in the hope of benefiting her health, Mr. Irving at length took for her a house at Clapham, where, though she would have less of his company, he thought she might, from being nearer her mother, enjoy more advantages, and be better amused than she had been in London. He also proposed to her keeping a one-horse chair, in which he told her he would occasionally drive her out. She replied, "she had no objection to his keeping a chair for his own accommodation, but he must not ask her to ride in it, as she had a particular objection to open carriages, and considered a one-horse chair a vulgar as well as an unsafe vehicle." "If that is your opinion," said Frederic, "I shall not have a chair, as it was entirely on your account that I proposed keeping one; for myself, I prefer riding on horseback: if you do the same, I will purchase for you a nag, as I know of one at present that has been used to carry a lady, and will in every respect just suit you." Louisa had, when single, learned to ride; she therefore, though but a poor horsewoman, acceded to this proposal; and the nag was accordingly purchased. Finding, on trial, that it was very gentle, she one evening consented to ride with Mr. Irving to ——, where he had occasion to go on some business connected with his profession. Unfortunately, they had not proceeded many miles on their road, before the horse on which Frederic was mounted took fright at some accidental circumstance, and set off at full speed. Louisa, terrified beyond measure, screamed aloud, and, by so doing, startled her own nag, which immediately broke into a gallop: she now lost all presence of mind, and would very soon have lost her seat, if the man-servant, who was riding behind them, had not hastened to her assistance. Frederic, who, after a short gallop, had checked his horse and turned him round, was also soon at his lady's side, whom, at her request, he assisted to alight: when she had a little recovered from the effects of her fright, Mr. Irving persuaded her to remount, but could not prevail on her to proceed on their intended journey. As she insisted on returning immediately, he was obliged, though very inconvenient to himself, to accompany her back. On their way home, having to go down a dull lane, Louisa was alarmed by the appearance of some horsemen, whom she mistook for highwaymen; and, to complete the disasters of the evening, before they reached their own gate it began to rain. Disconcerted by these trifling adventures, Mrs. Irving peevishly declared she would never mount again: she kept her word, and the nag was soon after disposed of to a more skilful rider; while, at her mother's request, a new and elegant chariot was bespoke for her daughter.

Mr. Irving's fortune was not large, and he had not hitherto increased it by his practice in the law; but, as he had no family, and expected an accession of property at the death of Mr. Randall, who had for some time past been in ill health, he did not much trouble himself about pecuniary matters, and left the entire settling of his establishment and other domestic arrangements to the sole management of the ladies. Louisa, whom her mother conceived to be entitled, by her fortune, education, and expectations, to every indulgence, was now surrounded by all the luxuries of nature and of art; yet she was still far from happy. Her music and drawing had long been given up; reading, as the mean of acquiring knowledge, she had no notion of, and books, when read merely for amusement, soon became insipid and tasteless; gardening was too laborious an employment; and her domestic concerns, to which she had never been much accustomed to attend, were now entirely intrusted to her housekeeper. She was not fond of cards; visiting fatigued her; and company at home she considered as a burden. She was not backward in drawing her pursestrings at the call either of benevolence or vanity; but for charities which required either personal attendance or mental exertion she had no great inclination. Frederic, whose pursuits called him to London, finding on his return home but little comfort or entertainment, now spent the greater part of his time in the metropolis, where men may always find occupation or amusement.

James Randall, who had now for some years been in partnership with his father, by no means resembled his sister, either in constitution, disposition, or temperament. Active, sanguine, and enterprising, he threw his whole soul, if soul it could be called, into whatever he took in hand. Anxious to acquire wealth, he urged his father, who had already realized a handsome fortune, to enlarge his business and extend his connexions. The old gentleman, very well satisfied with the success which had hitherto crowned his own steady industry, was at first unwilling to enter into any more extensive concerns; but was at length over-persuaded by his son to take his advice, and to trust to him the sole management of the business and warehouse.

Fortune, who, it is said, favours the bold, appeared for a time to smile on James Randall. Intoxicated by present success, and sanguine with regard to future gain, he set no prudent bounds either to his ambition or speculations; and considered the sage advice and angry remonstrances which his father would sometimes force upon him as the effects of old age and mental imbecility.

Trade, like the tide, is ever ebbing and flowing; and when any article of commerce has, by whatever means, been for any length of time kept up beyond either its intrinsic or relative value, it must necessarily, before it finds its proper level in the market, suffer a considerable and rapid depreciation. This was now the case in the manufactory in which the Randalls were principally engaged; and, in the course of a few months, they lost a great portion of what they had previously gained. James Randall, though much mortified, was not discouraged, trusting that time or a change in public affairs, of which he might take advantage in future speculations, would soon set all to rights again: but his father, now advanced in years, knowing and dreading the temerity of his son, not merely suffered from present disappointment, but trembled with anxiety in respect to the future.

But enough of these uninteresting details: suffice it to say, that James Randall, in the hope of retrieving what he had lost, ran[24] greater and greater hazards, till he nearly ruined both his father and himself.

Mr. Randall, whose health had for some time past been declining, did not long survive these repeated vexations. At his death Mr. Irving, finding that the ten thousand pounds which he had received with Miss Randall on his marriage was likely to prove her whole fortune, took an early opportunity of suggesting to his wife the necessity of reducing their expenditure: every indulgence, he added, which his income could afford, she might still command; but the carriage and their present house must be parted with, and the sooner the better. Economy, and a patient submission to existing circumstances, were things of which Louisa, previous to her marriage, had scarcely heard the names, and were virtues which, at present, she was but little qualified to practise. The giving up the carriage was to her not only a bitter mortification, but a real inconvenience; a carriage being a luxury to which she had been early accustomed, and, with her delicate health and indolent habits, could scarcely exist without; while the bare idea of living for a few years in chambers, which Frederic gently hinted to her as a plan which might at present be expedient, threw her into a paroxysm of mingled grief and rage. She did not, it is true, upbraid her husband; he had never given her any cause; but on her brother, between whom and herself there had not been much intercourse, and never any great affection, she poured forth, the most cutting and bitter invectives; while she bewailed her own hard fate in being obliged to make sacrifices, which she had no right to do, in consequence of his imprudence. Unmindful of the cares, the sorrows, and the severe trials, to which but too many of her sex are exposed, she called herself the most unfortunate of women; forgetting that no individual, however prosperous or however deserving, is born with any charter which can exempt him or her from adversity.

Mr. Irving, finding his wife deaf to reason, had recourse to Mrs. Randall, who, seeing with him the necessity of their reducing their establishment, assured him that she would endeavour to reconcile Louisa as well as she could to the present unpleasant change in their prospects, and make such arrangements with her as might be found prudent or eligible for the future.

Soon after this period Mr. Irving had the offer of a respectable and lucrative situation in the suite of ——, who, having been appointed one of the judges, was going out to India in that capacity. He immediately determined on accepting it; but, before he gave his final answer, consulted with Mrs. Randall and her daughter on the subject, and proposed to the latter her accompanying him to Madras, where it was most probable he should remain for some years.

Mrs. Randall, who could neither consent to Louisa's quitting England nor to her husband's going abroad without her, endeavoured to dissuade Frederic from accepting the situation which had been offered to him; but when Mrs. Irving declared that she was willing to accompany her husband to India, anything being preferable to reducing their establishment at home, Mrs. Randall gave up the point, though she frequently warned Mr. Irving of the danger of the seas, and of the risk which he incurred in taking her daughter to a foreign country and unhealthy climate. She also reminded him of what he but too well knew – how unequal poor Louisa was to struggle with any difficulties, should he, on his arrival at Madras, find his station there less pleasant than he at present anticipated.

Louisa, amused for a while by making purchases and procuring finery suited to a tropical climate, continued to express her determination to accompany her husband; but, when the time of embarkation drew near, her resolution began to fail: fears of the sea, an element on which she had never yet been induced to venture, even on a party of pleasure, began to haunt her imagination; which, added to other weak and nervous apprehensions of fancied perils and uncertain ills, induced her at length, after many changes of mind and much vacillation of conduct, to relinquish the plan of going to India with Frederic, who could not now, even if he were so disposed, give up the appointment. Mr. Irving, disgusted by her conduct, left England with many painful feelings, mingled with some tender regrets; for, though he had been disappointed in his union with Louis – not only in point of fortune, but in what is of much higher value, domestic felicity – he was still attached to her. His disposition was amiable and affectionate; if he had not been happy in the marriage state, it was not his own fault: this was his best consolation; he had done nothing wherewith Louisa could reproach him, and, what was still better, wherewith he could reproach himself.

After a safe and not unpleasant voyage, and without meeting with any accident or encountering with any particular inconvenience, Mr. Irving in due time arrived at Madras, from whence, finding his situation eligible, and likely to be permanent, he wrote to his wife, strongly pressing her to join him; adding, for the purpose of obviating any difficulty which might be started either by her or her mother, that he had written to a friend who was coming to Madras the next season on the subject, desiring him to call on Mrs. Irving, and settle with her everything preparatory to her voyage or necessary for her accommodation.

Louisa, who had, since the departure of Frederic, become more peevish and discontented than ever, was greatly agitated and much perplexed at the receipt of this letter. She now repented of not having accompanied her husband to India; but, though she worried and fretted from morning to night at the probability of his long absence from her, she could not summon sufficient courage to follow him. The gentleman to whom Mr. Irving had written called on her again and again, and, by representing to her in flattering colours the prospects which awaited them in India, vainly strove to persuade her to accede to her husband's wishes. But all would not do; she had no resolution, and was incapable of any mental exertion: miserable in the thought of her husband's protracted stay in India, and unequal to the task of following him, she at length determined on writing to him by the gentleman who was to have been her escort, pleading her own inability of exertion and delicacy of constitution as an excuse for her refusing to join him abroad, while she urged and entreated him to return to England, at all hazards, as soon as possible.

Mr. Irving, who had vainly flattered himself that Louisa, who had in her letters to him lamented his absence, would be prevailed on to follow him, was both mortified and disappointed by her refusal; but, though he still retained for her some remains of affection, he did not feel himself either disposed by inclination or bound by duty to give up his situation, and by so doing sacrifice his present interest and future prospects to a wife who had never, in any one instance since their marriage, accommodated herself to his circumstances, or consulted his wishes or convenience.

Years rolled on, but Mr. Irving did not return: engaged in the pursuit of fortune, and enervated by the enjoyment of eastern luxuries, he forgot that he had a wife in England, or remembered it only as a subject of regret. Mrs. Randall, now far advanced in years, paid the debt of nature; James Randall became a bankrupt; while *Louisa the Indulged*, a widowed wife, pined out the remainder of her days in retirement and solitude, a prey to *ennui*, discontent, regret, mortification, and disappointment.

Appendix C

LETTERS OF ELIZABETH HAYS LANFEAR

1. Elizabeth Hays, Gainsford Street, to Mary Hays, 30 Kirby Street, Wednesday morning, undated [*c.* January 1796].[1]

Dear Mary

John[2] brought me such an indifferent account of you yesterday – as makes me anxious concerning your health – send me word therefore how you are today, & whether you would wish me to acquaint my Mother of your indisposition, which I believe she is at present ignorant of – I read Rousseau yesterday from morn, till night, – & have return'd you the two first volumes – the others I have not quite done with – that it has interested me I need not say, the rapidity with which I have pursued it, is a sufficient proof – the farther I proceed, the more I am charm'd – yet I find in it a thousand things to disapprove, – many of their principles are false – their ideas of duty erronius – their sexual distinctions absurd – & their loves though trebly refined, the extreme of voluptuousness. It has enervated me beyond measure[3] – but this will soon be over, my mind will shortly regain its elasticity – I return to Helvetius[4] with new vigour. You sometimes reproach me with want of sensibility – in this you do me injustice – I much doubt whether my feelings are not equally strong with your own – though various circumstances may have rendered them less irritably acute, the only difference between you, & me, is this, – that terrified by your example, it has been the business of my life, to repress sentiments, which it has been too much yours, to indulge – in avoiding one extreme, I may sometimes have run into the other, – & vainly boasted of a philosophy which in an hour of temptation would have avail'd me nothing. You know my heart to be capable both of love, & friendship – though a more indiscriminate mixture with society than you experience, may have made me less romantic – I am neither cold – nor selfish – I am only more cheerful – more rational & not quite such a maniac as my unfortunate favourite sister –

M[r] Martin from Yarmouth[5] John [Hays] informs me is come to Town – he is a person of whom I have heard much, & should like to be introduced to – tell our friend Brown,[6] I wish he would bring him some afternoon to drink tea with us[7]

– that is if it is convenient to himself, & he thinks it would not be disagreeable to Mr Martin – not otherwise, for I do not wish to be troublesome.

I wish to say of my friendship, as St Paul says of the gospel – It is a law of liberty[8] – Adieu, I hope you will soon recover your health of body – would to God you could also recover your health of mind.[9] At any rate get well, & live – I thought Lord B—s[10] letter against suicide a good one, I would have you read it again before the books go home – yours affectionately

E. Hays

Should Browne bring Mr Martin to see us, I should like to know the day – lest I should be out, or engaged in frivolous company.

Wednesday morn
Gainsford Street

2. Elizabeth Hays, Chelmsford, Essex, to Mary Hays, 22 Hatton Street [Hatton Garden], Holborn, 4 February 1801.[11]

Feby 4 1801

Chelmsford

Though I have now no wish to change it, I perfectly agree with you in pronouncing a state of celibacy to be but little favourable either to virtue or happiness – I wonder not that old maids generally speaking have been objects of censure or ridicule – Perhaps there is no character, which it is so difficult for a woman to maintain with propriety. Her affections like a stream impeded in its course either run into irregular channels, or return into her own bosom where pent up, they ravage & destroy the soil they ought to have adorned & fertilized. In the first case unless her understanding is of the superior class (for understanding will always command respect) there is danger of her becoming contemptible, in the latter of growing unamiable. Pride (& it may be a want of that very soft sensibility which some of my sex possess) will now preserve me from one of those evils, whether I shall entirely escape the other time & future events must determine. There are more or less I should suppose in the life of every one particularly trying periods, periods in which the mind undergoes a sort of revolution. The last two or three years *has* been one of those to me. – The struggle is over, & now that I have resigned for ever the sweet illusions of youth, I shall endeavor to reconcile my mind to the world as it is, & daily more & more cultivate a taste for those rational & simple pleasures, which if they do not afford any very lively interest, leave no sting behind. It is well as you observe that each prefers his own burthen to that of his neighbor. I wish not to be again under the dominion of the passions, & would not for worlds exchange my situation for yours. Our dispositions though similar in some points, are in others materially different – I with you could have placed my happiness in the affections & for procuring or preserving the felicity of mutual attachment should have thought few sacrifices too great – but my heart was not formed to cherish the romantic disinterested sort of passion, which you have rather too much prided yourself on being capable of feeling – for without that pride I think your present attachment could not have lasted so long[12] – its commencement was whimsical, & its perseverance madness – But the dart has not corroded too long in your breast to be extracted with safety, & I do not wish to probe a wound I have not the power of healing. The subject is to me on various accounts a painful one – I do not say I shall love you more, (because my friendship for you is not the friendship of a day, nor founded on mere sensation) but I certainly should enjoy more pleasure in your society if your heart was at liberty. Apathy is a bad thing – but mental slavery is a worse, & equally if not more dangerous to virtue – Affectionate sorrows may have in them a species of sweetness, but I know by experience that all is bitter in the sensation which arises on the conviction "Of friendship unreturn'd, & unregarded love"[13] –

I [am] glad you have at least for the present given up your plan of taking a house,[14] for these are not times to make experiments – If I had one wish it should be for money though that is an article which in one sense I may be said never to have known the want of, & while I continue to live with my brother most likely never shall.[15] Of John I have nothing to complain, I believe he has a regard for me, & when we are together we are very friendly & comfortable – was I sure he would settle in the country & not marry I should be very well satisfied with my situation & make the best of it – I have no wish to live again in London – It is my lot, & in some degree my inclination now, to be a solitary, & the solitude of the Country where the distance is not too great to admit of occasional intercourse with our relations and friends is certainly preferable to the solitude of London.

& as we get more acquainted with the people in Essex, I have no doubt but we may find some agreeable society, & I do not wish for a great deal. Now that I have recovered the use of my arm & the weather is sufficiently good to admit of walking almost every day, I do not find my hours pass on heavily – solitude with an incapability of employment, & that in the very worst season of the year, with a mind always too ready to prey on itself was very bad, neither my health nor spirits could support it, but that is past, & I hope I shall never be again in a similar situation. You who have never experienced it, can have no idea of the weariness, & many inconveniences I suffered – My arm has much mended since I left Town, & I am trying by a liberal use of cold water to strengthen it as fast I can. Farewell & believe me

yours affectionately

E. Hays

*Letter continues on another loose sheet of paper,
with address on the back.*

On reading your letter again, I find I have not yet answered every part of it. I am ready to allow that there may be some positive, & much comparative happiness in the world, though I believe the state of society in England was never more unfavourable than at present to both, all I meant to affirm was, that realities but little resemble the fond pictures of imagination, & that every situation in life has its attendant evils, for where can we go "that the voice of complaint is not heard."[16] – I am sorry the unmerited calumny you have incurred should have given you a distaste to general society – The narrow cir[cles] to which most women are confined is [I] believe one great cause of their unhappiness and of their errors. I seldom go into company my self, however averse I may have been to making the effort, without finding my self the better for it. The more we see of, & compare the different lots of our fellow creatures, the less we are inclined to repine at our own & the more we expand our feelings in general benevolence, the less danger there is our becoming a prey to concentrated passion, or selfish misanthropy – both of which originate in the same source[17] – *Sickly & Distorted Sensibility.*[18]

It will give me pleasure to hear from you, what ever be the subject of your letters, when ever you have leisure & inclination to write.

3. Elizabeth Hays, Ingatestone, Essex, to Mary Hays, George Row [9 St. George's Place], Camberwell, 14 August 1803.[19]

August 14th 1803
Ingatestone

Dear Mary

Both my mind, & my feelings have for some months past been occupied by a subject which, till entire "certainty was mine," I did not like to mention to any one but my mother, but I now feel my self at liberty to communicate to you, what I trust your friendship for me will enable you to read with pleasure. In short I have at present the prospect of a change in my situation, which on the maturest reflection & deliberation entirely meets with my approbation – Perhaps you may have heard M[rs] Palmer[20] speak of her accidentally taking me while I was with her one morning into Cheapside where we saw, & spake to M[r] Lanfear.[21] The next day Martha[22] called on me in Aldermanbury & gave me an invitation to Islington by I have since found her uncle's desire. I did not go – the invitation was repeated by M[r] L himself whom I again met by accident one morning at M[r] Francis's[23] at whose house I called to enquire after his health. Since then M[r] L has tried every means in his power to be introduced to my acquaintance, & gain an interest in my esteem; & last friday morning he prevailed on me to consent to devote the remainder of my days to him & his. Yes, I will endeavour to perform every duty, & love those boys whom he so seriously, & so pathetically recommended to my attention.

M^r L appears to be a man of virtuous principles, liberal sentiments & good, though not a polish'd understanding but if I am not deceived in him he possesses what is still dearer to me, an excellent temper, & great sensibility of heart – goodness seems to be his characteristic, as I believe it is that of every branch of his family, to all of whom, M^{rs} J Dunkin[24] & Martha Lanfear in particular, I feel more than ever inclined to attach my self.

But enough on this subject & more perhaps than I ought to indulge my self with, in writing on to you who with my mother are at present much on my mind. My mother who thank God is greatly recovered in her health expresses her self as pleased with my prospects, & would not suffer any considerations on her account to interfere with my final determination –

Remember me to all friends, & to my sister Dunkin[25] in particular, to whom I wish you to show this letter, though I do not wish the subject of it to be yet made public. I shall at some future day tell M^r L that he is indebted to Mrs Dunkins[26] recommendation for some of the first serious & favourable thoughts which I bestowed on him.

And now my dear Mary what can I say to you. [W]ould to God that you were happy – calmly rationally happy, it is an alloy to my own satisfaction that you are not so. My heart is too full of complicated & various emotions to permit me to say any more

Farewell

Eliz^h Hays

NOTES

NOTES TO THE INTRODUCTION

1 Elizabeth Hays appears briefly in A. F. Wedd (ed.), *The Love-Letters of Mary Hays (1779–1780)* (London: Methuen, 1925), p. 2; M. L. Brooks (ed.), *The Correspondence (1779–1843) of Mary Hays, British Novelist* (Lewiston, ME: Edwin Mellen Press, 2004), pp. 472–4; and G. L. Walker, *The Idea of Being Free: A Mary Hays Reader* (Peterboro, Ontario: Broadview Press, 2005), pp. 310–11. Much more would be known of Elizabeth Hays after 1798 had A. F. Wedd not excised nearly every reference to her in *The Fate of the Fenwicks* (London: Methuen, 1927), Wedd's edition of the Fenwick-Hays correspondence is now residing at the New York Historical Society. Fortunately, Henry Crabb Robinson inserted several references to Elizabeth Hays Lanfear in his early diaries (pre-1811) and in his formal Diary after 1811. For a discussion of these references and the first detailed look at the life of Elizabeth Hays Lanfear, see T. Whelan, 'Elizabeth Hays and the 1790s Feminist Novel', *Wordsworth Circle* 48 (2017), pp. 137–51. For a new edition of all letters by, to, and about Mary Hays, belonging primarily to collections of Hays material at the Carl H. Pforzheimer Collection of Shelley and his Circle, The New York Public Library, Astor, Lenox and Tilden Foundations, New York; the Fenwick Family Correspondence, 1798–1855, MS 211, New York Historical Society, New York; and the A. F. Wedd Collection, shelfmark 24.93, Dr Williams's Library, London; along with texts of many of Hays's writings, and extensive genealogical material on the Hays family, see Timothy Whelan (ed.), *Mary Hays: Life, Writings, and Correspondence* (www.maryhayslifewritingscorrespondence.com) (hereafter Whelan, *Mary Hays*).
2 See Wollstonecraft to Hays, 15 and 20 September 1796, in Whelan, *Mary Hays*; Brooks, *Correspondence*, pp. 307–8; J. Todd (ed.), *Collected Letters of Mary Wollstonecraft* (Chichester, UK: Columbia University Press, 2003), pp. 364, 367.
3 See A. Smyth to Mary Hays, 21 February 1820, in Whelan, *Mary Hays*; Brooks, *Correspondence*, p. 539.
4 British Library, shelfmark C.186.b.7.
5 Scholars have generally focused on Mary Hays's feminism, her novels and life writings, and her friendships with Godwin and Wollstonecraft. Attention to her life as a religious Dissenter, however, has significantly increased since 1995 through the work of Marilyn Brooks, Gina Luria Walker, Mary Spongberg, Felicity James, and Timothy Whelan. See M. L. Brooks, 'Mary Hays: Finding a Voice in Dissent', *Enlightenment and Dissent* 14 (1995), pp. 3–24; G. L. Walker, *Mary Hays (1759–1843): The Growth of a Woman's Mind* (Aldershot, UK: Ashgate, 2006); and 'Energetic Sympathies of Truth and Feeling: Mary Hays and Rational Dissent', *Enlightenment and Dissent* 26 (2010), pp. 259–85; M. Spongberg, 'Mary Hays and Mary Wollstonecraft

NOTES

and the Evolution of Dissenting Feminism', *Enlightenment and Dissent* 26 (2010), pp. 230–58; and F. James, 'Writing Female Biography: Mary Hays and the Life-Writing of Religious Dissent', in D. Cook and A. Culley (eds.), *Women's Life Writing, 1700–1850* (Basingstoke, UK: Palgrave Macmillan, 2012), pp. 117–32; and T. Whelan, 'Mary Steele, Mary Hays and the Convergence of Women's Literary Circles in the 1790s', *Journal for Eighteenth-Century Studies* 38 (2015), pp. 511–24.

6 For biographical entries on many members of the Hays family, see Whelan, *Mary Hays*.

7 Hays once wrote to her fiancé, John Eccles, 'Sweet were the sensations I experienced on thursday whilst reviewing those scenes [in Greenwich and the park] where I had passed many of my early days – days of happiness and innocence' (Mary Hays to John Eccles, 7 August 1779; Whelan, *Mary Hays*; Wedd, *Love-Letters*, p. 37; Brooks, *Correspondence*, p. 55). Hays may be reminiscing about a boarding school experience in Greenwich, but more likely she is thinking about summer visits to family and friends living at that time in Greenwich, which may also explain why she returns there to live in the 1820s. Mr Hays's wealth was probably sufficient to provide his daughters with a boarding school education, but apparently it was not viewed as necessary.

8 Thomas Hays, grandfather of Mary and Elizabeth Hays, died *c*. 1735. His wife, Sarah Applegath Hays, married a second time to Capt. Thomas Hills, who died in 1774, the same year as John Hays. Thomas Hills, along with his wife, Sarah, son Thomas, and another relation, Dinah Hills, were all members of the Particular Baptist meeting in Carter Lane, Southwark, not far from the Gainsford Street chapel. In 1774, the younger Thomas Hills left Carter Lane and joined the new Baptist congregation in Dean Street that would soon be led by William Button. Most likely, this Thomas Hills was a cousin of the Thomas Hills who married Sarah Hays in 1776 and who lived in Gainsford Street in the 1760s and 1770s and attended the Baptist chapel there in Blackfields with his father (William Hills) and his brother and sister (William and Sarah), his two siblings attending the same Baptist boarding schools in Northampton as did John and Christopher Dunkin, William Button, Benjamin Flower, and Elizabeth Rutt, sister of John Towill Rutt. See Horsleydown and Carter Lane Church Book, MS Metropolitan Tabernacle, London, fols 10, 16, 23, 25, 29; T. Whelan, 'John Ryland at School: Two Societies in Northampton Boarding Schools', *Baptist Quarterly* 40 (2003), pp. 90–116.

9 See Baptism Book, White Row, Spitalfields, MS London Metropolitan Archives, microfilm X099/303, N/C025/001, 1756–1891; for Benjamin Flower's tribute to his education under Ryland at Northampton, see T. Whelan (ed.), *Politics, Religion, and Romance: The Letters of Benjamin Flower and Eliza Gould Flower, 1794–1808* (Aberystwyth, Wales: National Library of Wales, 2008), pp. 68–73.

10 See Whelan, 'John Ryland', pp. 90–116; also T. Whelan, 'Mary Hays and Henry Crabb Robinson', *The Wordsworth Circle* 46 (2015), pp. 178–80.

11 Eccles to Hays, 4 October 1779, Whelan, *Mary Hays*; Wedd, *Love Letters*, p. 36; Brooks, *Correspondence*, p. 54.

12 References to Elizabeth Hays can be found in letters by Eccles to Hays dated late July 1779, 1 August 1779, 2 August 1779, 4 August 1779, 27 September 1779, 2 October 1779, 11 October 1779, 23 October 1779, 25–26 October 1779; Hays to Eccles, 25 October 1779, 13 July 1780, *c*. October 1780; references also appear in letters by Hays to Mrs Collier, *c*. late July-early August 1780, and 21 October 1780. All can be found in Whelan, *Mary Hays*; and in Brooks, *Correspondence*.

13 Hugh Worthington to Mary Hays, in Whelan, *Mary Hays*; Brooks, *Correspondence*, p. 268.

14 Ann Robinson to Hays, 8 May 1792, in Whelan, *Mary Hays*; Brooks, *Correspondence*, p. 272.

15 Worthington to Hays, 17 August 1792, in Whelan, *Mary Hays*; Brooks, *Correspondence*, p. 275.

NOTES

16 Worthington to Hays, 3 September 1792, and 21 May 1793, in Whelan, *Mary Hays*; Brooks, *Correspondence*, pp. 275, 281. John Disney's letters to Mary Hays also comment on Elizabeth Hays, with Disney inviting both sisters to his Sloane Street home for Sunday dinner after church at Essex Street in May and August 1793. See Disney to Hays, 31 January, 7 February, 1 May, 21 June, 9 July 1793, and 26 March 1795, in Whelan, *Mary Hays*.

17 Dyer to Hays, 27 January 1793 and 28 February 1794, in Whelan, *Mary Hays*; Brooks, *Correspondence*, pp. 267, 286–7.

18 See Frend to Hays, 16 April 1792, in Whelan, *Mary Hays*; Brooks, *Correspondence*, pp. 268–70.

19 Hays to Godwin, 1 January 1795, in Whelan, *Mary Hays*; Brooks, *Correspondence*, p. 390.

20 Eleanor Coade (1733–1821) was a member of the Baptist congregation in Blackfriars, south London, during the ministry of James Upton (1759–1834). Coade established a firm in Lambeth, just across the Thames from Westminster Abbey, *c.* 1769 called 'Coade's Lithodipyra, Terracotta, or Artificial Stone Manufactory', which became known for its patented ceramic imitation of stone ('Coadestone'), some of which was used in the construction of Buckingham Palace, St George's Windsor, and the Royal Naval College, Woolwich. Searles also used her stone for his colonnades at the Paragon in Blackheath, Greenwich, where John Hays, Elizabeth's younger brother, lived between 1812 and 1819. See 'Coade, Eleanor', *Oxford Dictionary of National Biography* (hereafter *ODNB*); N. Rhind, *The Paragon and South Row Blackheath: A Triumph in Late 18th Century Unintentional Town Planning* (Blackheath, London: Bookshop on the Heath, 2012), pp. 18–19.

21 Christall's little known subscription list exhibits broad religious diversity. Subscribers included Wollstonecraft and her sister Everina, as well as George Dyer, William Frend, Anna Letitia Barbauld, Benjamin Flower, Amelia Alderson, Capel Lofft, and J. T. Rutt, all Unitarians; Robert Hall, Robert Robinson's successor at the Baptist congregation in St Andrew's St, Cambridge; a Mrs Wedd, most likely a future relation of the Hays sisters through the marriages of Peter and George Wedd to two daughters of John Dunkin, Jr; John Gurney (1768–1845), one of the Treason Trials' attorney in 1794–95, and a Miss Smithers, both members of the Baptist congregation at Maze Pond; and John Rippon (1751–1836), pastor at Carter Lane in Southwark, another Baptist congregation not far from the Blackfields chapel in Gainsford Street.

22 Though best known for his interactions with most of the leading literary figures of his day, Henry Crabb Robinson was an important writer and thinker in his own right, especially in the dissemination of German thought in England. He lived in Germany for most of 1800 through 1805, spending three years as a student at the University of Jena and writing pioneering articles on Kant, Schelling, and the rapidly developing field of aesthetics for publication in London. Though he briefly experimented with Godwinian scepticism in the 1790s, after his return from Germany he identified thereafter as a 'rational dissenter', worshipping among the Unitarians. After a brief stint covering the Peninsular war as a correspondent for the *London Times* (1808–9), Robinson spent 15 years as a solicitor (1813–28). In retirement, he took an active role in the University of London, in Unitarian affairs, and in the literary, artistic, and political life of London until his death in 1867. The Robinson archive, one of the most important collections belonging to Dr Williams's Library, London, contains 33 volumes of his Diary (1811–67), 29 volumes of Travel Diaries (1801–66), four volumes of Reminiscences (1775–1843), numerous pocket diaries, and more than 30 volumes of correspondence and other papers. Only a small portion of Robinson's literary remains have been published. Selections can be found in Thomas Sadler's *Diary, Reminiscences and Correspondence* (3 vols, 1869) and Edith Morley's *Henry Crabb Robinson on Books*

NOTES

and Their Writers (3 vols, 1938); see also John Milton Baker's Henry Crabb Robinson of Bury, Jena, The Times, and Russell Square (1937).

23 Sometime in 1798, Thomas Martin resigned his pastorate at the Great Meeting (Independent), Yarmouth (he had become a Unitarian), and removed to Liverpool, where he became a wealthy merchant, owner of Calderstones Park (1807–25), and eventually Secretary of the Royal Liverpool Institution. He was the author of *Zetemata Dianoetika: Or a View of the Intellectual Powers of Man* (Liverpool, 1819), a paper Martin delivered before the Literary and Philosophical Society of Liverpool. See J. W. Robberds (ed.), *A Memoir of the Life and Writings of the Late William Taylor of Norwich*, 2 vols (London: J. Murray, 1843), vol. 2, p. 297.

24 Elizabeth Hays specifically mentions Martin and Browne in her letter to Mary Hays *c.* January 1796 (see Appendix C, Letter 1). Stephen Weaver Browne (*c.* 1769–1832) was originally from Swaffam, Norfolk, near Norwich; he studied at Pembroke College, Cambridge, between 1785 and 1790. He served as curate at Harleston, Norfolk, but in the aftermath of the French Revolution, he left the Anglican communion and joined with other radicals advocating political reform in England. He moved in a circle in the mid- to late 1790s that included Godwin and many of his friends among the Romantic poets, as well as Mary and Elizabeth Hays, Amelia Alderson, Henry Crabb Robinson, and Mary and John Reid. After the Peace of Amiens in 1802, Browne went to France and was detained there for a time by Napoleon. Upon his return to England, he ministered to the French Protestant Church in Norwich, and briefly thereafter to a dissenting congregation on the Isle of Wight before becoming evening Lecturer to the congregation of the Old Meeting (Unitarian), Birmingham (Joseph Priestley's former church) in May 1819. He closed his ministry in London, first at the Presbyterian congregation in Monkwell Street, London (1821–24), and then for two years at a new Presbyterian congregation in York Street, St James's Square, preaching occasionally as well at the Unitarian chapel in Essex Street. He remained in London after his retirement, living in the Featherstone Buildings, Holborn, until his death on 13 January 1832. Among his publications are *Remarks on a Charge Delivered to the Clergy of his Diocese by the Lord Bishop of Lincoln* (1795), *The Duties of Christian Ministers* (1819), and *Corruptions of Christianity* (1819). See Browne's obituary in *Unitarian Chronicle* 1 (1832), p. 32; also G. Carter, *Unitarian Biographical Dictionary* (London: Unitarian Christian Publishing Office, 1902), p. 23.

25 See Reid to Hays, 23 January 1797, in Whelan, *Mary Hays*; Brooks, *Correspondence*, p. 504. In his novel *Edmund Oliver* (1798), Lloyd used Hays as his model for the naive, freedom-loving, *Emma Courtney* – quoting Lady Gertrude Sinclair, a character recast two years later as Bridgetina Botherim in Elizabeth Hamilton's *Memoirs of Modern Philosophers*. Not even a review by John Reid in the *Analytical Review* (June 1798, pp. 638–41) could provide cover for Hays. Despite Lloyd's harsh criticism of Hays, the two writers saw each other often during the summer of 1798 and resumed their interviews after Lloyd's return to London from Cambridge that December, about the same time the Reids arrived from Leicester. Not long thereafter the infamous escapade involving Hays, Lloyd, and Stephen Weaver Browne occurred, in which Lloyd accused Hays of making unwarranted advances upon him. Letters passed between them, which Lloyd claimed included passages showering him with sentimental pleas, tears, confessions – even declarations of love and sexual desire; to make matters worse, he publicly humiliated her by reading her letters to gatherings of his friends. For more on Lloyd and Mary Hays, see G. L. Walker, *Mary Hays (1759–1843): The Growth of a Woman's Mind* (Aldershot, UK: Ashgate, 2006), pp. 198–201; also T. Whelan, 'Mary Hays', pp. 181–5.

26 See his obituary notice in the *London Times*, 24 February 1795. He may have been the brother of William Cole, who died in 1802 and who was also for some 50 years Printer to the Bank of England (see *London Times*, 21 January 1803).

NOTES

27 All references to Godwin's diary in the above paragraph are taken from *The Diary of William Godwin*, eds. V. Myers, D. O'Shaughnessy and M. Philp (Oxford: Oxford Digital Library, 2010) (http://godwindiary.bodleian.ox.ac.uk) (hereafter *William Godwin Diary*).

28 Edward Palmer (1770–1831) was the son of Christopher Palmer (1741–1808), a hatter and feltmaker with the firm of Moxon, Palmer, and Norman at 40 Cannon Street, London. For much of his adult life, the elder Palmer lived at 19 Crosby Row, Walworth, not far from the Paragon, where John Dunkin, Jr, lived for much of the 1790s. Less than two years after the death of Marianna Hays Palmer, Edward Palmer remarried and became a successful druggist in the City of London, associating himself with the firm of Edward Palmer, his uncle, in Throgmorton Street. Nathaniel Palmer (1774–1840) married Joanna Dunkin on 21 June 1798 (she was living at that time with her parents in Champion Hill), after which the couple moved into his residence in Surrey Square, not far from the Paragon and Crosby Row; in 1803 they removed to Aldermanbury, London. His former residence at 42 Surrey Square passed to William Giles, who married Nathaniel's sister, Sarah Palmer, in 1803. In 1811, Nathaniel Palmer became a partner in the firm of Scott, Garnett and Palmer, where he remained until his death in 1840, becoming extremely wealthy, much like Elizabeth Hays's relations, John Dunkin, Jr, and John Hays. Edward Palmer's youngest brother, Samuel (1775–1848), was at various times a bookseller, teacher, and lay Baptist minister in Southwark and places outside London. He married Martha Covell Giles (1778–1818), sister of the William Giles mentioned above, in October 1803. He became a leading member of the Baptist congregation in East Street during the minister of Joseph Jenkins (1743–1819), not far from his home in Beckford Row, as well as an active member of the Camberwell Bible Society between 1813 and 1822. His wife died in January 1817 during their residency in Houndsditch; in the latter part of 1819 he removed to 10 Broad Street, Bloomsbury, where he operated a bookshop until his retirement (provided for him by his brother Nathaniel) *c*. 1827. At that time, he removed, with his two sons and nursemaid, to Shoreham, where Samuel Palmer, Jr (1805–1881), the future Romantic artist, flourished as a landscape painter. William Blake visited the Palmers at Shoreham and Crabb Robinson would later become friends with the younger Palmer. Prior to leaving for Shoreham, young Samuel Palmer often visited Greenwich, where several of Joanna Palmer's sisters, as well as Mary Hays, lived in the mid-1820s. William Bennett, husband of Joanna Palmer's younger sister, Marianne, purchased some of Samuel Palmer's earliest paintings in 1825. See Raymond Lister (ed.), *The Letters of Samuel Palmer*, 2 vols (Oxford, UK: Clarendon Press, 1974), vol. 2, pp. 9–10; see also Horsleydown and Carter Lane Church Book, MS Metropolitan Tabernacle, London; East Lane Church Book, 1806–19; Poor Rate Books for the parish of St Mary Newington, Southwark; and Minutes of the Camberwell Bible Association, 1813–22, MS William B. Hamilton Collection, David M. Rubenstein Rare Book and Manuscript Library, Duke University.

29 The Little John Street address first appears in the correspondence of Mary Hays on 14 December 1796; the final appearance is on 26 September 1797.

30 Marianna was buried on 9 December, at the age of 24 (Burial Book, St John Horsleydown, Bermondsey, 1797). Edward Palmer remarried in 1799 to Elizabeth Bates (d. 1812).

31 John Dunkin, Jr's, home was eventually matched by John Hays's impressive residence at the Paragon in Blackheath (1812–19), Michael Searles's second version of his original Paragon in Walworth. For more on Searles and his two Paragons, see Rhind, *The Paragon*.

32 See Appendix C, Letter 2. Eliza Fenwick viewed life similarly through the lens of a single woman, even though she was legally married to John Fenwick throughout her friendship with Mary Hays. She writes to Hays on 24 September 1812 about whether

NOTES

she should advise her daughter, Eliza, to marry Mr. Rutherford or 'live single': 'Live to be old neglected solitary joyless without natural ties to bind you to the flagging remnant of life while I unhappy in marriage yet feel hourly & momentarily mingled blisses & cares through my children and am stealing towards the grave without any of those blank lonely desolate feelings that you my dear Mary gifted with extraordinary resources & connected with a numerous & in a great degree kind & amiable family too often participate'. See Fenwick to Hays, 24 September 1812, in Whelan, *Mary Hays*; Wedd, *Fate of the Fenwicks*, p. 114; passage omitted in Brooks, *Correspondence*, p. 348.

33 Hays to Godwin, 13 October 1795, in Whelan, *Mary Hays*; Brooks, *Correspondence*, p. 403.
34 See Appendix C, Letter 3.
35 In 1809, Joseph Lanfear received a grant from the King to take his mother's name of Stanfeld and assume the family's properties in Middlesex.
36 See Appendix C, Letter 3.
37 See Appendix C, Letter 3.
38 Martha Lanfear was Ambrose Lanfear's niece and apparently had a connection with the Dunkin family prior to Elizabeth's engagement; she also appears in the subscription list to *Fatal Errors* in 1819. All the individuals in the above paragraph were known to Crabb Robinson and, except for Martha Lanfear, appear in his Diary and Reminiscences.
39 Both of Lanfear's sons died young: John in 1817 and Francis in 1830. Their early deaths suggest they may have been consumptive, a common sickness at that time. They were buried in the family plot in St Mary's parish church, Islington, where their mother is also buried.
40 See 1806 Survey Map of the Parish of St Mary, Islington, and the 1805–6 Poor Rate Book, St Mary, Islington, MS Local History Centre, Islington.
41 Hays to Robinson, 14 February 1806, in Whelan, *Mary Hays*; Brooks, *Correspondence*, p. 571.
42 George Dyer, Overbury, near Tewkesbury, to [Messrs Vernor and Hood], undated [*c*. 1805–6], MS Montagu d. 4, fol. 190, Bodleian Library, Oxford.
43 In 1819 John Evans and several members of his family subscribed generously to Lanfear's *Fatal Errors*.
44 See John Dunkin to Mary Hays, 3 and 23 March 1808, in Whelan, *Mary Hays*; Brooks, *Correspondence*, pp. 490–94.
45 Fenwick to Hays, 7 April 1806 and 26 October 1806, in Whelan, *Mary Hays*.
46 Crabb Robinson Notebook, November 1805–December 1806, fols 29, 32, Crabb Robinson Archive, Bundle 6.VIII, Dr Williams's Library, London. Quotations taken from materials in the Crabb Robinson Archive, as well as letters from the A. F. Wedd Collection, shelfmark 24.93, appear by permission of the Director, David Wykes, and the Trustees of Dr Williams's Library, London.
47 See Fenwick's letters to Mary Hays, April 1811–May 1812, in Whelan, *Mary Hays*.
48 Crabb Robinson Reminiscences, vol. 1, f. 416, Crabb Robinson Archive, DWL.
49 Fenwick to Hays, 23 July 1810, in Whelan, *Mary Hays*; not in Wedd, *Fate of the Fenwicks*; or Brooks, *Correspondence*. Fenwick refers again to 'poor Mrs Lanfear' in a letter to Hays on 8 February 1813 (from Lee Mount in Ireland), and offers her condolences to Hays after the loss of Lanfear's son in a letter dated 24 April 1818. Fenwick also knew Ambrose Lanfear, Jr, lamenting that on his visit to America in 1824 he was unable to visit her in New Haven. She was more hopeful in April 1828, declaring in her final surviving letter to Hays from New York City that she soon expected to see Ambrose and his wife as soon as they arrived in New York. See Whelan, *Mary Hays*.

50 John Hays and his family remained at the Paragon till 1819, when financial woes forced his removal by the end of that year to a smaller home in Doughty Street near King's Cross, not far from Mary Hays's rooms in Ann Cole's new residence at 1 Upper Cumming Street, just to the north of King's Cross, along the same road that led to Elizabeth Lanfear's home in Church Street, Islington. For sources related to the information in the above paragraph, see the Poor Rate Books at the Southwark Local Studies Library, John Harvard Library, Southwark; Lambeth Archives, Minet Library; Wandsworth Local History and Heritage, Battersea Library, Clapham Junction; Greenwich Heritage Centre, Royal Arsenal, Woolwich; Islington Local History Centre, Islington; and Camden Local Studies and Archives Centre, Holborn Library. See also subscription lists to Robert Robinson's *Ecclesiastical Researches* (London, 1792), Ann Batten Christal's *Poetical Sketches* (London, 1795), and Samuel Lowell's *Sermons on Evangelical and Practical Subjects* (Bristol, 1801), as well as a variety of *Directories* for London and its environs between 1777 and 1840.
51 See Will of Elizabeth Hays, Widow of St Mary, Islington, proved 20 January 1813, PROB 11/1540/448, Public Record Office, Kew.
52 See Whelan, *Politics*, p. 320; Whelan, 'Mary Hays', p. 179; Crabb Robinson Diary, 2 March 1835, vol. 16, fol. 67, MS Crabb Robinson Archive, DWL.
53 Crabb Robinson Diary, vol. 2, fol. 131, MS Crabb Robinson Archive, DWL.
54 Smyth to Hays, 4 November 1817, in Whelan, *Mary Hays*; Brooks, *Correspondence*, p. 532.
55 Smyth to Hays, 9 January 1818, in Whelan, *Mary Hays*; Brooks, *Correspondence*, p. 534.
56 Smyth to Hays, 21 February 1820, in Whelan, *Mary Hays*; Brooks, *Correspondence*, p. 539. Mary and Elizabeth Hays were not the only writers within their extended family. In 1783, John Dunkin, Jr (1753–1827), their brother-in-law, published *The Divinity of the Son of God, and the Complete Atonement for Sin . . . in a Letter to a Friend*, a critical response to Joseph Priestley's *An Appeal to the Serious and Candid Professors of Christianity* (1783). Four decades later, John Hays, Elizabeth's younger brother, published *Observations on the Existing Corn Laws* (1824), a topic to which he returned two decades later in *Remarks on the Late Crisis in the Corn Trade* (1847). His daughter, Matilda Mary Hays (1820–1897), a favourite niece of Mary Hays, became, like her aunt, an accomplished novelist as well as a translator, journalist, and outspoken feminist in a career that began shortly after Mary Hays's death in 1843 and carried on into the 1860s. Crabb Robinson used the same expression for her as he did for her more famous aunt – 'in advance of the age', a reference to their heterodox religious, social, and political views. See Crabb Robinson Reminiscences for 1819 [composed 31 July 1859], vol. 2, fol. 243, MS Crabb Robinson Archive, DWL.
57 Crabb Robinson Diary, vol. 8, fol. 31, MS Crabb Robinson Archive, DWL.
58 Fenwick to Hays, 10 December 1821, in Whelan, *Mary Hays*; Wedd, *Fate of the Fenwicks*, pp. 213–17; Brooks, *Correspondence*, pp. 353–7 (passage above omitted from both Wedd and Brooks). Fenwick would comment again on Lanfear in her letter to Hays on 1 March 1825, not knowing Lanfear had died a few weeks prior to her letter. 'I sympathize sincerely in all you feel for poor M[rs] Lanfear', she writes. 'I always admired her fortitude'. With a tone more expressive of evangelical culture than the scepticism she shared with Hays and the Godwin circle in the 1790s, she adds, 'May God encrease it, & reward her when she reaches that shore where pain sorrow & suffering are unknown' (Whelan, *Mary Hays*).
59 Crabb Robinson Diary, vol. 11, fol. 2, MS Crabb Robinson Archive, DWL.
60 Crabb Robinson Diary, vol. 11, fol. 27, MS Crabb Robinson Archive, DWL.
61 Crabb Robinson Diary, vol. 11, fol. 41, MS Crabb Robinson Archive, DWL.

NOTES

62 See records of St Mary's Church, Upper Street, Islington, MS P83/MRY1/1267–71, X085/106, London Metropolitan Archives, London; also Will of Elizabeth Lanfear, Widow of Islington, PRO, PROB 11/1701/344; her will was proved on 21 July 1825.
63 Hays to Godwin, 2–6 February 1796, in Whelan, *Mary Hays*; Brooks, *Correspondence*, p. 427.
64 After borrowing the first volume of *Political Justice* from Godwin, Hays wrote to him on 7 December 1794: 'I shou'd not have retain'd the volume I now return, with unfeign'd acknowledgements, so long, but from the wish of making a sister, who resides not with me but with whom I have long been united in habits of strict friendship from a similarity of mind & principle, a participater [sic] of the satisfaction experienc'd from the perusal of it' (Whelan, *Mary Hays*; Brooks, *Correspondence*, p. 388).
65 See Appendix C, Letter 1.
66 Hays's two letters on Helvétius (signed 'M. H'.) appeared in the *Monthly Magazine*, 1 (June 1796), pp. 385–7, and 3 (January 1797), pp. 26–8.
67 Hays to Godwin, 20 November 1795, in Whelan, *Mary Hays*; Brooks, *Correspondence*, pp. 410–11.
68 See Appendix C, Letter 1.
69 Hays to Godwin, 2–6 February 1796, in Whelan, *Mary Hays*; Brooks, *Correspondence*, p. 430.
70 Hays to Godwin, 11 May 1796, in Whelan, *Mary Hays*; Brooks, *Correspondence*, p. 458.
71 Wollstonecraft to Mary Hays, 15 September 1796, in Whelan, *Mary Hays*; Brooks, *Correspondence*, p. 307.
72 Wollstonecraft to Hays, 20 September 1796, in Whelan, *Mary Hays*; Brooks, *Correspondence*, pp. 307–8.
73 Fenwick to Hays, 4–5 July 1800, in Whelan, *Mary Hays*; Wedd, *Fate of the Fenwicks*, p. 9.
74 Fenwick voiced surprise and some dismay to Hays in October 1826 that Lanfear's publications had not yet crossed the Atlantic. Both of Lanfears's works are now extremely rare, with only one known copy remaining of *Fatal Errors* (British Library), two copies of the 1824 edition of *Letters to Young Ladies* (British Library and Harvard University), and one copy of the 1828 edition of the same volume (University of Utah). See Fenwick to Hays, 15 October 1826, in Whelan, *Mary Hays*.
75 For the above quotations, see Appendix B.
76 See Appendix C, Letter 3.
77 See Whelan, *Nonconformist Women Writers*, and T. Whelan, *Other British Voices: Women, Poetry, and Religion, 1766–1840* (New York, NY: Palgrave Macmillan, 2015).
78 D. E. White, *Early Romanticism and Religious Dissent* (New York and Cambridge: Cambridge University Press, 2006), p. 1.
79 See, for example, G. L. Walker, *Mary Hays (1759–1843): The Growth of a Woman's Mind* (Aldershot, UK: Ashgate, 2006); E. Ty, *Unsex'd Revolutionaries: Five Women Novelists of the 1790s* (Toronto and London: University of Toronto Press, 1993) provided an important early consideration of Hays's novels. A good survey of recent trends in criticism of Mary Hays, with a special focus on *Female Biography*, may be found in *Women's Writing* 25.2 (2018), a special issue edited by M. Spongberg and G. L. Walker.
80 Mary Wollstonecraft, *Mary and the Wrongs of Woman*, ed. Gary Kelly (Oxford: Oxford University Press, 2009), p. 107.
81 Samuel Richardson, *Clarissa, or the History of a Young Lady*, ed. Angus Ross (London: Penguin Classics, 1985), pp. 1371–2.
82 Sarah Pennington, *An Unfortunate Mother's Advice to Her Absent Daughters, in a Letter to Miss Pennington* (London: S. Chandler, 1761), p. 60.

NOTES

83 Pennington, *Unfortunate Mother's Advice*, p. 14.
84 Sophia Lee, *The Recess; Or, a Tale of Other Times*, ed. April Alliston (Lexington, KY: University of Kentucky Press, 2000), p. 137.
85 Wollstonecraft, *Wrongs of Woman*, p. 107.
86 Amelia Opie, *Adeline Mowbray, or, The Mother and Daughter; A Tale*, ed. Anne McWhir (Peterborough, Ontario: Broadview Press), p. 255.
87 G. Kelly, *Women, Writing, and Revolution, 1790–1827* (Oxford: Clarendon Press, 1993), p. 89.
88 Kelly, *Women, Writing, and Revolution*, p. 89.
89 N. J. Watson, *Revolution and the Form of the British Novel, 1790–1825: Intercepted Letters, Interrupted Seductions* (Oxford: Clarendon Press, 1994), p. 26.
90 Mary Hays, *The Memoirs of Emma Courtney*, 2 vols (London: G. G. and J. Robinson, 1796), vol. 2, p. 68.
91 W. Godwin, *Memoirs of the Author of A Vindication of the Rights of Woman*, eds. P. Clemit and G. L. Walker (Peterborough, Ontario: Broadview Press, 2001), p. 105.
92 Mary Hays, *The Victim of Prejudice*, ed. E. Ty (Peterborough, Ontario: Broadview Press, 1995), pp. 213–14.
93 T. Castle, '"Sublimely Bad": Review of "Secresy; or, The Ruin on the Rock", by Eliza Fenwick, edited by Isobel Grundy', *London Review of Books* 17.4 (1995), pp. 18–19. (www.lrb.co.uk/v17/n04/terry-castle/sublimely-bad). Accessed 20 April 2019.
94 Watson, *Revolution*, p. 41.
95 M. Reeves, *Pursuing the Muses: Female Education and Nonconformist Culture 1700–1900* (London and Washington: Leicester University Press, 1997), p. 5.
96 G. L. Walker, 'I Sought & Made to Myself an Extraordinary Destiny', *Women's Writing* 25.2 (2018), p. 142.
97 A. O. Winckles and A. Rehbein, *Women's Literary Networks and Romanticism: 'A Tribe of Authoresses'* (Liverpool, England: Liverpool University Press, 2017), p. 4.

NOTES TO *FATAL ERRORS*

1 Lines from Wordsworth's 'Simon Lee: The Old Huntsman', which originally appeared in the *Lyrical Ballads* (1798). The date of this poem suggests that Lanfear continued to work on her novel after 1797, though the exact time of her decision to forego publication remains unclear.
2 Lines from 'Written in a Cottage Garden, at a Village in Lorrain' (ll. 35–36), by John Langhorne (1735–1779). Originally from Winton, Westmoreland, Langhorne served as a clergyman in London and Blagdon, Somerset. His *Poetical Works* appeared in 1766, followed by a popular edition (assisted by his brother) of Plutarch's *Lives* (1770) and his long poem, *The Country Justice* (1774–7).
3 Lanfear's niece, Emma Dunkin Hills (b. *c.* 1792), was the daughter of John Dunkin, Jr, and Joanna Hays Dunkin, eldest sister of Mary and Elizabeth Hays. After the death of her mother, Emma joined her sisters Sarah and Marianne in Islington, living with and being tutored by Mary Hays at her Park Street residence in Islington, *c.* 1806–08. On 7 December 1810 she married her cousin, William Hills (b. 1784), son of Thomas and Sarah Hays Hills, at Hazeleigh Church, Maldon. After their marriage, Emma and William settled into a townhome in newly developed Canonbury Square in Islington, opposite Park Street (Park Place where Mary Hays had lived was at the end of Park Street) on the east side of Upper Street, not far from where William's mother, Sarah Hays Hills, would soon reside at 5 Felix Terrace, and where Elizabeth Lanfear, living then at 4 Upper Terrace, Islington, would later reside in nearby Church Street. William Hills's sister, Mary (1792–1832), was a bridesmaid at the wedding of George Wedd (1785–1854) and Sarah Dunkin (1793–1875) on 20 August 1812 at Hazeleigh Church,

Maldon, Essex. They all appear in Crabb Robinson's diary on 5 September 1812, when William and his sister attended a dinner at George Wedd's. On 22 March 1813 Robinson had tea at the home of the Hills in Islington, with Mary Hays, and mentions the Hills again on 8 November 1817 and on 1 January 1825. William Hills partnered with William Wheeler, his brother-in-law, as corn merchants at 8 Haydon Square (*Post Office Directory* for 1812). By 1823 the firm was operating at 34 Mark Lane. After Elizabeth Lanfear's death in 1825, the Hills (followed shortly thereafter by Sarah Hills) moved to a large home at Maze Hill, next to Greenwich Park and adjacent to Vanbrugh Castle, where Mary Hays and several of Emma Hills's relations lived at that time: William and Marianne Dunkin Bennett, Henry Francis (his wife and her sister, the former Elizabeth Dunkin Francis, had died in 1825); and George and Sarah Dunkin Wedd. Crabb Robinson visited Maze Hill often to see Hays and her many family members living there. As he writes in his Diary on 10 April 1828: "Walked to Greenwich and visited Mrs Hays there'. After a short walk with Hays, he visits some other friends nearby and then 'returned to Mrs Hills with whom Mrs Hays lives – and dined with Mr Hills & young Wheeler. Old M^{rs} H: is turned of 70 – quite an invalide – Hills is a respectable man – But the afternoon was rather unpleasant – M^{rs} H: could not help reproaching me with drowsiness and she was as usual disputatious and rude in disputing' (vol. 13, fol. 115, MS Crabb Robinson Archive, DWL). The Hills would remain at their Maze Hill residence into the 1840s.

4 Lanfear's son, John, died in August 1817, at the age of 12, and was buried in the cemetery at St. Mary's Church, Islington.

5 Mary Wollstonecraft and Mary Hays first read Lanfear's manuscript c. 1796–7, about 20 years prior to the death of her son.

6 In the previous 20 years, Lanfear had witnessed the death of Thomas Hills, her brother-in-law, in 1803; Joanna Dunkin, her eldest sister, in 1805; her husband's suicide in 1809; and the deaths of her mother and her son in 1812 and 1817, respectively.

7 Given the rise in popularity of didactic fiction for young and old readers, a field dominated by women writers (including Mary Hays, whose publications in 1815 and 1817 were prime examples of this genre), Lanfear was fully aware her novel, written during her Jacobin phase amidst her friendship with Wollstonecraft, Alderson, Mary Robinson, and Eliza Fenwick, would seem a stark contrast to contemporary tastes in fiction.

8 Given that Lanfear shared her manuscript with Wollstonecraft, Fenwick, and Mary Hays, it seems likely she intended publishing the novel at that time. Fenwick's aside in a letter to Mary Hays from early July 1800 suggests that Elizabeth was still contemplating publication. Fenwick writes, 'I wish it were possible for you to avoid giving your sister my opinion of her manuscript. I respect her too much to not be reluctant to give her that pain,' that final phrase slightly ambiguous as to whether 'pain' was related to Fenwick's critique of Elizabeth's manuscript or Fenwick's awareness of the inevitable reception such a novel would provoke at that time. For whatever reason, Elizabeth Hays decided against publication and stored the manuscript in her desk drawer. By 1819 she had placed considerable distance between herself and her radical literary friends within the Godwin circle of the late 1790s, separated further by her creation of a fictional persona as *editor* rather than author.

9 The British Library copy has an asterisk affixed to the end of this sentence, with an accompanying note in pencil at the foot of the page that reads 'by RS', a tantalizing thought that the 'gentleman' might have been Robert Southey, who became acquainted with Mary and Elizabeth Hays in the early months of 1797.

10 How much Lanfear altered the original manuscript by 1819 cannot be known, but it may be that her original text possessed passages of sentimental language and

heightened emotion common to many of the romantic novels of the 1790s, whether Jacobin or Gothic, that Lanfear no longer deemed proper for public consumption. By 1819, literary tastes had changed, and Lanfear appears to have adjusted accordingly. On the other hand, her letters to her sister in 1796 and 1801 suggest that she was more emotionally reserved than her sister at that time, and it could be that the somewhat negative critiques by Wollstonecraft (Elizabeth's novel 'displays more rectitude of mind than warmth of imagination') and Fenwick suggest that her lack of such heightened language and 'high-wrought characters' may have been viewed as a fault.

11 Most likely a relation of the Mrs Allen mentioned in a letter from Benjamin Seymour, Elizabeth's cousin, to Mary Hays, 15 December 1794. He writes: '[I]t will give a sincere pleasure to hear of the health and happiness of Mrs Hays, and your sisters and their connections, pray let me know if my dear Mrs Allen is happy; her generous and affectionate sensibility on my first interview with her on my return from Russia, has made an impression on my mind, never to be effaced by time; or absence' (Whelan, *Mary Hays*; Brooks, *Correspondence*, p. 479).

12 The Applegaths were a prominent South London Baptist family. Elizabeth Lanfear's grandmother was Sarah Applegath, who married Thomas Hays. After his death *c*. 1735, she married Capt. Thomas Hills (d. 1774), establishing a connection between three South London families – Applegath, Hays, and Hills – that continued for more than a century. The Applegaths worshiped primarily in the Baptist congregation at Carter Lane, during the ministries of John Gill (1697–1771), the famed Calvinist theologian, and John Rippon (1751–1836). On 14 October 1784, Ann Lepard, a member at Carter Lane and Mary Hays's close friend during her teenage years, married Augustus Joseph Applegath (*c*. 1753–1816) (it was her second marriage) at St. Mary Woolnoth. His father was, like Capt. Hills, for a time a sea captain employed with the East India Company. Their son, also named Augustus Applegath (1788–1871), would later become a prominent Baptist layman best known for inventing the vertical printing press. Applegath joined the printing firm of Cornish and Sons, in Southwark, in 1813, and soon partnered with Edward Schickle Cowper (1790–1859), printing banknotes for the Bank of England and then as printing engineers for the London *Times*. Despite his success in advancing printing technology, Applegath experienced bankruptcies in 1826 and 1842. His brother, Joseph Applegath (1792–1859), married Mary Lepard (most likely a sister or relation of Ann Lepard) and later emigrated to Edwardsville, Illinois. His sister, Ann Applegath (1794–1836), married his partner, Edward Cowper; he later served for many years as head of the Department of Engineering at King's College, London. His son, Edward Alfred Cowper (1819–1893), became one of the leading mechanical engineers of his day, supervising the redesigning of the Crystal Palace between 1852 and 1854. See Church Book, Horsley-down and Carter Lane, 1719–1808, MS Metropolitan Tabernacle, London, fols 10, 16, 23, and 25; also entries for August Applegath and Edward Cowper in the *ODNB*.

13 Mrs Atkinson was either the mother or sister-in-law of Elizabeth Atkinson Breese, who married John Hays, Lanfear's brother, in 1812.

14 Most likely the daughter of Thomas Belsham (1750–1829), a Unitarian minister who served for a time as Headmaster of Daventry Academy. Belsham assisted Joseph Priestley in the formation of the Unitarian college at Hackney in the early 1790s. After Priestley's emigration to America in 1794, Belsham assumed the pastoral duties of the Unitarian congregation at Gravel-Pit in Hackney. In 1805 he succeeded John Disney at the Essex Street (Unitarian) Chapel, London, where he remained until his death in 1829. His most popular work was *A Summary View of the Evidence and Practical Importance of the Christian Revelation* (1807). He was a frequent contributor to the *Quarterly Review*, *Gentleman's Magazine*, and the *Monthly Repository*.

15 Marianne Dunkin Bennett (b. *c.* 1795) was the youngest of the eight daughters of John Dunkin, Jr. She and her sisters Elizabeth and Sarah boarded with and were tutored by their aunt Mary Hays *c.* 1806–8 in Islington. Marianne married William Bennett (b. 1790) of Faringdon House, Berkshire, in 1817 (he later became High Sheriff of Berkshire, where his family held large estates). By the time of the publication of *Fatal Errors* (two years after their marriage), the Bennetts had moved into Vanbrugh House (sometimes called 'Mince-pie House') on the grounds of Vanbrugh Castle at Maze Hill in Greenwich. That same year her sister, Elizabeth Dunkin Francis (1787–1825), moved with her family into one of the other large houses on Maze Hill. In 1823 they were joined by Mary Hays, who took rooms in Vanbrugh Castle itself, which at that time was a school operated by Robert Browne and his wife. The Bennetts had five children: Daniel, William, John Dunkin, Elizabeth Emma, and Marianne. Marianne Bennett's eldest sister, Joanna Dunkin Palmer, married Nathaniel Palmer in 1798. Her nephew, Samuel Palmer (1805–1881), the Romantic artist, during visits to see her and her sisters on occasion at Greenwich, arranged with William Bennett for a set of drawings and paintings in 1828 (see above, Notes to the Introduction, n. 28).

16 Stephen Weaver Browne (*c.* 1769–1832) was originally from Swaffam, Norfolk, near Norwich, and studied for the Anglican ministry at Pembroke College, Cambridge, between 1785 and 1790. In the aftermath of the French Revolution, he left the Anglican communion and joined with other radicals advocating political reform in England. He moved in a circle in the mid- to late 1790s that included Godwin, as well as Mary and Elizabeth Hays, Amelia Alderson, Crabb Robinson, Mary and John Reid, and several of the Romantic poets. After the Peace of Amiens in 1802, Browne went to France and was detained there for a time by Napoleon. Upon his return to England, he ministered to the French Protestant Church in Norwich, and briefly thereafter to a dissenting congregation on the Isle of Wight before becoming evening Lecturer to the congregation of the Old Meeting (Unitarian), Birmingham (Joseph Priestley's former church) in May 1819. He closed his ministry in London, first at the Presbyterian congregation in Monkwell Street, London (1821–4), and then for two years at a new Presbyterian congregation in York Street, St James's Square, London, preaching occasionally as well at the Unitarian chapel in Essex Street. He remained in London after his retirement, living in the Featherstone Buildings, Holborn, until his death on 13 January 1832. Among his publications are *Remarks on a Charge Delivered to the Clergy of His Diocese by the Lord Bishop of Lincoln* (1795), *The Duties of Christian Ministers* (1819), and *Corruptions of Christianity* (1819). See Browne's obituary in *Unitarian Chronicle* 1 (1832), p. 32; also G. Carter, *Unitarian Biographical Dictionary* (London: Unitarian Christian Publishing Office, 1902), p. 23.

17 James Collins, an attorney at 33 Spital Square (*Holden's 1805 London Directory*).

18 Most likely an unmarried daughter or sister of the James Collins listed above.

19 John Dunkin, Jr, married Joanna Hays in 1774. Like the Hays family, the Dunkins worshiped at the Baptist meeting in Gainsford Street, Blackfields, during the ministries of John Dolman, John Langford, and Michael Brown, though they appear to have left by the late 1780s. In the late 1760s, Dunkin, along with his brother Christopher, attended the Baptist academy in Northampton under the tutelage of the Baptist minister John Collett Ryland (1723–1792). Among his classmates were Ryland's son, John Ryland, Jr (1753–1825), a brilliant scholar and later Baptist minister at Northampton and Bristol and leader in the Baptist Missionary Society; William Hills, most likely a cousin of Mary Hays and a member at the Gainsford Street chapel; William Button (1754–1821), later the Baptist minister at Dean Street, Southwark, and publisher of one of Mary Hays's novels in 1815; William Lepard, brother of Mary Hays's close friend, Ann Lepard; Thomas Rutt, brother of J. T. Rutt (whose nephews would marry two of John Dunkin's daughters); and

NOTES

Benjamin Flower (1755–1829), later a prominent Unitarian writer, printer, and newspaper editor whose wife was a close friend of the wife of John Dunkin's younger half-brother, Summerhays Dunkin (1779–1823). After John Dunkin's marriage to Joanna Hays, the couple moved into the house adjacent to the Hays family on Gainsford Street. Mr Hays had died three months previously, and Dunkin, though only 21 at the time, served as guardian thereafter to the Hays children. He became a wealthy cornfactor and helped establish Elizabeth's brothers, Thomas and John, and several of his sons and sons-in-law as cornfactors. The Dunkins appear often in the correspondence that passed between Mary Hays and her fiance, John Eccles, *c*. 1779–80. By 1792 the Dunkins had moved to the Paragon at Walworth, the spacious town home where Mary Hays would live *c*. 1794–95. In 1798 the Dunkins moved to a mansion in Champion Hill, Camberwell, and in 1804 to the Lodge at Mortimer Woodham, Essex. After his wife's death in 1805, Dunkin lived in spacious homes in Buckinghamshire and Bath prior to his death in 1827.

20 This Mrs Dunkin is most likely the former Sarah Francis, who married John Hays Dunkin (1775–1858), eldest son of John Dunkin, Jr, on 16 May 1799. She was the sister of Henry Francis (see below), who married her husband's sister, Elizabeth Dunkin, in May 1803. The younger Dunkins lived for some time in Beeleigh where the Dunkin family had purchased a mill in the 1790s. They had at least five children: Henry Hays Dunkin (b. 1800), to whom Mary Hays dedicated her novel, *Harry Clinton*; Joanna Dunkin; Elizabeth Dunkin (b. 1802); Emma Dunkin (b. 1804); and John Hays Dunkin (*c*. 1807–1824). See Nonconformist Registers, RG4-4663, MS Public Record Office, Kew; see also John Hays Dunkin's obituary in the *Gentleman's Magazine* 135 (1824, part 1), p. 93.

21 George Dyer (1755–1841) was educated at Christ's Hospital, London, and Emmanuel College, Cambridge, leaving with a B.A. in 1778. After spending several years (1779–1785) as a Baptist tutor (both for Robert Robinson at Cambridge and at J. C. Ryland's academy at Northampton) and Baptist minister (Oxford, 1781–2), Dyer became a Unitarian. A final attempt at the ministry, this time as an assistant to John Prior Estlin at the Unitarian chapel at Lewin's Mead, Bristol, failed in 1791. Shortly thereafter, Dyer left Cambridge for London, employing himself in a variety of literary labours the rest of his life. A gentle but eccentric scholar who composed a considerable amount of poetry (not always appreciated by his friends Charles Lamb, S. T. Coleridge, and Robert Southey), Dyer nevertheless produced several noteworthy writings, especially his early political works – *Inquiry into the Nature of Subscription to the Thirty-nine Articles* (1789); *The Complaints of the Poor People of England* (1793); *Dissertation on the Theory and Practice of Benevolence* (1795); *Memoirs of the Life and Writings of Robert Robinson* (1796); and *An Address to the People of Great Britain on the Doctrine of Libel* (1799). Dyer came to know Mary and Elizabeth Hays in 1792 through their friendship with Robert Robinson's daughters, Mary and Ann, both of whom he had formerly tutored. He also introduced Mary Hays to William Frend that year and may have been instrumental in bringing the two sisters into a circle of Unitarian ministers that included John Disney, Theophilus Lindsey, Hugh Worthington, and John Evans, all of whom corresponded with Mary Hays between 1792 and 1794. Dyer's letters to Mary Hays can be found in collections at Dr Williams's Library and the Pforzheimer Collection, New York Public Library. Dyer also mentions Elizabeth Hays in his undated (*c*. 1806) letter to Messrs Vernor and Hood about some periodical pieces she had sent Dyer for publication in the *Lady's Monthly Museum* (see above, Notes to the Introduction, n. 42). For more on Dyer's life and career as a Dissenter, see T. Whelan, 'George Dyer and Dissenting Culture, 1777–1796', *Charles Lamb Bulletin* N.S. 155 (2012), pp. 9–30.

NOTES

22 John Evans (1767–1827), General Baptist minister and schoolmaster, was a descendant of the Evans family of Radnorshire, Wales. He was the grandson of Caleb Evans (d. 1790), a Baptist preacher and schoolmaster in Wales, who was the half-brother of Hugh Evans (1712–1781), President of Bristol Baptist Academy and minister at Broadmead in Bristol, 1758–81. John Evans was educated for the ministry at Bristol Academy, where Robert Hall served as his tutor. He then became a Ward scholar at the Universities of Aberdeen and Edinburgh, graduating from the latter with an M.A. in 1790. While in Scotland, he openly adopted Unitarianism. He was ordained in 1792 by the General Baptist congregation at Worship Street, London, remaining there as pastor until shortly before his death in 1827. He lived in a large house in Pullen's Row, Islington, for most of his career, operating a successful school there for boys and young ministers from 1796 to 1821. Not far away, at 1 Upper Terrace (the same street in which Elizabeth Lanfear lived after her marriage in 1804), Alice Flowerdew, a member of Evans's congregation, operated a school for young girls. It is likely, as suggested in Dyer's letter *c.* 1806, that Lanfear worked for a time in Flowerdew's school. Evans met Mary Hays in 1792 and corresponded with her for a time. He published some 40 works in his lifetime, including his influential *A Sketch of the Denominations of the Christian World* (1795). Besides himself, Evans's wife and four of his children also subscribed to *Fatal Errors*.

23 Elizabeth Dunkin (1787–1825) married Henry Francis (1781–1847) of Aldermanbury, London, at St. Giles, Camberwell, on 17 May 1803, when she was 16. The Francises, like the Dunkins, were a prominent Dissenting family in Southwark in the latter part of the eighteenth century and into the nineteenth. In 1801, a Henry Francis, living at the Paragon, Walworth, subscribed, along with John Dunkin and Dunkin's eldest son and father, to Samuel Lowell's *Sermons on Evangelical and Practical Subjects*. This is probably the father of Henry Francis, since the younger Henry Francis would only have been 21 at that time, and too young to have had his own residence among the plush town homes of the Paragon, the former residence of John Dunkin and, for a time, Mary Hays. Elizabeth Francis was joined in Lanfear's subscription list by a Mrs Francis, Maldon, and a Mrs R. Francis of Finsbury, relations of her husband most likely. By the summer of 1823, the Francises (Henry was a solicitor, like Crabb Robinson) were living at Maze Hill, adjacent to Vanbrugh Castle, Blackheath, Greenwich, where Mary Hays was living, and along the same street where the family of Elizabeth's sister, Marianne Dunkin Bennett, were living. Elizabeth Francis died on 22 January 1825, just a few days prior to Elizabeth Lanfear's death (6 February 1825), leaving Henry Francis with 11 children.

24 Mrs Harvey was the wife of Daniel Whittle Harvey (1786–1863), MP for Colchester (he would serve that borough several times thereafter as well as the borough of Southwark). He was a political radical and was often opposed to the Whig government, his views eventually aligning with many of the positions in Chartism. In 1821 he founded the Sunday paper, *The New Observer*, which the following year became the *Sunday Times*. In 1840 he became London's first Chief of Police, remaining in that capacity until 1863 (*ODNB*).

25 John Hays (1768–1862) was the youngest brother of Mary and Elizabeth Hays. At the time of the publication of *Fatal Errors*, he was living in Doughty Street, opposite the house that would later be occupied by Charles Dickens and not far from Mary Hays's former residences in Kirby Street and John Street. John Hays was joined in the subscription list by his wife, Elizabeth; Mary Hays (listed as 'Mrs. M. Hays', a common title given to older unmarried women), living then with the family of John Fenn in Peckham; and his brother Thomas, living in Bermondsey, near the old family home in Gainsford Street. Surprisingly, Sarah Hays Hills,

NOTES

older sister to Mary and Elizabeth, did not subscribe to the novel. On 4 May 1812 John Hays married Elizabeth Atkinson Breese (*c.* 1781–1832) at St. Bride, Fleet Street, London (it was her second marriage). After his marriage, he moved his new family into a spacious town home at No. 3 Paragon in Blackheath, not far from Greenwich Park. In 1819, after some commercial setbacks, he returned to central London, residing in a newly developed section of Doughty Street. He would later live at Norwood Lodge, South London (1832–9), and then at 11 Grosvenor Place, Camberwell. Like the Dunkins, Hays was a cornfactor, partnering for much of his career with George Wedd (his wife was Mary Hays's niece, Sarah Dunkin) and operating out of warehouses and offices in Gainsford Street, Shad Thames, Billiter Square, Mark Lane, and Riches Court (Camberwell). John Hays was also connected with Hills Mills at Bromley, Middlesex, part of the business of William Hills, a nephew of Mary and Elizabeth Hays who lived for several years in Canonbury Square. Like his two sisters, John Hays was a published writer. His *Observations on Existing Corn Laws* was published in 1824 (a second edition appeared in 1828, and another edition in 1847, titled *Revised Observations on Existing Corn Laws*). John and Elizabeth Hays had six children: Elizabeth (b. 1813), Anna (b. 1814), Henry (b. 1817), Susanna (b. 1818), Matilda Mary (1820–1897), and Albert (b. 1823). Mary Hays lived with John and his family almost exclusively between 1832 and 1839, during the formative years of Matilda Mary Hays, most likely serving as her primary tutor, just as she had done for her three Dunkin nieces *c.* 1806–8. Like Mary Hays, Matilda Mary Hays became a writer and a radical voice for social and political reform. Her first novel, *Helen Stanley*, appeared in 1846, and a second novel, *Adrienne Hope*, two decades later. She is best known for introducing the novels of George Sand into English, her translations appearing in six volumes in 1847, published by Churton. Her last translation of Sand was *Le Petite Fadette*, which appeared in 1851. She co-founded the *English Woman's Journal* in 1858 and lived openly as a lesbian at a time when few public figures dared to do so. Crabb Robinson wrote in his Diary on 24 May 1844 that Matilda, then 24 years old, had written to him asking advice 'about the character of a publisher of a novel she has written' (the novel was *Helen Stanley*). He later adds this telling comment about her in his Reminiscences for 1819, composed on 31 July 1859: 'It is a curious fact, that a niece of Mary Hayes (a daughter of her Brother John,) is become an authoress, being as her aunt was, in advance of the age – if advance be the proper term, which it is to be hoped, it is not; for that implies that the age is to follow = She is the translatress of several of George Sand's novels!!!' See Crabb Robinson Dairy, vol. 19, fol. 273, and Crabb Robinson Reminiscences, vol. 2, fol. 243, MS Crabb Robinson Archive, DWL; Church of England Births and Baptisms, 1813–1917, Public Record Office, Kew.

26 Thomas Hays (*c.* 1772–1856) married Elizabeth Dunkin (*c.* 1775–1832), John Dunkin, Jr's, younger half-sister, in 1796, remaining in the Gainsford Street/Bermondsey area of Southwark for many years before moving into a spacious home on Wandsworth Common, near Clapham, where he lived *c.* 1808 to 1817. Mary Hays lived with her brother at Wandsworth from 1809 to 1813, assisting in the education of his children and, for a time, Eliza Fenwick's son, Orlando, who attended a nearby boarding school *c.* 1811–12. Like his brother John, his brother-in-law John Dunkin, Jr, his nephew William Hills, and his relation Nathaniel Palmer, Thomas Hays was a cornfactor, operating for many years in Mill Street, Dockhead, directly across the narrow inlet of wharves at the end of Gainsford Street and Shad Thames. A commercial setback forced him to leave Wandsworth in 1817 and move into a house on Mill Street near his warehouse and wharf, where he remained for many years. He

partnered for a time with a Mr. Clulow at the Mill Street address, but by 1820 he was partnering with a Mr. Wheeler, most likely the brother of William Wheeler, the brother-in-law of William Hills. For most of the 1820s and 1830s, Hays and Wheeler operated at Meriton's wharf, Mill Street, Dockhead. Thomas Hays appears often in Crabb Robinson's diary, for Robinson was a frequent guest of Mary Hays during her residence at Wandsworth and at dinners at Thomas Hays's residence in Mill Street after Mary Hays's return from Bristol in 1817. The following obituary appeared in the *Gentleman's Magazine*, New Series 45 (April 1856): 'At Seaton, Kent, the residence of his son-in-law, R. C. Kingsword, aged 84, Thomas Hays, esq. late of Bermondsey' (p. 436).

27 Mary Hays, who moved to Cross Street, Islington, *c*. August 1819.
28 Emma Dunkin Hills (see above, Notes to *Fatal Errors*, n. 3).
29 John Jeaffreason was a surgeon in Upper Street, Islington (see *Holden's 1805 London Directory*).
30 Rev. Sampson Kingsford (1740–1821) was the primary minister at the General Baptist meeting in Black Friars, Canterbury, from 1771 until his death on 27 August 1821. Connections between the Hays and Kingsford families existed as early as the late 1790s, when Mary Hays visited the Kingsfords at their home in Wepham near Canterbury in the summer of 1799 (see Eliza Fenwick to Mary Hays, 30 August 1799, in Whelan, *Mary Hays*). How these connections originated, however, is not clear. Elizabeth Kingsford (b. 1783) of the Vicarage at Kensworth was the daughter of William and Elizabeth Kingsford and most likely a relation of Sampson Kingsford. A 'W K' appears in a letter of John Dunkin, Jr, to Mary Hays on 29 November 1807, most likely a reference to William Kingsford, another indication of the varied Hays-Dunkin connections shared with the Kingsfords. Dunkin was later connected with the family of Mrs Kennett Kingsford of Beeleigh, Essex, whose husband purchased the Beeleigh Steam Mill from him in 1822. Beeleigh is the same village in which several of Elizabeth Lanfear's relations on the Dunkin side lived (some of whom also subscribed to *Fatal Errors*), in particular, John Hays Dunkin (see above, Notes to *Fatal Errors*, n. 20). For the Dunkins, Kingsfords and the Beeleigh Mill, see *History of Beeleigh Mill* (Maldon, UK: Maldon Archealogical and Historical Group, n.d.), pp. 11–12.
31 Beebeigh] 1819 text.
32 Ambrose Lanfear, Jr (1787–1870) was the son of Ambrose Lanfear, Sr, from his first marriage (see above, Introduction). The younger Lanfear married his cousin, Mary Hills (1792–1832), on 28 September 1826 at Islington. He had already visited New York in 1824 and in 1828 immigrated with his wife to America (see Eliza Fenwick to Mary Hays, 24 March 1824, and 15 April 1828, in Whelan, *Mary Hays*). Mary Lanfear died in New York City in September 1832, about eight months after the birth of Emily Francis Lanfear, Elizabeth Hays Lanfear's step-granddaughter; Emily Lanfear married Gordon Norrie (1830–1909) and died in New York City in 1917. At some point after 1832, Ambrose Lanfear removed to New Orleans, where he became a banker. He was joined on the subscription list by many members of his family, most of them having primary residences in Berkshire. See Whelan, 'Mary Hays', p. 179.
33 Most likely this is the wife of Joseph Lanfear (b. 1792), half-brother to Ambrose Lanfear from his father's second marriage to Sarah Stanfield (*c*. 1767–1802). In 1809, after his father's suicide, Joseph was granted the legal right to take his mother's name of Stanfield and assume properties belonging to her family in Middlesex.
34 Anne Dunkin Lee (b. *c*. 1785), another daughter of John Dunkin, married John Wyatt Lee at Maldon, Essex, on 17 October 1805, about ten months after the death of her mother, Joanna Dunkin. Her father had moved the year before from Champion Hill, Camberwell, to Mortimer Woodham, Essex. Anne Lee had at least one daughter,

Joanna Dunkin Lee, who was christened on 15 August 1813 at the Mundon Church in Essex, near Maldon. By 1819, the Lees were living once again in London. Discussions of John Lee's financial situation prior to his marriage to Anne Dunkin can be found in John Dunkin, Jr's, letter to Mary Hays on 3 March 1808 (Whelan, *Mary Hays*; Brooks, *Correspondence*, p. 489).

35 Two choices are possible here. William Lepard III worked with his brother, John Pelly Lepard (1758–1796), and his father, William Lepard, Jr (1730–1805) in the family business in Newgate Street as stationers, rag merchants, paper makers, and printers. In 1789 John Pelly Lepard moved to 91 Newgate Street, and his father joined him there the next year. That same year William Lepard and James Smith, the latter most likely a member of the Baptist congregation in Little Wild Street, opened a printing and bookselling business at 14 Bridges Street, Covent Garden, with Smith remaining with Lepard at that location until 1798. William Lepard, Sr, joined the Baptist meeting in Carter Lane, under John Gill, in 1717; he died in 1799 at the age of 99; William, Jr, joined at Carter Lane in 1755. Among the junior Lepard's earliest printing jobs (1758–66) were various works by Gill and, in the 1770s and early 1780s, works by Robert Robinson. During that time, Ann Lepard, sister of William Lepard, Jr, became a close friend of Mary Hays and appears often in the Hays-Eccles correspondence, 1779–1780, as does her father. The other subscriber listed above, a Mrs Lepard living in the Strand, may be the widow of John Pelly Lepard or William Lepard, Jr.

A second possibility for the above subscriber is John Lepard, most likely a son of William II, who in the early 1820s was a partner in the firm of Sheppard, Thomas & Lepard, Solicitors, 9 Cloak Lane, London. In January 1826 John Lepard and a Joseph Harding were listed as the assignees for a contract concerning the sale of 900 copies of William James's *Naval History*, with Augustus Applegath (his mother was the same Ann Lepard mentioned above) also listed as one of the assignees. The document was signed by Joseph Harding, John Lepard, Augustus Applegath, and William James. Mary Hays's fiancé John Eccles, during his time in Gainsford Street, worked for John James, a cornfactor who attended the same Baptist chapel where the Hays worshiped. This William James, given his connections with the Applegaths and Lepards, may be the son of that John James. For more on the Lepards, see *Universal British Directory*, vol. 1 part 2, p. 211; Horsleydown and Carter Lane Church Book, 1719–1808 (MS Metropolitan Baptist Tabernacle, London), fols 22, 27, 33–35; I. Maxted, *The London Book Trade 1775–1800: A Preliminary Checklist of Members* (Kent: [n.p.], 1977), pp. 137, 208; C. Woollacott, *A Brief History of the Baptist Church in Little Wild Street, Lincoln's-Inn Fields, from 1691 to 1858* (London: Houlston and Wright, 1859), p. 41; and John Lepard to W. James, 1826, Add. MS. 46612 (now bound separately), ff. 210–12, Bentley [Richard] Papers, vol. 53, British Library.

36 Endfield] 1819 text.
37 Endfield] 1819 text. In the 'N' section of the 'List of Subscribers', 'Laytonstone' has been silently corrected to 'Leytonstone'.
38 Joanna Dunkin Palmer (b. c. 1777), another of the many nieces of Elizabeth Hays Lanfear, married Nathaniel Palmer (1774–1840), son of Christopher Palmer (1741–1808) of Crosby Row, Southwark, on 21 June 1798. They lived for five years in Surrey Square before moving to Aldermanbury in 1803. In the early 1830s they removed to a spacious mansion at Norwood Grove, near Streatham Common, and then c. 1840 to Mongewell House near Wallingford, Berkshire, just prior to Nathaniel Palmer's death. Joanna Palmer appears in Elizabeth Hays's letter to Mary Hays on 14 August 1803 (Appendix C, Letter 3); in letters from John Dunkin to Mary Hays, 15 December 1807, and Mary Hays to Crabb Robinson, 26 November 1814 (Whelan, *Mary Hays*; Brooks, *Correspondence*, pp. 490, 573). In Robinson's Diary entry for 21

May 1820 he comments about a conversation over tea on 21 May 1820 at the home of John Hays in Doughty Street, Bloomsbury, with the Palmers (though he is in error about Nathaniel Palmer being a 'solicitor'): 'Mrs P. [Joanna Dunkin Palmer, Mary Hays's niece] [is] a lively pretentious woman – He rather a shewy and I sho^d think a sensible man. . . . Conversation ab^t law and lawyers. P. is a solicitor of eminence in the city – quite out of my way certainly' (Crabb Robinson Diary, vol. 8, fol. 29, MS Crabb Robinson Archive, DWL).

39 Storford] 1819 text.
40 John Reid (1763–1822) was the son of Matthew and Mary Atchison Reid of Leicester. He had another brother, Matthew, a Leicester merchant, and a sister, Mary (1769–1839), who became a close friend of Mary and Elizabeth Hays. John Reid was baptized at the Great Meeting, Leicester, on 9 February 1773; he later studied at Daventry Academy (1788–89) and at New College, Hackney (1789–94) in preparation for a career as a Dissenting minister. He grew disenchanted with his prospects as a minister and turned to medicine, completing his degree at Edinburgh in September 1798. He soon settled in London, bringing his mother and sister Mary with him. Crabb Robinson wrote that it was 'my friend Reid' who wrote an epigram about George Dyer's poems 'that I fear was thought just – ' (Crabb Robinson Reminiscences, vol. 1, fols 111, 109, MS Crabb Robinson Archive, DWL). John Reid was known to Dr Richard Pulteney (1730–1801), apothecary, botanist, and biographer of Linnaeus who settled at Blandford, Dorset, in 1765, a friendship gained through Reid's parents and another Leicester family, the Coltmans, all of whom worshiped at the Great Meeting with Pulteney prior to his departure for Blandford from Leicester. While in Blandford, Pulteney formed a friendship with the poet Mary Scott that earned him a place in *The Female Advocate* (Whelan, *Nonconformist Women Writers*, vol. 4, pp. 45–6). Reid received a substantial legacy from Pulteney after the latter's death in 1801. Once established in London, Reid became a friend of numerous Romantic literary figures, including Coleridge, Lamb, and Godwin. He married twice, the second time to Elizabeth Jesser Reid (1789–1866), daughter of William Sturch and founder of Bedford College for Women in London in 1849 (later a part of the University of London). Among his writings are *A Treatise of Consumption* (1806), *Essays on Insanity* (1816), and *Essays on Hypochondriasis and other Nervous Affections* (1821). He was a regular contributor for many years on medical issues to the Richard Phillips's *Monthly Magazine* and after 1800 lived in Grenville Street, Brunswick Square.

Mary Reid, like her brother, was raised in the Great Meeting, Leicester, but in 1807, after the arrival of the celebrated Robert Hall, she moved her membership to his Baptist congregation in Harvey Lane. She never married, rejecting numerous suitors, including the poet James Graham. After the death of her mother and her brother John, she inherited a considerable amount of property, both in Leicester and Glasgow, where her family originated. According to the Glasgow historian Robert Reid, 'Miss Mary Reid was a literary lady, and was spoken of as a blue stocking in my early days'. She was a close friend of the writers Elizabeth Coltman and Susanna Watts of Leicester, Mary Steele of Broughton, Mary Scott of Milborne Port, and Elizabeth Benger of London. 'She was also', Robert Reid adds, 'a keen politician, of the Foxite school', which would have placed her in good company in the mid-1790s with Mary Hays and many of her friends. Though never a writer herself, Reid maintained close friendships with literary women throughout her adult life. Her connection with Richard Phillips, the radical Leicester bookseller/newspaperman who moved to London late in 1795 to commence publication of the *Monthly Magazine*, may have been the source of Hays's introduction to and subsequent working relationship with Phillips. Her friendship with Hays began that same year and continued into the 1830s, a friendship often noted in the Diary and Reminiscences of Crabb Robinson. For more on the Reids, see Robert Reid [Senex], *Old Glasgow and Its Environs* (Glasgow, UK: David Robertson; London: Longman, 1864), p. 55; 'Times Stepping Stones', The Journal of Samuel Coltman, MS 15D56/449, Leicester, Leicestershire, and Rutland Record Office; and Crabb Robinson Diary, 29 February 1820, vol. 7, fol. 79, MS Crabb Robinson Archive, DWL. For Mary Reid's letters to Mary Hays (1797 and 1808), see Whelan, *Mary Hays*; and Brooks, *Correspondence*, pp. 504–6.

41 Nathaniel Rutt of Coleman Street was a great-nephew of J. T. Rutt and a relation of Mary and Elizabeth Hays and Crabb Robinson by way of marriage.

42 Richard Sharp (1759–1835), widely known as 'Conversation Sharp', was at various times a hat-maker, banker, merchant, poet, critic, MP, and conversationalist. He was, like Mary and Elizabeth Hays, immersed in the radical politics of the 1790s, and probably met the two sisters during that decade. He joined the Committee for the Society for Effecting the Abolition of the Slave Trade in 1788, and several other reformist societies in the next decade. He befriended both Coleridge and Wordsworth at various times, and was a close friend of the poet Samuel Rogers, with whom he shared, as he did the Hays sisters, a strong interest in Unitarianism. He served as MP for Castle Rising (1806–12), Portarlington (1816–19), and Ilchester (1826–27).

43 Some connections existed between the Hays and Dunkin families and the Shuter family of Gainsford Street, for one of Sarah Dunkin Wedd's children was named Susan Shuter Wedd, born 17 June 1818 and christened 9 July 1818 at the Adelphi Independent Chapel in James Street, London. See 'England and Wales Non-Conformist Record Indexes' (microfilm RG4, 4207), Public Record Office, Kew.

44 William Smith (1756–1835) served as an MP from 1784 to 1830, primarily as a representative of Norwich. His political life was more successful than his mercantile interests, for his family firm faced bankruptcy the year Lanfear's novel appeared and was liquidated in 1823. Smith was a staunch defender of the rights of Dissenters, especially the Unitarians, with whom he became associated in the early 1790s.

45 William Tooke (1777–1863) was a prominent legal, political, and cultural figure in London throughout the first half of the nineteenth century. He became a solicitor in 1798, working out of his offices in 39 Bedford Row, eventually forming the firm of Tooke, Son, and Hallowes. Like his friend Crabb Robinson, he played a central role in the founding of London University (now University College) in the mid-1820s, serving as its treasurer until 1841, and in the formation of the Society for the Diffusion of Useful Knowledge in 1826. He became friends with Mary Hays in the 1790s and helped mediate her contracts with Richard Phillips between 1800 and 1806, most likely becoming known to Elizabeth Hays at that time as well. The Tookes and the Hayses had met as early as 1796, for on 9 June Godwin writes in his diary that he had tea that day at the home of Mary and Elizabeth Hays, joined by Amelia Alderson, Mary Wollstonecraft, and the Tookes. Most likely William Tooke, Sr, joined the younger Tooke that day, but other members of the Tooke family were known to the Hayses as well. Mary Hays writes to Tooke on 19 May 1803 (she was living in Camberwell at the time), reminding him that 'The ladies of your family, to whom present my respects, have promised a visit to my little retreat. Your father & yourself will, I hope, accompany them'. The Miss Tooke who appears in the subscription list to *Fatal Errors* may be his sister, but mostly likely the two names that follow his own are those of his wife and daughter, who were joined by William's older brother, Thomas Tooke (1774–1858), and his wife. For the Hays-Tooke correspondence from 1799, 1803, and 1807, see Whelan, *Mary Hays*; Brooks, *Correspondence*, pp. 323, 336, 342–6; see also *William Godwin's Diary*.

NOTES

46 Abraham John Valpy (1787–1854) was a London printer and publisher. He was the son of Richard Valpy, Headmaster of the Reading School. He is best known for his publishing ventures in the area of classical literature, most noticeably the monumental series, Delphin Classics (143 volumes), primarily under the editorship of George Dyer, a friend of Lanfear and Mary Hays and a fellow subscriber to *Fatal Errors*.

47 Sarah Dunkin Wedd (1793–1875), one of the many daughters of John Dunkin, Jr, married George Wedd (1785–1854), at that time living in Gainsford Street, at Hazeleigh Church, Church, Maldon, in August 1812 (*Monthly Magazine*, vol. 34, 1812, part 2, p. 280). He was a nephew of J. T. Rutt and a distant relation of Crabb Robinson; she was one of Mary Hays's favourite nieces and the recipient of most of Mary Hays's letters and other papers. Possibly the primary reason Mary Hays lived with the Dunkins at the Paragon *c.* 1794–96 was to assist her elder sister after Sarah's birth in 1793. Hays remained close to her Dunkin nieces thereafter, and *c.* 1806–8 taught three of them in her home in Islington, including Sarah. After their marriage, the Wedds may have taken over the original Hays residence in Gainsford Street (Mrs Hays had died shortly before their marriage), for Wedd was a business partner of John Hays, Elizabeth Lanfear's younger brother. By the mid-1820s the Wedds had moved to Maze Hill, Greenwich, where they joined Mary Hays and her sister, Sarah Hills, and several of Sarah's sisters and their families. The Wedds worshiped after their marriage in various Congregational churches, including the Adelphi Chapel and the Congregational church in Maze Hill. By the 1841 Census, the Wedds had moved to Grove Street, Hackney, not far from Mary Hays, who was living in a boarding house in Clapton at that time. Sarah Dunkin Wedd died on 8 May 1875 at Leinster Square, Bayswater, London. Her granddaughter, Anne Frances Wedd (1875–1958), inherited Mary Hays's papers and in the 1920s published two volumes from that collection, one containing the letters of Hays and John Eccles and the other the letters of Eliza Fenwick to Hays.

48 Sarah Hills Wheeler (b. 1777) married William Wheeler at Islington on 21 April 1808. William Wheeler joined with William Hills, his brother-in-law and neighbour in Canonbury, to form the firm of Hills & Wheeler, Corn merchants, 8 Haydon Square (*London Post Office Directory*, 1812, p. 151). A 'young Wheeler' appears in Crabb Robinson's Diary on 10 April 1828, possibly their son (see vol. 13, fol. 115, MS Crabb Robinson Archive, DWL).

49 Sarah Dennet had recently married a Mr. Woodfield. Mary-Anne will pay her a visit later in the novel, describing their marriage as surprisingly happy and equitable.

50 London does not have a Berner Street, but there is (and was at that time) a Berners Street, located on the north side of Oxford Street between Wells Street and Newman Street. Later in the novel Lanfear spells it with the 's', but for consistency, we have left the spelling throughout as 'Berner'.

51 Ecclesiastes 1:14.

52 Linking sexual distinctions in character and manners to women's education was a frequent topic of discussion among the women writers in the Godwin circle in the 1790s, especially Mary Hays and Mary Wollstonecraft. It is one of the major themes in Hays's *Memoirs of Emma Courtney*, emerging from Hays's reading of the French philosopher Helvétius (1715–1771). Hays's initial comments on Helvetius first appeared in her letter to the editor of the *Monthly Magazine* in June 1796, pp. 385–7.

53 Lanfear's language here overlaps closely with Wollstonecraft's use of chains, slavery, and imprisonment in connection with relationships between the sexes, such as 'the mind shapes itself to the body, and, roaming round its gilt cage, only seeks to adore its prison', or her assertion that in becoming 'the slave of her own feelings', a woman's reason is employed 'rather to burnish than to snap her chains'. See Mary

Wollstonecraft, *A Vindication of the Rights of Woman*, Everyman's Library Edition (London: David Campbell, 1992), pp. 48, 109.

54 Mary Hays addressed this topic in her letter on female education in the *Monthly Magazine* for March 1797, during the period of Elizabeth Hays's composition of *Fatal Errors*: 'Female education, as at present conducted, is a complete system of artifice and despotism; all the little luxuriances and exuberances of character, which individualise the being, which give promise of, and lay the foundation for, future powers, are carefully lopped and pruned away; sincerity and candor are repressed with solicitude; the terrors of *opinion* are set in array, and suspended over the victim, till the enfeebled and broken spirit submits to the travels, and, passive, tame, and docile, is stretched or shortened (as on the frame of the tyrant Procustes) to the *universal standard*. From woman, thus rendered systematically weak and powerless, on whom truth and morals have been confounded, inconsistent and contrary qualities are absurdly expected: for *principle*, it is attempted to substitute *rule* and dogma, while prejudice is combated only by other prejudices, equally, if not still more pernicious. The majority of human beings have yet to learn, notwithstanding a daily and melancholy experience, the dangerous tendency of every species of imposition and falsehood: one erroneous idea, entangling itself with others, from the nature of association and mind, is sufficient to destroy the whole character, nay more, to poison a community. Not an action nor a thought can be entirely inconsequential; nothing is stationary; truth or error rapidly and incessantly propagates itself.' See Mary Hays, 'Improvements Suggested in Female Education', *Monthly Magazine* 3 (1797), pp. 193–5; quotation from pp. 193–4.

55 Mary Hays most likely composed an essay on women's education and equality in 1792 (*Appeal to the Men of Great Britain*) but did not publish it until 1798. The ideas expressed in it are present in her correspondence with Godwin and in *Emma Courtney* and would have been the source of many conversations between her and her sister, Elizabeth. The *Appeal* argues that 'it is obvious, and frequently lamented by thinking people, that both the mental and bodily strength of women, even taking them as they are; – an oppressed, – a degraded, – and an excluded portion of the human race; – are fully equal to the perfecting of many of the arts, from which they are by the tyranny of fashion debarred'. A later passage reads, 'In short, I cannot perhaps explain myself better, than by saying that it appears to me, that women, with respect to mental abilities, compared with men . . . possess a capability of every thing useful and agreeable, or great and good'. Hays's pleas for a more 'equal' education did not bear the fruit she desired at that time, a lament echoed near the end of the *Appeal*: 'it is a melancholy truth, that the whole system raised and supported by the men, tends to, nay I must be honest enough to say hangs upon, degrading the understandings, and corrupting the hearts of women; and yet! they are unreasonable enough to expect, discrimination in the one, and purity in the other'. See *An Appeal to the Men of Great Britain in Behalf of Women* (London: J. Johnson and J. Bell, 1798), pp. 40, 44, 59.

56 The Royal Academy of Arts was founded in 1768 by George III. Its initial exhibitions were held in a small building in Pall Mall before moving to larger quarters in 1780 in a new wing of the Somerset House, located in the Strand. In 1868 it moved to Burlington House on Piccadilly, where it remains to this day.

57 Most likely the reference here is to *Observations on the River Wye: And Several Parts of South Wales, &c. Relative Chiefly to Picturesque Beauty; Made in the Summer of the Year 1770* (1782) by William Gilpin (1724–1804), a travel writer popular among the Romantics for his love of the picturesque. A title closer to the one mentioned in the text would be *Observations on the Western Parts of England, Relative Chiefly to Picturesque Beauty, Also the Isle of Wight* (1798), but given the date of the novel's composition (*c.* 1797) and the date of the narrative itself (*c.* 1786–90), the earlier title is more probable.

NOTES

58 The particular painting discussed above may or may not be based upon the work of a known artist, but the comments are pertinent to the 1790s, the time of the composition of *Fatal Errors*. Numerous artists associated with the Royal Academy, such as Henry Fuseli (an acquaintance of Elizabeth and Mary Hays), Thomas Stothard, James Barry, Richard Westall, Thomas Lawrence, Richard Corbould, Edward Dayes, Edward Francis Burney, and, of course, William Blake, were instrumental in transforming previous images of Satan as a hideous, horned creature into the romanticized, Promethean Lucifer, the arch-revolutionary fallen angel and deceiver of mankind – one possessing deadly power encased in a beautiful human form.

59 'None without hope e'er lov'd the brightest fair, / But love can hope where reason would despair', a popular epigram by George, Lord Lyttleton (1709–1773).

60 Lines from Act IV of Edward Young's tragedy, *The Revenge* (London: J. Bell, 1792). It was originally published in 1721 and revived for the stage at Drury Lane in 1792.

61 feel] 1819 text

62 Lines taken from *An Epistle to a Friend* (1798) by Samuel Rogers (1763–1855), addressed to Richard 'Conversation' Sharp. This allusion offers further insights into the dating of Lanfear's final manuscript, which clearly had emendations after Wollstonecraft's 1796 reading of the novel.

63 fourth] 1819 text

64 Line taken from Act II of *Rosina, A Comic Opera* (1782), by Frances Brooke (1724–1789), a writer and friend of Mary Hays's close friend, Mrs Collier, who appears often in the Hays-Eccles correspondence *c*. 1779–80, and on one occasion (July 1780) in Brooke's company at Tinwell (see Whelan, *Mary Hays*; Brooks, *Correspondence*, pp. 216–17). Numerous quotations from Brooke's novel, *The History of Emily Montague*, 4 vols (London: Dodsley, 1769), appear frequently in the Hays–Eccles correspondence. Collier may have passed on some manuscript poems by Brooke to Hays, for in the *Monthly Magazine* for February 1797 (p. 141), Hays published five odes by Brooke.

65 An irresistible echo of Austen's *Pride and Prejudice* (1813), suggesting Lanfear might have continued her reading of contemporary novels. The similarity suggests interesting parallels to the ways in which Austen revised her 1790s plots in the 1810s, dealing, albeit in a very different mode, with similar questions concerning the difficulties faced by unmarried women.

66 Glitterred] 1819 text.

67 to, –.] 1819 text.

68 Source unknown. A similar expression can be found in *Hamlet*, IV.vii.172–76, as Queen Gertrude recounts the drowning of Ophelia, when among the willows by the river 'here on the pendant boughs her coronet weeds / Clambring to hang, an envious sliver broke, / When down her weedy trophies and herself / Fell in the weeping brook, her clothes spread wide, / And mermaid-like, a while they bore her up'.

69 Lines from a poem by the Italian poet Metastatio and translated by Robert Merry and subsequently quoted by Hester Lynch Piozzi in *Observations and Reflection in the Course of a Journey Through Italy, and Germany*, 2 vols (London: T. Cadell, 1789), vol. 1, p. 275; the lines also suggest echoes of Milton's 'pendant shades' in *Paradise Lost*, IV.239.

70 Taken from Shakespeare's *Macbeth*, I.iii.145.

71 Werther is the highly emotional protagonist of Goethe's famous work, *The Sorrows of Young Werther* (1774). One of Mary Hays's earliest published pieces is a review of *Werther* in *The Universal Magazine* 76 (1784), pp. 317–18.

72 From 'The Passions: An Ode for Music', in *Odes on Several Descriptive and Allegorical Subjects* (1747), by William Collins (1721–1759); second quotation in the sentence is taken from Helen Maria Williams's 'Sonnet: To Disappointment', in *Poems,*

NOTES

Moral, Elegant and Pathetic (London: E. Newbery, 1796), p. 214; the sonnet first appeared in Williams's *Paul and Virginia* (London: G. G. and J. Robinson, 1795), a translation of Bernardin de Saint-Pierre's *Paul et Virginie*.

73 Madona] 1819 text
74 Iago's famous line in Shakespeare's *Othello*, III.iii.171.
75 Smuggle] 1819 text
76 Press-gangs were commonly employed by the Royal Navy (and even some merchant ships) to acquire able-bodied sailors for duty about warships both during times of war and peace. Though the practice was often criticized, it was consistently validated by the British courts in the seventeenth and eighteenth centuries as necessary to maintaining the massive numbers of sailors required for the ever-expanding British navy and merchant marine. By 1819, the year *Fatal Errors* was published, press-gangs had largely ended, but during the time of the novel's composition in the late 1790s, the practice was still widely in use.
77 Elizabeth Lanfear and Mary Hays lived in an age known for its philanthropic efforts to improve living conditions, wages, and literacy among the poor and working classes. These efforts were aided by the work of the Sunday School Society, a joint venture of evangelical Anglicans and Dissenters to establish schools (they met on Sunday afternoons) to teach writing and reading (primarily biblical texts, Isaac Watts's hymns and catechism, and short religious and heavily didactic prose pieces) to the poor children of each parish. Founded in 1786 through the leadership of William Fox (1736–1826), a Baptist merchant, and Robert Raikes (1735–1811), an Evangelical Anglican, 30 schools were established the first year, and over 147 by January 1787. A decade later, the Sunday School Society had helped establish nearly 1,100 Sunday schools, educated 70,000 scholars, and distributed over 5,700 Bibles, 26,000 Testaments, and 110,000 spelling books. By 1805, the numbers had more than doubled.

Susanna Morgan of Bristol, a friend of Mary Hays, in her *Hints Toward the Formation of a Society for Promoting a Spirit of Independence Among the Poor* (Bristol: E. Bryan, 1812), reinforced the importance of education as a means of benevolence toward the poor: 'But the more enlightened the mind, and enlarged the ideas, the more likely are these lessons of prudence, as well as those of religion and virtue to be understood and practiced. And as education is necessarily the first step towards enlightening the mind, active benevolence can never employ itself more usefully than in the establishment and superintendence of schools. Happily for the best interests of mankind, these are truths which are now almost universally acknowledged: and the exertions making in consequence of it, afford to the philanthropic mind, long wearied by the din of war, and appalled by the horrors and the extensive ruin of which it is productive, a hope, which like a speck of light in a gloomy horizon, gives a faint promise of a brighter day' (pp. 17–18). She also posited in her essay, however, the need for the poor to find a way to achieve a state of independence, wondering 'how the Poor, can more effectually, and less injuriously to their moral character, be assisted – and how that salutary spirit of independence, which injudicious established and private charities have almost annihilated, can in some measure be restored' (p. 14). Mary Hays served with Susanna Morgan as a member of the Committee for the Poor Man's Friend Society in Bristol in 1815 and 1816.

In *The Brothers* (London: W. Button, 1815), published as a dramatic elaboration of Morgan's *Hints*, Hays continued this same theme, with further elaborations in her 'Postscript' and in 'A Short Essay on Savings Banks', an anonymous piece affixed to the end of the second edition of Hays's *The Brothers* (London: G. & W. B. Whittaker, 1818) but most likely written by Hays. Just as Morgan did in her *Hints*, Hays argues for 'independence' as one of the major benefits of a proper benevolence bestowed upon the poor. Acquiring 'independence' had been one of the major objectives of

NOTES

Hays's adult life, and the 'Essay' implores readers (which would have included the fictional Mr. Howard and Mary-Anne Southerdon of *Fatal Errors*) to consider that 'One of the greatest blessings in this world is independence; not merely that independence of mind, which puts a man above the performance of a bad action, at the command of another; but that independence of property, by which he is placed above many of the little chances and temptations of this life. Let a man think with himself in what condition he should be, if, by being out of employment of some time, or by the sickness of nay part of his family, he should be put to such expense, as might render it impossible for him to say the rent of his little cabin. His wife, his children, and himself tuned out to the open air, perhaps in nakedness and hunger. – Let him think what must be his feelings then, while he is convinced that a little economy on his part, a little saving, the putting by every week, even of a sixpence, would have saved them and him from such misfortune. The small sums, which were thrown away – or worse, were spent in the public-house, if they had been saved, would then be of great service to him; instead of having his heart torn at seeing the misery of his wretched family, and all of it occasioned by himself, he would have the comfort of seeing them sitting about him at his fire side, in his own cottage, from which no one has the power to turn him, because he has the means of meeting every demand which may be made upon him. Wretched indeed is the man who must crouch at the feet of another, must tremble at his very nod, when, by a little saving, he might have put himself above all such meanness!' (*The Brothers*, 2nd ed., pp. 100–101). For more on the Sunday school movement, see T. W. Lacquer, *Religion and Respectability: Sunday Schools and Working Class Culture 1780–1850* (New Haven and London: Yale University Press, 1976).

78 A line from Shakespeare's *Macbeth*, II.ii.36.
79 Taken from William Wordsworth's 'Lines written near Richmond, upon the Thames, at Evening', which first appeared in *Lyrical Ballads* (1798), another indication that Lanfear continued to work on her novel after 1797.
80 We] 1819 text
81 A line from the song, 'To the woods, to the winds, to the waves I complain', from Thomas Holcroft's translation of Beaumarchais's *The Follies of a Day; or, The Marriage of Figaro* (London: G. G. J. and J. Robinson, 1785).
82 Line taken from Shakespeare's *Merchant of Venice*, V.i. Jessica is the daughter of the Jewish merchant, Shylock; she runs off with Lorenzo, a Christian, taking with her a bounty of her father's ducats and family heirlooms.
83 Either *Twelve Canzonets* (1770) or *A Second Set of Twelve Canzonets* (c. 1782), by William Jackson (1730–1803), chief musician at Exeter Cathedral, 1777–1803.
84 Lines taken from Sanchio's closing speech in Beaumont and Fletcher's *Love's Pilgrimage* (1711), II.i.
85 landscape – Black] 1819 text
86 Taken from William Shenstone's 'Pastoral Ballad' (1755), ll. 15–16.
87 From 'Evening: Gertrude', in *Poetical Sketches* (1795), by Anne Batten Christall (1769–1848). Both Elizabeth and Mary Hays, as well as one of their brothers, either John or Thomas, were subscribers to Christall's volume (see above, Notes to the Introduction, n. 21).
88 Compare this passage with one from Mary Hays's 'Letter to Amasia, on a Future State' from *Letters and Essays, Moral, and Miscellaneous* (1793), in which Hays writes that the 'next world will not materially differ' from this life, suggesting 'that we may be obliged to labour for our subsistence'. More importantly, she contends, 'An unquenchable thirst after perfection, an ever ardent and restless pursuit after something – 'higher, more powerful, more living than visible nature' – surely point to a nobler destination!' (p. 203).

NOTES

89　Reference is to the expulsion of Adam and Eve from the Garden of Eden, after which the entrance was guarded by the Cherubim and a flaming sword. Lanfear would have known the story from both the biblical text of Genesis 3 as well as the scene from Milton's *Paradise Lost*, Book XII.
90　Mrs Blount is referring to the common notion embedded in much eighteenth-century sentimental fiction, beginning with Samuel Richardson's *Pamela; or Virtue Rewarded* (1740), that the 'reformed rake makes the best husband', a notion the rational Mary-Anne regards with considerable scepticism.
91　Bedford Square, one of London's best preserved Georgian squares, was built between 1775 and 1783, its title taken from the surname (Russell) of the Dukes of Bedford, who owned most of the land in what is now Bloomsbury.
92　Lines from 'Autumn' (ll. 235–36) in James Thomson's popular poem, *The Seasons* (1730).
93　Berners] 1819 text
94　as] 1819 text
95　your's] 1819 text
96　Lines from Book III of Richard Blackmore's *Prince Arthur: An Heroick Poem* (1695).
97　Lines spoken by Brutus in Shakespeare's *Julius Caesar*, IV.ii.
98　An expression derived from I Samuel 16:7 – 'But the Lord said unto Samuel, Look not on his countenance, or on the height of his stature; because I have refused him: for *the Lord seeth* not as man seeth; for man looketh on the outward appearance, but the Lord looketh on the heart'.
99　A small mask covering only the area around the eyes and bridge of the nose, frequently worn at masquerades in the eighteenth century.
100　This scene is reminiscent of Wollstonecraft's desertion by Gilbert Imlay in Paris in 1794 and her discovery upon her return to London (with her infant daughter, Fanny) the following year that he was living with an actress.
101　Taken from Alexander Pope's *Eloisa to Abelard*, l. 317: 'I come, I come! prepare your roseate bowers'.
102　Lines from John Donne's 'Elegy on Mistress Elizabeth Drury', ll. 4–6.

NOTES TO APPENDIX A

1　*Letters and Essays*, pp. 124–38.
2　*Letters and Essays*, pp. 138–59.
3　Quotation from Ch. XXV of Samuel Johnson's prose tale, *The History of Rasselas, Prince of Abyssinia* (1759). Nekayah was Rasselas's sister who accompanies him on his travels from the Happy Valley to Cairo.
4　conduct; Gay. . .] 1793 text
5　Josepha confessing her love to Clermont foreshadows Mary Hays's declaration to William Frend in 1795 and Emma's letter to Harley in *Emma Courtney* (pp. 199–203). Not long after her affair with Frend abruptly ended, Hays confessed to Godwin, 'My heart was unreservedly open before him [Frend] I coverd my paper with its emotions & transmitted them to him' (Hays to Godwin, 2–6 February 1796, in Whelan, *Mary Hays*; Brooks, *Correspondence*, p. 430). Mary Hays had expressed similarly frank sentiments more than a decade earlier to her fiancé John Eccles, declaring to him on November 5, 1779, that 'if it is indelicate to avow an attachment so warm, so animated, yet so pure – of what indecorum have I been guilty! – But it is not! – it cannot be so! . . . I never yet have had cause to repent my frankness – nor do I think I ever shall' (Whelan, *Mary Hays*; Brooks, *Correspondence*, p. 183). Hays was not alone among Dissenting women writers in questioning established roles of men and women during courtship. Having committed herself to feminist ideals in *The Female Advocate* (1774), the West Country poet Mary

NOTES

Scott brought similar ideals to her courtship with the Presbyterian minister John Taylor. 'Decorum prescribes a Thousand absurd modes of conduct to our Sex', she explained to Taylor on 26 May 1777, 'from which you are happily exempted; one of these is that a Woman ought not to acknowledge her affection for a Man, whatever his merit or attachment to her may be, till she is married to him'. Under normal conditions, she should have told him 'a Thousand falsehoods, & endeavor'd to inspire ye World with a belief of my thinking lightly of y^o'. The 'claims of honor, truth & humanity', however, are 'infinitely superior to ye rules of *Decorum*', a stance that links the West Country's Scott and London's Hays sisters in their common quest for 'artless simplicity' and 'virtuous love' (Whelan, *Nonconformist Women Writers*, vol. 4, p. 275).

6 These lines appear near the end of 'Spring' in James Thomson's popular poem, *The Seasons* (1730).
7 Line is by Imlac the poet, from Ch. XXX of Samuel Johnson's *Rasselas*.
8 Phrase is loosely taken from I Peter 5:8.

NOTES TO APPENDIX B

1 An announcement of the forthcoming publication of Elizabeth Hays Lanfear's *Letters to Young Ladies* appeared in *The Edinburgh Magazine and Literary Miscellany; a New Series of the Scots Magazine*, vol. 93, for February (p. 234), with a formal notice of the publication appearing in the June issue (p. 747).
2 Lines from the poem, 'Advice to a Lady' (1733), by Lord George Lyttelton, 1st Baron Lyttelton (1709–1773). The first edition of *Letters to Young Ladies* contains a frontispiece by the celebrated watercolourist Thomas Uwins (1782–1857) and engraved by P. Thomson, titled 'Maternal Affection', from Letter IX of the book.
3 *Letters to Young Ladies*, pp. 1–9.
4 Like her sister, Lanfear maintained close ties to many of her numerous nieces and nephews, including the three daughters of John Dunkin, Jr, who lived with Mary Hays in Islington in close proximity to Lanfear, *c.* 1806–8.
5 Mary Hays expressed similar sentiments in her 'Letter to Amasia' when she opined: 'In this world, intellectual pleasures afford the most elevated and real gratification, – the pursuit after truth, the benevolent affections . . . may we not then suppose, that in a superior degree, and in constant progression and improvement, such will be the sources of our felicity in the next?' (Letter XV, *Letters and Essays*, p. 204).
6 Lanfear had previously commented on female education in Letter VII of *Fatal Errors*, suggestive of similar comments and opinions she shared with Mary Hays that appeared in the latter's correspondence with William Godwin *c.* 1795–96, in *Memoirs of Emma Courtney*, and in Hays's previously cited essay from the *Monthly Magazine* (1797), 'Improvements Suggested in Female Education', all composed about the same time as *Fatal Errors*.
7 Here Lanfear declares her continued allegiance to the central doctrine of Unitarianism, a belief held no less dear by Mary Hays, who would have seconded Lanfear's insistence, as expressed later in the above letter, that Christians should focus on espousing beliefs 'essential to salvation' and not those solely governed by 'party spirit' or 'prejudice'.
8 *Letters to Young Ladies*, pp. 10–15.
9 effcoted] 1824 text
10 attaching] 1824 text
11 *Letters to Young Ladies*, pp. 16–23.
12 Lines from *The Fair Penitent* (1703), III.i.98–9, by Nicholas Rowe.
13 Lanfear speaks from personal experience here, having lost her husband to suicide in 1809 and her eldest son, John, in 1817 at the age of 12.
14 Job 16.2.

NOTES

15 Reference to the parable of Jesus about two men, one who built a house on sand and the other upon rock, found in Matthew 7:24–27 and Luke 6:47–49.
16 Source unknown.
17 Lines taken from Thomas Gray's 'Ode on a Distant Prospect of Eton College' (1747).
18 *Letters to Young Ladies*, pp. 54–63.
19 Lanfear made similar comments in her letter to Mary Hays on 4 February 1801 (see Appendix C, Letter 2).
20 *Letters to Young Ladies*, pp. 129–54.
21 A short street that begins near the rear of St. Paul's Cathedral and leads to Queen Victoria Street in the City of London.
22 A fashionable section of south London not far from Wandsworth Common where Elizabeth Lanfear's brother, Thomas Hays, lived for about a decade (see above, Notes on *Fatal Errors*, n. 26).
23 This line, most likely adapted from two lines in Alexander Pope's *Rape of the Lock*, Canto I, had become a cliché by 1824. The line eventually provoked a popular anonymous poem, as found in *Who Wrote It? A Dictionary of Common Poetical Quotations in the English Language* (London: G. Bell, 1878), p. 117:

> Oft great events from trifling causes spring.
> A few explosive grains will rend apart
> The flinty cliff, or level the proud tower;
> A little worm destroys the mighty oak,
> A little drop – drop – drop will wear away
> The key-stone of an arch that holdeth up
> A stately fabric bridge, or firm-trod road;
> And from a little spark will spring to life
> A fierce devouring flame: so a small word
> Breathed by the lips of slander may destroy
> A noble reputation. Have a care
> Of what you say, and more of what you do,
> For great effects from little causes spring.

24 run] 1824 text

NOTES TO APPENDIX C

1 Whelan, *Mary Hays*; Brooks, *Correspondence*, pp. 481–2.
2 John Hays (1768–1862), Elizabeth's younger brother (see above, Notes to *Fatal Errors*, n. 25).
3 Reference here is to Rousseau's important pre-romantic novel, *Julie, ou la nouvelle Héloïse* (1761), which appeared in London in its English translation in 1784 as *Eloisa: or, A Series of Original Letters*.
4 By the mid-1790s, the sensationalist philosophy of Claude Adrien Helvétius (1715–1771), especially his views on the natural equality of the sexes expressed in his important work, *De l'esprit: or, Essays on the Mind* (Paris, 1758; London, 1759), had significantly influenced the opinions of Elizabeth and Mary Hays on the gendered nature of human experience and education. Discussions linked to central concepts of Helvétian philosophy appeared in *The Memoirs of Emma Courtney*, positions Hays had previously set forth in her 1796 essay, 'Improvements Suggested in Female Education'.
5 For Martin, see above, Notes to the Introduction, n. 23.
6 For Browne, see above, Notes to the Introduction, n. 24.
7 Thomas Martin (see above) supped with Godwin at the Alderson home on 28 June 1794, along with Bartlett Gurney, Taylor, Charles Marsh, William Firth, Dr Southwood

Smith, and Robert Merry, several of which were from Norwich. Most likely it is Stephen Weaver Browne who has tea with Godwin and Holcroft at Mary Hays's house in Kirby Street on 2 December 1795, at which time they talked of 'causes'. He has tea again at Hays's apartment on 20 January 1796, with Godwin and Rev. Draper, the same person Hugh Worthington had mentioned in a letter from 1794. This reference may be the most helpful in dating this letter. Browne appears often in Godwin's diary in the spring of 1796, and most noticeably on 9 June 1796, when he writes: 'Tea Hayes's, with Wolstencraft, A A [Amelia Alderson], Brown, Tookes & Hayes's'. The last reference is helpful in dating the above letter, for Godwin seems to imply multiple 'Hayes' in his use of the term, which is most likely Mary and Elizabeth, who appears to have received the answer to her request in the same letter. However, the fact that the letter originated from the family home in Gainsford Street, with Mrs Hays also there, suggests that if they did live with John Dunkin, Jr, for a time at the Paragon, they had returned to Gainsford Street by January 1796 (see *William Godwin's Diary* for the above references). Alderson also brought Catherine Buck to see Godwin on 17 May, 21 May, 3 June, and 11 June 1795. At this same time Robinson was writing an essay in defence of Godwin that appeared in the *Cambridge Intelligencer* on 1 August 1795. See T. Whelan, 'Mary Steele, Mary Hays and the Convergence of Women's Literary Circles in the 1790s', *Journal for Eighteenth-Century Studie*s 38 (2015), pp. 511–24; and T. Whelan, 'Henry Crabb Robinson and Godwinism', *Wordsworth Circle* 33 (2002), pp. 58–69.

8 Paul's important passage discussing the doctrine of the 'law of liberty' is found in Romans 14:1–13.
9 This letter arrived about a month after Hays's rejection by William Frend (see Introduction).
10 See Eloisa, Letter CXIV. Whether Elizabeth Hays had suggested such a remedy to her sister over her despondency concerning William Frend is not known.
11 Whelan, *Mary Hays*; Brooks, *Correspondence*, pp. 482–4.
12 Reference here is to Mary Hays's affair with Frend, which, though it had officially ended by January 1796, resurfaced several times until 1808, when he married Sara Blackburne, daughter of Francis Blackburne of Brignall and granddaughter of Archdeacon Francis Blackburne, dashing Hays's hopes forever.
13 Line is from Oliver Goldsmith's poem, 'Edwin and Angelina' (often known as 'The Hermit'), which first appeared in his novel, *The Vicar of Wakefield* (1766) and in his *Poems for Young Ladies* in 1767.
14 In 1800 Hays moved into Ann Cole's new residence at 22 Hatton Street, Holborn; the two women had previously lived together at 30 Kirby Street, near Hatton Garden, since 1795 except for Hays' year-long stay in the home of Edward and Marianna Hays Palmer in John Street. Hays remained with Cole in Hatton Street through May 1803, after which she did indeed take her own house at 9 St George's Place, Camberwell, staying there through early 1806, when she removed to 3 Park Street [Place], Islington. She maintained herself as an independent woman with one servant at both residences, but for part of her time at Islington she boarded and tutored three of her Dunkin nieces after the death of Joanna Hays Dunkin in December 1805. Hays would return to live with Cole at 1 Upper Cumming Street, Pentonville, *c.* 1819–20.
15 By this time John Hays, like his brother Thomas, had become a cornfactor, most likely assisted in his early years by John Dunkin, Jr. Dunkin's attention to the establishment of John and Thomas Hays was part of his extraordinary legacy as guardian of the Hays children after the death of their father, John Hays, in 1774, the year Dunkin married Joanna Hays. In the late 1790s John Dunkin (whether Sr or Jr is not clear) purchased a mill at Beeleigh, Essex; the Dunkins already owned or would soon own large farms as well in the area around Maldon and Chelmsford, Essex, where John Hays was living

NOTES

in 1801 and appears to have remained for some time. Dunkin eventually settled his family, just prior to the death of his wife in 1805, at Mortimer Woodham, Essex, not far from Maldon and his mill at Beeleigh.

16 Source unknown.
17 sourse] MS
18 Compare this passage with similar sentiments in *Letters to Young Ladies*, Letter VII, 'On the Single Life' (see Appendix B).
19 Whelan, *Mary Hays*; Brooks, *Correspondence*, 485. Ingatestone was about three miles to the southwest of Chelmsford, where Elizabeth's 1801 letter was composed. Previously she had been living with her brother John, but she appears to be visiting friends or other relations at the time of this letter. Mary Hays was living on her own in Camberwell at this time, and Mrs Hays was more than likely living with the Dunkins in their large home in Champion Hill (she appears to have left Gainsford Street for good in 1803).
20 For more on Joanna Dunkin Palmer, niece of Mary Hays and Elizabeth Hays Lanfear, see above, Notes on *Fatal Errors*, n. 38.
21 For more on Ambrose Lanfear, see Introduction. He apparently had previous connections with several of Elizabeth Hays's nieces and nephews.
22 Martha Lanfear, niece of Ambrose Lanfear.
23 For more on Elizabeth Francis and her family, see above, Notes on *Fatal Errors*, n. 23.
24 Mrs John Hays Dunkin (1775–1858) (see above, Notes on *Fatal Errors*, n. 20).
25 Joanna Dunkin, Lanfear's eldest sister. The Dunkins had not yet removed from Champion Hill, Camberwell, to Mortimer Woodham in Essex.
26 Possibly the elder Joanna Dunkin, but most likely Mrs John Hays Dunkin.